Failure Management

Failure Management

Malfunctions of Technologies, Organizations, and Society

William B. Rouse

OXFORD
UNIVERSITY PRESS

OXFORD
UNIVERSITY PRESS

Great Clarendon Street, Oxford, OX2 6DP,
United Kingdom

Oxford University Press is a department of the University of Oxford. It furthers the University's objective of excellence in research, scholarship, and education by publishing worldwide. Oxford is a registered trade mark of Oxford University Press in the UK and in certain other countries

First Edition published in 2021

Impression: 1

Published in the United States of America by Oxford University Press
198 Madison Avenue, New York, NY 10016, United States of America

British Library Cataloguing in Publication Data
Data available

Library of Congress Control Number: 2020952229

ISBN 978–0–19–887099–9

DOI: 10.1093/oso/9780198870999.001.0001

Printed and bound by
CPI Group (UK) Ltd, Croydon, CR0 4YY

Preface

I have spent my career concerned with human behaviors and performance in complex systems; with particular emphasis on how to support people to best fulfill their roles. I was first concerned with operators and maintainers of complex systems such as aircraft, ships, and power plants. My interests evolved to focus on managers, executives, and policymakers in complex organizations in healthcare, education, national security, transportation, and urban systems.

My earliest interest was in people's abilities to predict futures states of their system, e.g., air traffic controllers predicting where aircraft would be. This evolved to focusing on how people decided what to do next when faced with multiple tasks competing for their attention. We researched how computers could help people with prediction and multi-task decision making.

After about a decade of such pursuits, I became fascinated with people's abilities to address failures, i.e., cope with things going wrong. How do they decide that something has gone wrong? How do they determine the source(s) of the problem? How do they compensate for the loss of an engine, reactor coolant, or product sales?

My overall concern is with how best to support people to succeed in dealing with such situations. How should they be trained to have the potential to perform as needed? How can aiding, usually computer-based, best directly augment their performance? What roles do the organization and marketplace play in all this? Can the organization itself be supported?

Failure Management addresses these questions in the context of 18 case studies of failures of complex technologies, organizations, and society. These well-known failure case histories are employed to synthesize an integrated approach to failure management, including the conceptual design of an integrated decision support system. I also consider the factors likely to affect acceptance or rejection of this approach in any particular context.

My overall argument is that we can think about all these failures within a single conceptual framework. The proximate causes of failures differ substantially across these 18 case studies. However, the distal and ultimate causes of these failures have much in common. Consequently, the overall approach to failure management can be enriched by all these cases.

Scores of people have influenced my thinking in this arena and contributed to the lines of reasoning that I relate in this book. This influence has come from colleagues, sponsors, and students, but also from thousands of books, journal articles, and reports. With over 50 years of experiences, acknowledging everyone who has played a part is impossible. I would easily be at risk of forgetting people who played important roles. Thus, I will keep this simple. Thank you.

I am also thankful for the ecosystems that supported me, including the University of Rhode Island, MIT, Tufts University, University of Illinois at Urbana-Champaign, Delft University of Technology, Georgia Institute of Technology, Stevens Institute of Technology, and Georgetown University, as well as my corporate experiences at Raytheon, Search Technology, Enterprise Support Systems, and Curis Meditor. The experiences with the 100+ companies and agencies with whom I have worked have been critical to the perspectives presented in this book.

As I am writing this Preface, the coronavirus pandemic is surging through the United States. This is a compelling instance of a failure of a complex ecosystem, likely exceeding the impacts of the AIDS and opioids epidemics addressed in this book. It is clear that failure management should not be a "pickup game," where we assemble various competencies and resources at the last minute. We need to make failure management a core competency of organizations and society. Failures will happen. They key is our resilience in addressing them.

William B. Rouse

Washington, DC
March 2020

Contents

List of Illustrations ix
List of Tables xi

1. Introduction and Overview **1**
Introduction 1
Definitions 2
Types of Failures 3
Case Studies of Failure 5
Framework for Analysis 6
Arguments That Follow 8
Chapter Overview 10

2. Multi-Level Framework **12**
Introduction 12
Background 13
Application Examples 17
Methodology 24
Conclusions 27
References 27

3. Failures of Complex Systems **32**
Introduction 32
Three Mile Island and Chernobyl 32
NASA Challenger and NASA Columbia 44
Exxon Valdez and BP Deepwater Horizon 53
Comparison across Case Studies 60
Anticipating Failures 60
Higher-Order Consequences 64
Conclusions 64
References 65

4. Failures of Complex Organizations **67**
Introduction 67
Kodak and Polaroid 68
Digital and Xerox 72
Motorola and Nokia 79

Comparison Across Case Studies 84
Anticipating Failures 84
Creative Destruction 97
Conclusions 99
References 99

5. Failures of Complex Ecosystems **103**
Introduction 103
AIDS and Opioids Epidemics 105
Great Depression and Recession 112
Population and Climate 118
Comparison Across Case Studies 128
Anticipating Failures 132
Conclusions 138
References 139

6. Multi-Level Analyses **143**
Findings 143
Observations 149
Amended Multi-Level Framework 150
Computational Modeling 150
Interactive Visualizations 153
Conclusions 158
References 159

7. Failure Management **161**
Background 161
Failure Management Tasks 162
Failure Surveillance and Control 166
Integrated Decision Support 171
AI For Failure Management 174
Conclusions 175
References 176

8. Enabling Change **178**
Introduction 178
Decision Making 179
Decision-Making Vignettes 182
Reflections on Maintenance 184
Broader Perspectives 185
Enabling Change 187
Conclusions 193
References 194

Index 197

List of Illustrations

1.1	Addressing point vs. distributed failures	4
2.1	Architecture of healthcare delivery enterprise	13
2.2	Generalization of multi-level framework	17
2.3	Population health services in the United States	19
2.4	Multi-level architecture of academic enterprises	20
2.5	Hybrid multi-level architecture of academia	21
2.6	Multi-level model of traffic congestion	21
2.7	Multi-level model of air transport system	22
2.8	Multi-level model of urban systems	23
2.9	Revised multi-level model of urban systems	23
2.10	Further generalized multi-level framework	24
4.1	Fortune 500 rankings of Kodak and Polaroid	69
4.2	Fortune 500 rankings of DEC and Xerox	74
4.3	Fortune 500 rankings of Motorola and Nokia	80
4.4	Context of enterprise transformation	89
4.5	Transformation framework	90
4.6	Evidence-based story for Nokia for 2001–2011	94
4.7	Strategy framework for enterprise decision makers	95
5.1	World population projections	119
5.2	Earth as a system	127
5.3	Addressing point vs. distributed failures	137
6.1	Amended multi-level framework	151
6.2	Multi-level simulation dashboard	155
6.3	Ecosystem and organization levels of model	156
6.4	Simulation of New York City health ecosystem	157
7.1	Model-based predictive control	167

7.2 Integrated decision support for failure management 172
7.3 Example dashboard for population control 173
8.1 Factors affecting decision making and consequences 181
8.2 Simulation of New York City health ecosystem 190

List of Tables

1.1	Domains of case studies	5
1.2	Ranges of perspectives and concerns	9
2.1	Modeling and visualization methodology	25
3.1	Consequences of failures of complex systems	33
3.2	Multi-level analysis of failures of six complex systems	61
4.1	Consequences of failures of complex enterprises	68
4.2	Multi-level analysis of failures of six complex organizations	85
4.3	Ten archetypal market situations	86
4.4	Strategic delusions	87
5.1	Consequences of failures of complex ecosystems	104
5.2	Causal chains of ecosystem failures	129
5.3	Multi-level analysis of failures of six complex ecosystems	130
5.4	Measures monitored by the US Federal Reserve	138
6.1	Case studies versus people, products, and technologies	144
6.2	Case studies versus processes and operations	145
6.3	Case studies versus organizations, management, and markets	147
6.4	Case studies versus society, government, and industry	148
6.5	Example phenomena to represent in computational models	152
6.6	Example issues, concerns, and models	153
7.1	Failure management tasks for point and distributed failures	163
7.2	Broad elements of failure management	165
7.3	Interventions vs. types of failures	167
7.4	Surveillance and control strategies	168

1
Introduction and Overview

Introduction

Failures are common phenomena in civilization. Things fail and society responds, often very slowly, sometimes inappropriately. What kinds of things go wrong? Why do they go wrong? How do people and organizations react to failures? What are the best ways to react? This book addresses these questions.

My analytic approach to these questions is case based. Chapter 2 briefly reviews 10 cases of past applications of a multi-level analytic framework. Chapters 3–5 review 18 well-known cases of failures using this analytic framework. Chapter 6 integrates across the case studies. Chapters 7–8 employ these findings to outline a conceptual approach to integrated failure management.

Beyond the evidence provided by these 28 cases, I report on my experiences working with the organizations highlighted as a member of advisory boards, recipient of grants and contracts, and as a consultant. These experiences have been important to my understanding their organizational contexts in terms of priorities, incentive and reward systems, and cultural values and norms.

My overarching conclusion is that the conceptual design of an integrated approach to failure management can encompass all of the 18 case studies. They all would have benefitted from the same conceptual decision support architecture. This enables cross-cutting system design principles and practices, assuring that failure management in every new domain and context need not start with a blank slate.

Failure Management: Malfunctions of Technologies, Organizations, and Society. William B. Rouse, Oxford University Press (2021). © William B. Rouse. DOI: 10.1093/oso/9780198870999.003.0001

The central themes of this book include:

- Failures are inevitable at physical, human, economic, and social levels of systems ranging from engineered organizations to corporate enterprises to societal ecosystems
- Detection, diagnosis, compensation, and remediation are core competencies for addressing failures at all levels and managing their consequences; improved investment, design, and operational practices are key to this.
- Distinguishing among point and distributed failures of systems, enterprises, and ecosystems enables selecting and employing appropriately different approaches to surveillance and control.
- These approaches can be integrated into an overall concept for decision support of failure management that enables anticipating failure scenarios and being prepared to mitigate failures that eventually emerge

Definitions

A few terms are used pervasively throughout this book and warrant clear definitions:

Failure

Failures are malfunctions that cause the system of interest to reach undesirable states with substantially negative and unacceptable consequences. Failures can be abrupt such as pump or sensor failures, but may be more gradual due to physical or human fatigue. Failures can slowly emerge such as product failures in the marketplace and infectious disease transmission over time. Succinctly, failures are abrupt events or emergent events that one would rather had not happened.

System

Complex systems, enterprises, and ecosystems are contrasted in this book. They are all systems, albeit differing in their technological, organizational, and societal aspects. They also differ in the extent to which they were engineered or designed. Chapter 3 addresses highly engineered systems. Chapter 4 considers organizational systems that may have been designed; although values and norms often just emerged. Chapter 5 deals with social, economic, and environmental ecosystems that emerged over time, seldom with any overarching design.

Management

Management includes the set of investment, design, and operational activities associated with developing and operating systems. This includes the set of investments, activities, and outcomes associated with detection, diagnosis, compensation, and remediation of system failures. Finally, it includes fostering and sustaining the values and norms of the organization associated with the system, including value and norms related to safety.

Types of Failures

The distinction between point failures and distributed failures is important in terms of how failures propagate and how they are addressed (see Figure 1.1). Point failures are latent in engineered systems due to their design, development, and deployment, as well as how they are operated, maintained, and managed. Point failures are much more quickly recognized, typically leading to immediate responses and eventual remediation.

Distributed failures are usually not readily apparent until their consequences have been manifested over time. Recognition and

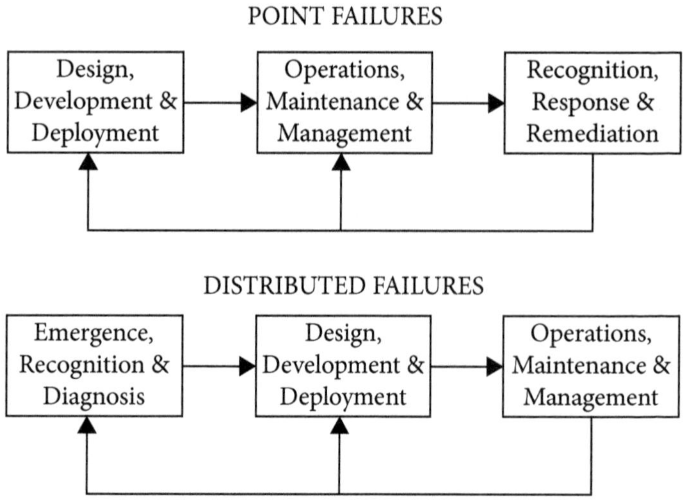

Figure 1.1 Addressing point vs. distributed failures

diagnosis are often quite delayed. Design, development, and deployment are in reaction to such failures. Operations, maintenance, and management relate to delivery of interventions intended to remediate the failures.

Thus, point failures tend to manifest themselves relatively quickly, while distributed failures emerge over time and are slowly recognized as failures. This difference significantly affects methods for addressing failures, including approaches to surveillance and control. It also tends to affect the breadth of stakeholders involved in addressing failures.

It is useful to elaborate the difference between point and distributed failures in terms of causes and consequences. A pump may be the cause of failure in a complex engineered system, but consequences may be distributed across the facility. An epidemic such as AIDS or coronavirus likely begins with one person—patient zero. However, it is not a failure until this infectious disease is distributed among a population of people. Thus, both the cause and consequences are distributed.

Failures of complex enterprises tend to be hybrids of point and distributed failures. Specific things may go wrong, e.g., releases of poorly received product offerings. However, this usually occurs in the context of overall corporate cultures and rules of the game. Consequently, it may require considerable time before the enterprise realizes a point failure has morphed into a distributed failure in terms of its pervasive impact on the enterprise.

Summarizing, engineered systems usually anticipate the possibilities of failures, e.g., of pumps, but they are not really expected; the consequences are initiated at one point, e.g., the pump. Social systems, e.g., healthcare, anticipate infectious diseases but usually do not know what specifically to expect, e.g., AIDS and opioids, and the consequences are distributed over time across populations.

Case Studies of Failure

Chapters 3–5 address 18 case studies of failure. The nine domains addressed by these case studies are summarized in Table 1.1. Clearly, the range of domains covered is quite broad.

The proximate, distal, and ultimate causes of the 18 failures are elaborated in Chapter 6 in terms of causal chains across the multiple levels of the framework introduced Chapter 2. As is discussed, humans interact with physical phenomena in the context of organizational and economic phenomena, all within the broader rules of the game set locally by firms and more largely by society. Chapters 7 and 8 then address the nature of failure management and approaches to surveillance and control.

Table 1.1 Domains of case studies

Domain	Case studies
Energy	Three Mile Island and Chernobyl
Space	NASA Challenger and NASA Columbia
Ocean	Exxon Valdez and BP Deepwater Horizon
Photography	Polaroid and Kodak
Computing	Digital and Xerox
Communications	Motorola and Nokia
Health	AIDS and the Opioid Epidemic
Economy	Great Depression and Great Recession
Environment	Population Growth and Climate Change

It is reasonable to ask why I chose 18 case studies rather than just a few. In effect, each of the 18 case studies provides one data point to support my line of reasoning. My thinking is that 18 data points are pretty compelling, not statistically, but in terms of repeated evidence of similar phenomena that illustrate management or mismanagement of failures.

With two types of failures and nine domains, one might think there would be some type of 2x9 design matrix, or perhaps 2x3 if we define domains as complex systems, enterprises, and ecosystems. However, only one type of failure is addressed in each domain. Further, the analytic framework employed in this book is case based rather than statistical.

Framework For Analysis

We need an analytic framework to address the diversity of these 18 case studies. Otherwise, they are just a set of disparate stories. Fortunately, these cases are very well documented via accident reports, business cases, and news reports. We need to make sense of this wealth of material in way that enables comparisons across technologies, organizations, and ecosystems.

A breakthrough in my thinking, discussed in Chapter 2, was the realization that such cases could be approached on more than one level of analysis. After several projects, also discussed in Chapter 2, I settled on four levels of abstraction: people, processes, organizations, and society. Sometimes these labels change depending on the context, but the four levels of abstraction remain fairly similar. Further, human phenomena arise on all four levels, but differ in terms of the most useful abstractions.

It is useful to contrast levels of abstraction and aggregation. Society, culture, the economy, etc. are not just aggregated individuals. Levels of aggregation are best illustrated in terms of the decomposition of a system, for example, an automobile. At the abstraction level of physical form, the vehicle can be decomposed into power train, suspension, frame, etc. The power train can be decomposed into engine, transmission, drive shaft, differentials, and wheels. The engine can be decomposed into block and cylinders, pistons, camshaft, valves, etc. These levels of aggregation are all represented within the same level of abstraction—physical form.

This four-level framework is employed throughout this book to differentiate proximal, distal, and ultimate causes of failures, as well as causes of inadequate failure management once consequences ensued. Failures often originate at the lowest level of people or physical components. Pumps fail, valves stick, viruses infect people, consumers dismiss new products offerings, people make risky investments, and people consume energy.

At the process level, consequences of failures propagate and interventions are introduced to thwart these consequences. The nature and capacities of these processes reflect organizational investment decisions, or lack of investments. Organizations make such decisions in the context of society's priorities, incentives, values, and norms.

Decisions, consequences, and constraints flow up and down. If society does not prioritize failure management, organizations may not invest, processes may not exist, or their capacities may be inadequate. Consequences may propagate more easily and interventions may be delayed and not meet demands. Thus, the physical failure for example, is the proximate cause, but poor or inadequate failure management are due to distal and ultimate causes at the process, organizational, and societal levels.

The four-level analytical framework is needed to enable comparisons of what might seem, on the surface, to be rather disparate cases. Any disparities are most evident in terms of proximate causes of failures, e.g., pump failures leading to loss of coolant versus humans eating monkeys leading to human immunodeficiency virus. However, common distal and ultimate causes are uncovered by comparisons at the levels of process, organization, and society.

Flawed management decision making regarding operations in general and safety in particular are a good example. Society's values and norms regarding investments in maintenance and safety are another example. At these higher levels, the common causes across case studies become very clear.

Arguments That Follow

There are several lines of argument woven throughout this book. These arguments emerge and evolve as the chronicles of failure case studies progress throughout the analyses of these cases. My goal is to assure that all the ingredients for model-based failure management are clear and the recipe for success is compelling.

Failures are pervasive phenomena in complex systems. Failures can be explained in terms of proximate, distal, and ultimate causes. Multi-level explanations enable articulating such causal chains, and differentiating multiple causes. Understanding multiple causes provides opportunities for multi-faceted interventions to manage the consequences of failures.

Dynamic "bubbles" can emerge across levels such that failures are inevitable. These bubbles can burst abruptly or deflate via steady decline. This can seriously threaten and perhaps destroy organizations or enterprises. The transformation of the enterprise may ultimately be necessary, although "creative destruction" often awaits those who try to avoid change.

Change depends on vision, leadership, strategy, planning, and communications. "Stewards of the status quo" are not good change agents. When such stewards occupy top leadership positions, they can hinder the impetus and capacities for change. Leaders with this stewardship orientation tend to doggedly pursue business as usual, at least until creative destruction eventually reigns.

Model-based decision support can enable sharing data and information, creating a balanced portfolio of near-term and long-term failure management capabilities, and empowering key stakeholders to explore the complexity of their domains and contexts. The conceptual design of model-based decision support is common across all the domains and contexts of the case studies in this book.

I expect the readers of this book will come with a variety of perspectives. Some readers will be people who operate, maintain, manage, or lead complex systems, enterprises, or ecosystem agencies. Representative concerns of these people are summarized in the top half of Table 1.2. They are concerned with performance goals, safe

Table 1.2 Ranges of perspectives and concerns

Perspective	Representative concerns
Operators	High performance, safe operations; appropriate training; steady, quality employment
Maintainers	High performance, safe maintenance; appropriate training; steady, quality employment
Clinicians	Safe, quality, affordable care; population risk management
Managers	Performance goals, achieved safely; recruiting and training qualified workers
Executives	Returns on investments in failure management; avoiding bad publicity associated with failures
Engineers	Design, development, and deployment of safe systems with integrated failure management capabilities
Economists	Capital and operating costs of failure management; human capital requirements and development
Behavioral scientists	Workers' risk behaviors, human factors, ergonomics, safety, and training
Social scientists	Individual and population behaviors in organizations and society; social responses to risks
Policy scientists	Policies that economically enhance safety, while not undermining competitiveness
Politicians	A healthy, educated, and productive population that supports legislation, regulation, and policies

operations, good jobs, quality care, investment returns, corporate reputations, and so on. This book shows them that enhanced failure management can contribute to enhancing these outcomes.

The bottom half of Table 1.2 provides representative concerns of a wide range of specialists. Many of these specialists will work in complex systems, enterprises, or ecosystem agencies. This book addresses their concerns across a panorama of case studies. Many others of these specialists will work in academia. Their focus is on concepts, principles, models, methods, and tools associated with the academic disciplines.

These readers may find this book a bit frustrating in that its breadth inevitably has resulted in less depth than academics typically desire. By focusing on how to put together all the puzzle pieces, I have spent less time on how to create puzzle pieces. There are ample references to more academic sources, but very limited detailed exposition. Hopefully, the juxtaposition of the concerns of a wide range of perspectives will help each specialty to better see how they can contribute to the overall endeavor of failure management.

Chapter Overview

Chapter 1, "Introduction and Overview," provides a broad discussion of the nature of failures and introduces the themes of the book. The 18 case studies are introduced and discussed quite briefly. The need for a framework for analysis across the 18 case studies is discussed. A brief overview of the book is provided.

Chapter 2, "Multi-level Framework," broadens the perspective on causes of failures, enabling the deeper analyses of subsequent chapters. The rich history of multi-level analysis and modeling is briefly reviewed. Numerous applications of the multi-level framework in a variety of domains are discussed. An overall methodology for applying this framework is presented and its application to the line of reasoning throughout this book is summarized.

Chapter 3, "Failures of Complex Systems," addresses failures in the nuclear power industry (Three Mile Island and Chernobyl), NASA space operations (Challenger and Columbia), and the maritime industry (Exxon Valdez and BP Deepwater Horizon). Multi-level analyses are used to provide comparisons across case studies. I briefly review how these industries anticipate and manage failures. Higher-order consequences of these types of failures are discussed.

Chapter 4, "Failures of Complex Organizations," addresses failures in the photography market (Kodak and Polaroid), computer market (Digital and Xerox), and communications market (Motorola and Nokia). Multi-level analyses are used to provide comparisons across case studies. I briefly review how these types of companies anticipate and manage failures. The notion of "creative destruction" is elaborated.

Chapter 5, "Failures of Complex Ecosystems," addresses failures in healthcare (AIDS and Opioids Epidemics), the economy (Great

Depression and Recession), and the environment (Population and Climate). Multi-level analyses are used to provide comparisons across case studies. I briefly review how these types of domains anticipate and manage failures.

Chapter 6, "Multi-level Analyses," summarizes the findings from Chapters 3–5 and provides a range of observations on these findings, articulating common elements across the three domains. An amended multi-level framework is discussed. The use of computational models and interactive visualizations is introduced.

Chapter 7, "Failure Management," addresses the notion of failure management in depth, proposing an overall integrated approach to failure management via surveillance and control. Failure management tasks are defined, and failure surveillance and control are discussed. The conceptual design of an integrated decision support is presented. The role of artificial intelligence (AI) in failure management is considered.

Chapter 8, "Enabling Change," provides a pragmatic perspective on enabling the changes needed to substantially enhance failure management practices. The behavioral and social nature of human decision making is reviewed. Decision-making vignettes are provided to illustrate the general human phenomena of interest. Societal views and practices of system maintenance are considered. Broader perspectives on economic, legal, political, and social aspects of change are reviewed. Numerous examples of computational approaches to change are summarized.

2
Multi-Level Framework

Introduction

In April 2008, I co-chaired a Workshop on Engineering the Learning Healthcare Delivery System hosted by the National Academy of Engineering and the Institute of Medicine (now National Academy of Medicine). On the morning of the second day of the workshop, my task was to summarize the findings of the first day. The speakers on the first day had included clinicians, informaticists, engineers, and computer scientists. It was clear to me that these various experts were talking about different levels of the system.

Figure 2.1 was the essence of my report that morning (Rouse, 2009; Rouse and Cortese, 2010; Rouse and Serban, 2014). The efficiencies that can be gained at the lowest level (clinical practices) are limited by nature of the next level (delivery operations). For example, functionally organized practices are much less efficient than delivery organized around processes.

Similarly, the level above (system structure) limits efficiencies that can be gained in operations. Functional operations are driven by organizations structured around specialties, e.g., anesthesiology and radiology. And, of course, efficiencies in system structure are limited by the healthcare ecosystem in which organizations operate. Differing experiences of other countries provide ample evidence of this.

The fee-for-service model central to healthcare in the United States assures that provider income is linked to activities rather than outcomes. The focus on disease and restoration of health rather than wellness and productivity assures that healthcare expenditures will be viewed as costs rather than investments. I argued that

Failure Management: Malfunctions of Technologies, Organizations, and Society. William B. Rouse, Oxford University Press (2021). © William B. Rouse. DOI: 10.1093/oso/9780198870999.003.0002

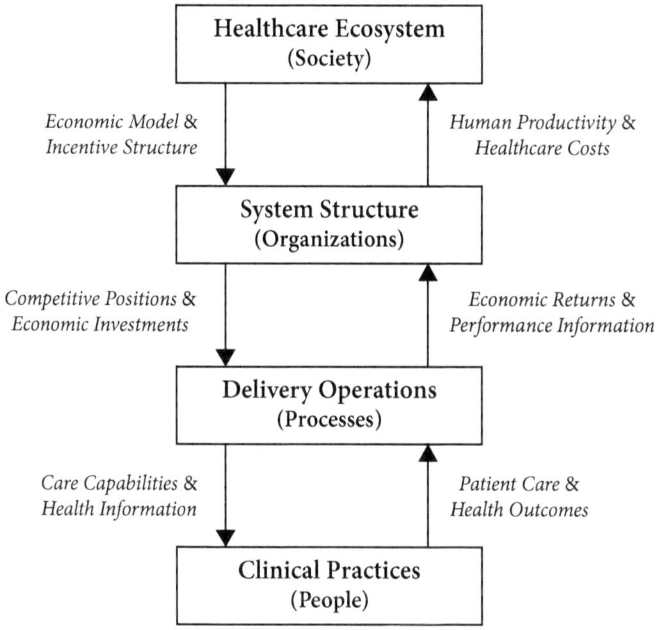

Figure 2.1 Architecture of healthcare delivery enterprise

recasting of "the problem" in terms of outcomes characterized by wellness and productivity may enable identification and pursuit of efficiencies that could not be imagined within our current frame of reference.

We have extended and applied this framework to a variety of domains. I discuss examples of these applications later in this chapter. First, however, it is useful to review the intellectual underpinnings of this approach to understanding complex systems. Why is multi-level analysis of complex systems warranted and useful?

Background

Multi-level analysis of complex systems has a long history of at least five decades. I first encountered the topic in *Theory of Multi-level Hierarchical Systems* (Mesarovic, Macko, and Takahara, 1970). The mathematics was impressive, but it was not clear to me how one could practically address other than fairly simple problems, unless one were to venture beyond strict mathematical formulations with closed form solutions.

Robert Rosen (1978) approaches the topic from the perspective of a theoretical biologist. Rosen's relational biology maintains that organisms have a distinct quality called organization, which is not part of the language of reductionist science. He argues that approaching organisms with reductionist scientific methods and practices ignores the functional organization of living systems and just studies the parts.

I find Rosen's arguments quite compelling. In a recent National Academies' study of cancer control (Johns et al., 2019), we concluded that the levels of the phenomena of interest ranged from cells to society. Cancer itself has organizational elements, e.g., in how it deceives the immune system. A higher level is the human organism that exists in a social system and accesses care delivery processes. These processes are operated by organizations that comply with rules, values, and norms provided by society.

Tolk (2013) addresses the epistemology of modeling. This involves the questions of what is knowledge, how can it be acquired, and what can be known. The empiricism branch of epistemology emphasizes the value of experience. The idealism branch sees knowledge as innate. The rationalism branch relies on reason. The constructivism branch seeks knowledge in terms of creation. These branches differ in terms of how they represent knowledge, in particular how this knowledge is best modeled and simulated.

There have been many broad applications of multi-level modeling. Davis has addressed national security (Davis et al., 1986, 2019; Davis and Huber, 1992; Davis and Bigelow, 1998). Hall (1989) incorporates multi-level analysis into systems engineering. Haimes (2004) applies this approach to risk management. Recent books by Davis and Tolk address modeling socio-technical systems (Davis, O'Mahony, and Pfautz, 2019; Tolk et al., 2018). Wallerstein (2004) pursues the enormously ambitious idea of modeling the whole of society throughout history to contemporary times.

In general, the multiple levels differentiate levels of abstraction and aggregation. Rasmussen (1983, 1986) and Rasmussen, Pejtersen, and Goodstein (1994) argue that information at different levels of abstraction and aggregation best support different modes of human decision making and problem solving, e.g., (Rouse et al., 2016). He proposed the following abstraction hierarchy:

- Functional Purpose—production flow models, system objectives
- Abstract Function—causal structure; mass, energy, and information flow topology, etc.
- Generalized Functions—standard functions and processes, control loops, heat transfer, etc.
- Physical Functions—electrical, mechanical, chemical processes of components and equipment
- Physical Form—physical appearance and anatomy, material and form, locations, etc.

Thus, the purpose of a system is a more abstract concept than how it functions. In turn, the systems' abstract and generalized functions are more abstract than its physical functions and form. Similarly, an economy is a more abstract concept than an individual consumer.

Levels of aggregation are best illustrated in terms of the decomposition of a system, for example, an automobile. At the abstraction level of physical form, the vehicle can be decomposed into power train, suspension, frame, etc. The power train can be decomposed into engine, transmission, drive shaft, differentials, and wheels. The engine can be decomposed into block and cylinders, pistons, camshaft, valves, etc. As noted, these levels of aggregation are all represented within the same level of abstraction—physical form.

Harvey and Reed (1997) provide a valuable construct for a broad perspective on behavioral and social systems. They articulate a compelling analysis of levels of abstraction of social systems versus viable methodological approaches. At one extreme, the evolution of social systems over long periods of time is best addressed using historical narratives. It does not make sense to aspire to explain history, at any meaningful depth, with a set of equations. At the other extreme, it makes great sense to explain physical regularities of the universe using predictive and statistical modeling.

Abbott (2006, 2007) considers how levels relate to each other and the possibilities of unforeseen higher-level phenomena emerging from lower levels. He argues "emergence occurs when a system is constrained in ways that produce macro entities whose behavior can be described in their own terms." Further, "to implement a level of abstraction is to impose constraints." Consequently, "a concept that comes into being at a given level of abstraction is typically inexpressible at lower levels of abstraction."

Pennock and Gaffney (2018) address the epistemic uncertainty associated with multi-level modeling. They argue that highly detailed models can hide epistemic uncertainties—bifurcations—phase, structural, and ontological uncertainties. They conclude that "it may be better to build a low fidelity multi-model to identify the existence of bifurcations that be managed by adaptations and hedges."

Heydari and Pennock (2018) consider the behavior of socio-technical systems. They articulate how agent-based models can best serve as elements of multi-level models of socio-technical systems. Lempert (2019) addresses robust decision making using complex models. He argues for a combination of "decision analysis, assumption-based planning, scenarios, and exploratory modeling to stress test strategies over myriad plausible paths into the future, to identify policy-relevant scenarios and robust adaptive strategies."

There are a variety of computational issues associated with multi-level modeling. Tolk (2003) addresses levels of conceptual interoperability. Being able to connect two models and have them jointly compute some outputs does not assure that these outputs are valid and meaningful. The issue here is one of "assumption management." Are the assumptions of the two or more interconnected models compatible? This is straightforward when the modelers are the creators of all the component models, but far from easy when some of the component models are legacy software codes.

Winsberg (2010) addresses multi-scale simulation in terms of "when theories shake hands." He shows that algorithms are often necessary to mediate between otherwise incompatible frameworks. He uses a compelling example of crack propagation in solid structures, where he has to bridge conflicting representations. Clearly, multi-level modeling is seldom "plug and play."

This brief review of the roots of multi-level modeling and the issues raised by this approach is intended to illustrate the richness of the topic and how it has been addressed by a wealth of researchers. This book primarily employs multi-level modeling as an analytic framework. The potential for computational modeling is discussed in Chapter 6, but not pursued in enough depth to raise several of the issues outlined in this brief review.

Application Examples

Figure 2.1 provided a framework for analysis of healthcare delivery that enabled multi-level explanations across people, processes, organizations, and society. Figure 2.2 provides a generalization of the framework applicable to many domains. This framework is employed in this book to help distinguish proximate, distal, and ultimate causes of failures. Remediation of solely the proximate causes often results in failures reoccurring.

Humans interact with processes that are enabled by economic investments that are made within the context of society's values,

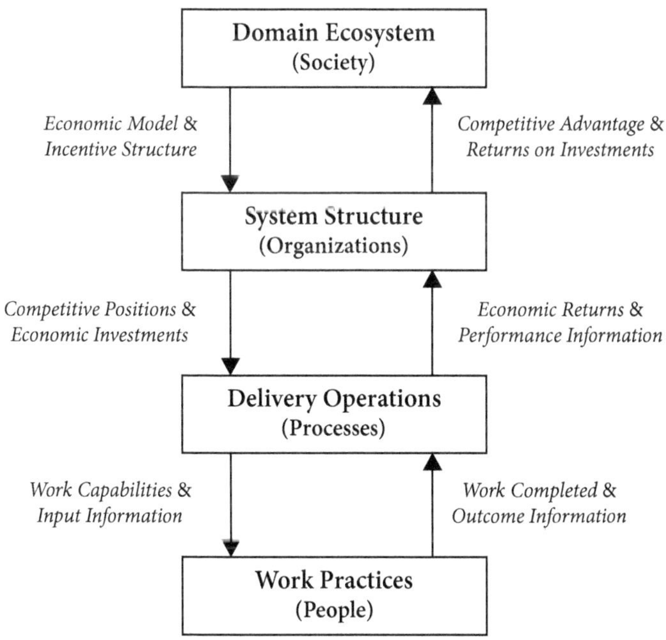

Figure 2.2 Generalization of multi-level framework

norms, and incentives. Failures in processes are often due to poor design, inadequate evaluation, or mismanagement. These unfortunate choices can often be traced to the higher levels of Figure 2.2.

This framework is applied in Chapters 3–5 to a significant set of 18 case studies, both historical and emerging. Six cases studies relate to technological and organizational failures, what might be termed point failures of engineered systems. Six case studies relate to failures of complex enterprises to adapt to changing technologies and markets. Finally, six case studies concern broader social, economic, and environmental failures, which can be termed distributed failures in the sense of their being more pervasive. Domain-specific versions of Figure 2.2 are discussed in these chapters. Chapter 6 provides an integrated multi-level analysis of the 18 case studies, articulating common elements across the three domains.

Applications

We have developed multi-level models for a variety of applications in healthcare, national security, higher education, transportation, and urban systems. I briefly review these applications in this section.

The framework in Figure 2.1 was used to create a multi-level model of Emory University's employee prevention and wellness program, with emphasis on reducing risks of diabetes and heart disease (Park et al., 2012). We were able to computationally redesign this program to assure a positive return on investment as it was scaled up. This model is discussed in more detail in Chapter 6.

We worked with the Aging Brain Care Center at Indiana Health to develop a multi-level model of their interventions for Alzheimer's disease (Boustany et al., 2016). The model was used to assess the issues associated with scaling this intervention from 2,000 to 100,000 patients. A variety of inefficiencies were identified and their impacts projected.

Penn Medicine developed a Transitional Care Model to help elderly patients avoid hospital readmissions, particularly readmissions that would be penalized by Medicare. We employed a version of Figure 2.1 to develop a computational model that enabled tailoring this intervention to each of the 3,000 Medicare hospitals in the United States. The model projected both the health and economic impacts of this intervention in each hospital (Pennock et al., 2018; Rouse et al., 2019).

A recent National Academies report on cancer control (Johns et al., 2019) leveraged a version of Figure 2.1 (Madhavan et al., 2018) to define a dashboard suitable for monitoring cancer prevention, screening, treatment, survivorship, and end of life care. This dashboard is discussed in Chapter 7.

Population health involves integration of health, education, and social services to keep a defined population healthy, to address health challenges holistically, and to assist with the realities of being mortal (Rouse, Johns, and Pepe, 2017, 2019). Figure 2.3 portrays who is involved in providing many of the services associated with population health and the inherent difficulty of accessing these services in the United States. This illustrates how Figure 2.1 has to morph for addressing different questions.

As mentioned earlier, when we ventured beyond healthcare, the framework in Figure 2.1 had to be generalized. The result was shown in Figure 2.2. The first application of this generalized framework was to understand the flow of counterfeit parts in the supply

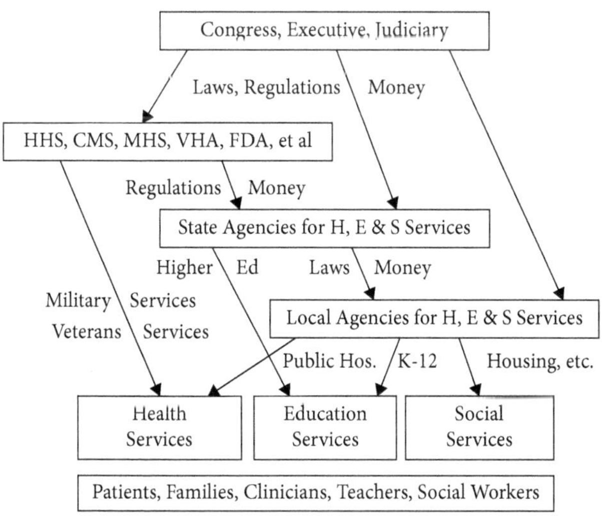

Figure 2.3 Population health services in the United States

chain of military communications systems (McDermott et al., 2013). The model was used to explore alternative policies for acquisition, intellectual property, and immigration.

Many people suggested that we should apply multi-level thinking to ourselves—the academic enterprise. We employed Figure 2.4 to understand relationships within universities. Considering relationships among universities led to Figure 2.5. The hierarchical structure of Figure 2.4 dovetails with the heterarchical nature of academic disciplines in Figure 2.5. The dotted rectangle in Figure 2.5 represents how faculty disciplines both compete and define standards across universities. This model was elaborated in great detail to explore the current tuition bubble in the United States and various technological and social forces affecting academia (Rouse, 2016; Rouse, Lombardi, and Craig, 2018).

We developed proposals for applications in transportation. The model in Figure 2.6 was developed to address congestion pricing in traffic networks. Figure 2.7 focused on the US air transport system and the impacts of the pace of deployment of new technologies.

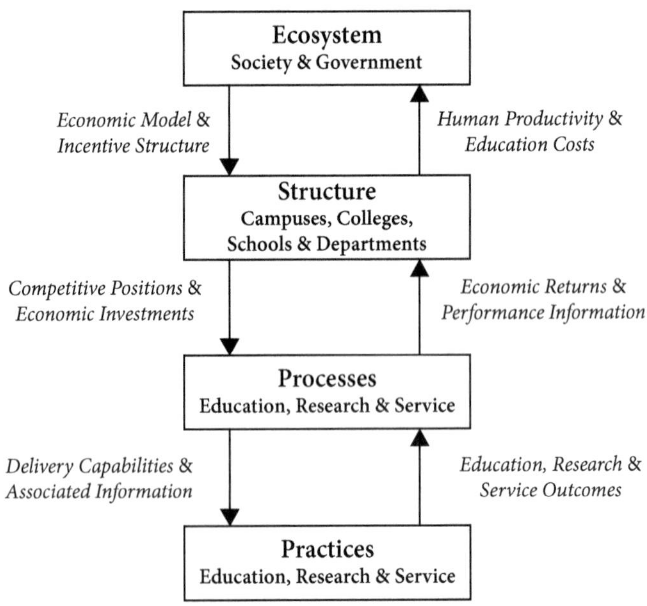

Figure 2.4 Multi-level architecture of academic enterprises

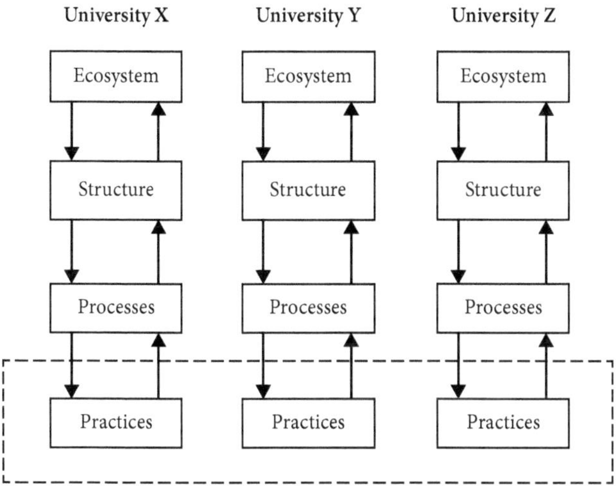

Figure 2.5 Hybrid multi-level architecture of academia

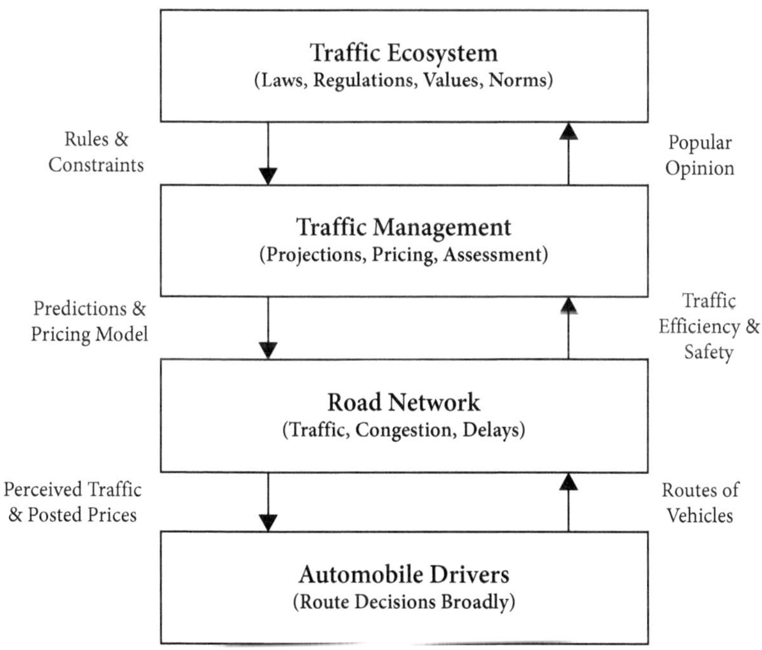

Figure 2.6 Multi-level model of traffic congestion

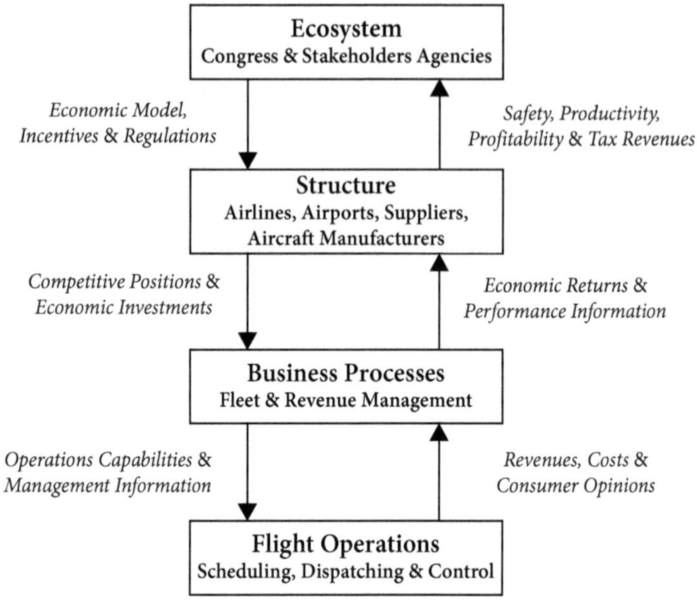

Figure 2.7 Multi-level model of air transport system

Both proposals were well received, but encountered push back from stakeholders who were sure they already knew all the answers. Such phenomena are discussed in Chapter 8.

Hurricane Sandy in October of 2012 led us to team with transportation specialists and urban oceanographers to understand how all the elements of urban systems interact. Figure 2.8 was our first draft. It was inadequate in two ways. First, the environment (e.g., weather) and physical infrastructure (e.g., public transit) needed to be explicitly separated. Second, the nature of urban decision making needed to reflect the interactions of decision makers and populations. These insights led to Figure 2.9.

The 10 examples briefly reviewed here provide important insights into multi-level modeling. First, the framework provides a template for discussion and debate. Second, the resulting model need not strictly reflect the standard framework. Insights are much more important than adherence to a fixed structure. Chapters 3–5 clearly illustrate how multi-level thinking can be adapted to a wide range of contexts and provide generalizable insights.

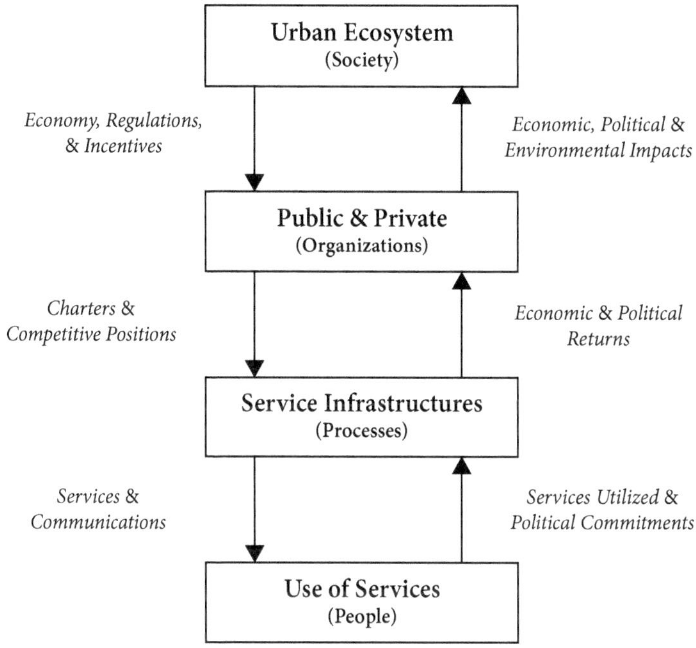

Figure 2.8 Multi-level model of urban systems

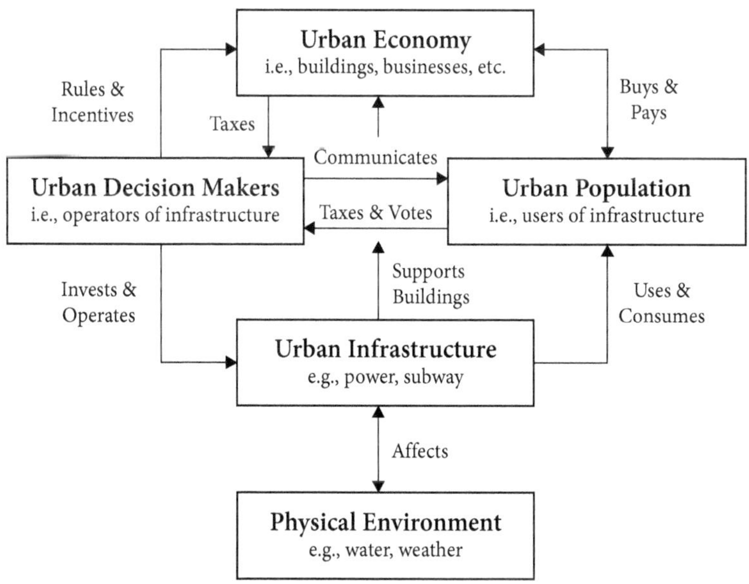

Figure 2.9 Revised multi-level model of urban systems

Methodology

Experiences with the above applications led to the development of an overall methodology for modeling and visualization of complex systems and enterprises (Rouse, 2015). The overall framework was further generalized as shown in Figure 2.10, in part to better align with the guidance provided in the book.

I hasten to emphasize the many variations among the versions of this figure that were tailored to the 10 examples in this chapter, as well as the 18 case studies in later chapters. The generalization of Figure 2.10 has to be tailored to each context and the questions of interest. For example, the physical level may enable human activity, e.g., in cities, or human activity may affect the physical environment, e.g., in climate change. Further, each version of Figure 2.10 is simply the starting point for a problem solving process that always results in morphing the representation to fit the problem.

A 10-step methodology was developed as shown in the left column of Table 2.1. The right column indicates how this methodology was applied in this book to the 18 case studies. Of particular note, the

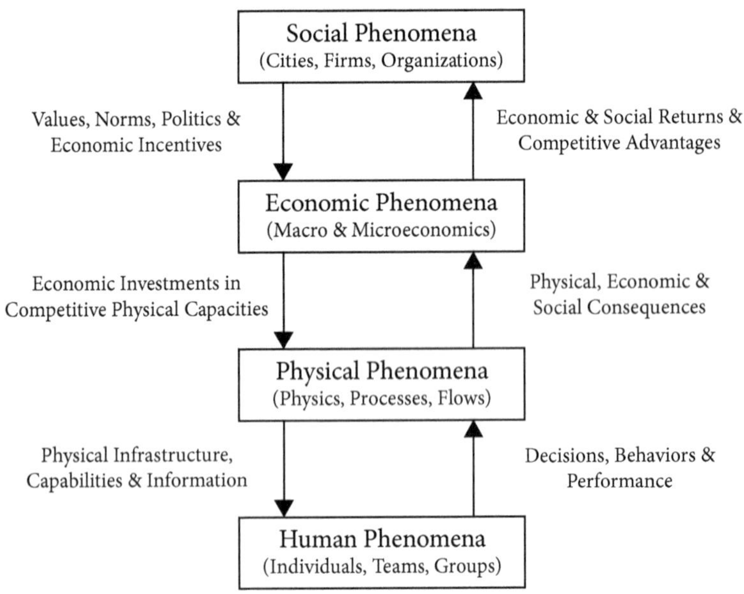

Figure 2.10 Further generalized multi-level framework

Table 2.1 Modeling and visualization methodology

Steps of methodology	As used in this book
Decide on the central questions of interest	What were the proximate, distal, and ultimate causes of failures?
Define key phenomena underlying these questions	Determination of phenomena at each level that contributed to failures
Develop one or more visualizations of relationships among phenomena	Comparisons of causes of failures across case studies
Determine key tradeoffs that appear to warrant deeper exploration	Interaction of causes of failures across levels and phenomena
Identify alternative representations of these phenomena	Alternative computational models that might be employed
Assess the ability to connect alternative representations	Model composition issues addressed and issues outlined
Determine a consistent set of assumptions	Not applicable
Identify data sets to support parameterization	Formal investigative reports of failures and related news publications
Program and verify computational instantiations	Not applicable
Validate model predictions, at least against baseline data	Assessment of extent to which causal explanations apply across case studies

Source: Rouse (2015).

methodology was used to guide multi-level analyses of the case studies, rather than development of computational models and associated visualizations. Chapters 6 and 7 discuss possible computational instantiations of the findings in this book, but such pursuits are well beyond the scope of this book.

Computational Modeling

There are several aspects of modeling. First, there is conceptual design of a multi-level model. This is the aspect addressed in this book in the context of the 18 case studies. Other aspects include detailed design and programming. These aspects are addressed in my recent books on modeling (Rouse, 2015, 2019).

Central decisions in conceptual design involve choosing computational representations. These choices are driven by what you want to predict, which is highly influenced by how the "state" of the system is conceptualized. Choices of representations are also constrained by what you are willing to assume, e.g., independence of successive events.

Multi-levels models usually involve combining representations within and across levels. This involves either literally integrating multiple representations or determining how variable values are communicated between levels. This can raise a variety of complicated composition issues as discussed earlier in this chapter, e.g., Pennock's bifurcations.

Once an initial conceptual design is available, attentions shifts to computational instantiations. This might involve software programming, but more often commercial modeling tools are employed. These tools usually include user-friendly interfaces, visualization functions, and debugging capabilities.

Interactive Visualization

My colleagues and I developed a simple methodology for designing visualizations (Rouse et al., 2016). Succinctly, one first identifies information use cases, including determination of knowledge levels of intended users. One then elaborates these use cases in terms of trajectories in an abstraction-aggregation space as discussed earlier in this chapter.

Next, one designs visualizations and controls for each point in the abstraction-aggregation space. Then, one integrates across visualizations and controls to dovetail the multiple representations. Finally, one integrates across use cases to minimize total number of displays and controls.

Immersion Laboratory

We use this methodology to create immersive experiences for decision makers. Hands-on immersion is essential to getting key stakeholders to buy into the multi-level modeling approach (Yu et al., 2016). We call these immersive environments policy flight simulators (Rouse, 2014), as suggested by several stakeholders from healthcare. They indicated that our original terminology—multi-level enterprise models—was meaningless to them. Flight simulators they understood. Two examples of policy flight simulators are discussed in Chapter 6.

Conclusions

This chapter began with relating my motivation in 2008 for adopting a multi-level modeling approach to understanding healthcare delivery. We then briefly explored the very rich history of this approach, including the nature of levels, relationships between levels, and computational issues.

This led to a rather terse review of 10 examples of previous applications in healthcare, national security, higher education, transportation, and urban systems. My goal was to illustrate the broad applicability of the approach, including how it needs to be adapted to the nature of the questions of interest and domain of application.

A methodology we have developed for multi-level modeling was quickly reviewed, showing how the steps of the methodology are pursued in this book. My intent was to show that modeling of complex systems and enterprises can be approached quite systematically. Thus, we are building upon some well-reasoned rigor.

The next step is to apply these concepts, models, methods, and tools to the 18 case studies in Chapters 3–5. Upon completion of these chapters, you will have perused 28 examples of multi-level modeling. This will hopefully have provided you with perhaps more than enough background to digest the concepts articulated in Chapters 6–8.

References

Abbott, R. (2006). Emergence explained: Abstractions. *Complexity*, 12 (1), 13–26.

Abbott, R. (2007). Putting complex systems to work. *Complexity*, 13 (2), 30–49.

Boustany, K., Pennock, M.J., Bell, T., Boustani, M., and Rouse, W.B. (2016). *Leveraging Computer Simulation Models in Healthcare Delivery Redesign*. Indianapolis, IN: Indiana University Health, Aging Brains Care Center.

Davis, P.K., Bankes, S.C., and Kahan, J.P. (1986). *A New Methodology for Modeling National Command Level Decision Making in War Games and Simulations*. Santa Monica, CA: Rand Corporation.

Davis, P.K., and Bigelow, J.H. (1998). *Experiments in Multi-Resolution Modeling*. Santa Monica, CA: Rand Corporation.

Davis, P.K., and Huber, R.K. (1992). *Variable-Resolution Combat Modeling: Motivations, Issues, and Principles*. Santa Monica, CA: Rand Corporation.

Davis, P.K., McDonald, T., Pendleton-Julian, A., O'Mahony, A., and Osoba, O. (2019). *Updating the Teaching of Policy Analysis to Better Address Complex Adaptive Social Systems*. Santa Monica, CA: Rand Corporation.

Davis, P.K., O'Mahony, A., and Pfautz, J. (eds) (2019). *Social-behavioral Modeling for Complex Systems*. New York: Wiley.

Haimes, Y.Y. (2004). *Identifying Risk through Hierarchical Holographic Modeling*. New York: Wiley.

Hall, A.D. (1989). *Metasystems Methodology: A New Synthesis and Unification*. New York: Pergamon.

Harvey, D.L., and Reed, M. (1997). Social science as the study of complex systems. In L.D. Kiel and E. Elliot, eds, *Chaos Theory in the Social Sciences: Foundations and Applications* (Chap. 13). Ann Arbor, MI: University of Michigan Press.

Heydari, B., and Pennock, M.J. (2018). Guiding the behavior of sociotechnical systems: The role of agent-based modeling. *Journal of Systems Engineering*, 21 (3), 210–26.

Johns, M.M.E., Madhavan, G., Nass, S.J., and Amankwah, F.K. (eds) (2019). *Guiding Cancer Control: A Path to Transformation*. Washington, DC: National Academies Press.

Lempert, R.J. (2019). Robust decision making (RDM). In V.A.W.J. Marchau et al., eds, *Decision Making under Deep Uncertainty* (Chap. 2). Berlin: Springer.

Madhavan, G., Phelps, C.E., Rouse, W.B., and Rappuoli, R. (2018). A vision for a systems architecture to integrate and transform population health. *Proceedings of the National Academy of Sciences*, 115 (50), 12,595–602.

McDermott, T., Rouse, W.B., Goodman, S., and Loper, M. (2013). Multi-level modeling of complex socio-technical systems. *Procedia Computer Science*, 16, 1132–41.

Mesarovic, M.D., Macko, D., and Takahara, Y. (1970). *Theory of Multi-level Hierarchical Systems*. New York: Academic Press.

Park, H., Clear, T., Rouse, W.B., Basole, R.C., Braunstein, M.L., Brigham, K.L., and Cunningham, L. (2012). Multi-level simulations of health delivery systems: A prospective tool for policy, strategy, planning, and management. *Journal of Service Science*, 4 (3), 253–68.

Pennock, M.J., and Gaffney, C. (2018). Managing epistemic uncertainty for multimodels of sociotechnical systems for decision support. *IEEE Systems Journal*, 12 (1), 184–95.

Pennock, M.J., Zhongyuan Yu, Z., Hirschman, K.B., Pepe, K.P., Pauly, M.V., Naylor, M.D., and Rouse, W.B. (2018). Developing a policy flight simulator to facilitate the adoption of an evidence-based intervention. *IEEE Journal of Translational Engineering in Health and Medicine*,6 (1), 1–12.

Rasmussen, J. (1983). Skills, rules, and knowledge: Signals, signs, and symbols, and other distinction in human performance models. *IEEE Transactions on Systems, Man, and Cybernetics*, 14 (3), 257–66.

Rasmussen, J. (1986). *Information Processing and Human–Machine Interaction*. New York: North-Holland.

Rasmussen, J., Pejtersen, A.M., and Goodstein, L.P. (1994). *Cognitive Systems Engineering*. New York: Wiley.

Rosen, R. (1978). *Fundamentals of Measurement and Representation of Natural Systems*. New York: North Holland.

Rouse, W.B. (2009). Engineering perspectives on healthcare delivery: Can we afford technological innovation in healthcare? *Journal of Systems Research and Behavioral Science*, 26, 1–10. Reprinted in Grossman, C., Goolsby, A., Olsen, L.A., and McGinnis, J.M. (eds) (2011). *Engineering a Learning Healthcare System: A Look at the Future* (pp. 65–75). Washington, DC: National Academies Press.

Rouse, W.B. (2014). Human interaction with policy flight simulators. *Journal of Applied Ergonomics*, 45 (1), 72–7.

Rouse, W.B. (2015). *Modeling and Visualization of Complex Systems and Enterprises: Explorations of Physical, Human, Economic, and Social Phenomena*. Hoboken, NJ: John Wiley.

Rouse, W.B. (2016). *Universities as Complex Enterprises: How Academia Works, Why It Works These Ways, and Where the University Enterprise Is Headed*. New York: Wiley.

Rouse, W.B. (2019). *Computing Possible Futures: Model-based Explorations of "What If?"* Oxford: Oxford University Press.

Rouse, W.B., and Cortese, D.A. (eds) (2010). *Engineering the System of Healthcare Delivery*. Amsterdam: IOS Press.

Rouse, W.B., Johns, M.M.E., and Pepe, K. (2017). Learning in the health-care enterprise. *Journal of Learning Health Systems*, 1 (4). https://doi.org/10.1002/lrh2.10024.

Rouse, W.B., Johns, M.M.E., and Pepe, K. (2019). Service supply chains for population health: Overcoming fragmentation of service delivery ecosystems. *Journal of Learning Health Systems*, 3 (2), https://doi.org/10.1002/lrh2.10186.

Rouse, W.B., Lombardi, J.V., and Craig, D.D. (2018). Modeling research universities: Predicting probable futures of public vs. private and large vs. small research universities. *Proceedings of the National Academy of Sciences*, 115 (50), 12,582–9.

Rouse, W.B., Naylor, M.D., Yu, Z., Pennock, M.P., Hirschman, K.B., Pauly, M.V., and Pepe, K.P. (2019). Policy flight simulators: Accelerating decisions to adopt evidence-based health interventions. *Journal of Healthcare Management*, 64 (4), 231–41.

Rouse, W.B., Pennock, M.J., Oghbaie, M., and Liu, C. (2016). Interactive visualizations for decision support: Application of Rasmussen's abstraction-aggregation hierarchy. *Journal of Applied Ergonomics*, 59, 541–53.

Rouse, W.B., and Serban, N. (2014). *Understanding and Managing the Complexity of Healthcare*. Cambridge, MA: MIT Press.

Tolk, A. (2003). The levels of conceptual interoperability model. *Proceedings of the Fall Simulation Interoperability Workshop*. Orlando, Florida, September.

Tolk, A. (ed.) (2013). *Ontology, Epistemology, and Teleology for Modeling and Simulation*. Berlin: Springer-Verlag.

Tolk, A., Diallo, S., and Saurabh Mittal, S. (eds) (2018). *Emergent Behavior in Complex Systems Engineering: A Modeling and Simulation Approach*. New York: Wiley.

Wallerstein, I.M. (2004). *World Systems Analysis: An Introduction*. Durham, NC: Duke University Press.

Winsberg, E. (2010). *Science in the Age of Computer Simulation*. Chicago, IL: University of Chicago Press.

Yu, Z., Rouse, W.B., Serban, S., and Veral, E. (2016). A data-rich agent-based decision support model for hospital consolidation. *Journal of Enterprise Transformation*, 6 (3/4), 136–61.

3

Failures of Complex Systems

Introduction

This chapter employs six case studies as a basis for exploring failures of complex systems. As indicated in Table 3.1, these case studies are drawn from domains of energy, space, and the ocean. All of these case studies involve failures of physical elements of these systems. However, as will be seen, the causes and consequences of these failures were much more pervasive than simply physical failures.

Note that this chapter addresses failures of complex systems, while Chapters 4 and 5 address failures of complex enterprises and failures of complex ecosystems, both of which are also exemplars of complex systems. All three chapters—and all 18 case studies—involve systems laced with behavioral and social phenomena that make it difficult to predict what *will* happen (Rouse, 2015) and, consequently, results in our relying on predictions of what *might* happen (Rouse, 2019). As these case studies illustrate, this complexity makes failure management rather difficult.

Three Mile Island and Chernobyl

The heat source in a nuclear power plant is a nuclear reactor rather than, for example, coal. This heat is used to generate steam. This steam drives a turbine connected to a generator that produces electricity. The operation and maintenance of nuclear plants, as well as its fuel costs, are relatively low and make them useful suppliers of a utility's base load. The cost of dealing with spent fuel, however, remains a challenge.

Failure Management: Malfunctions of Technologies, Organizations, and Society. William B. Rouse, Oxford University Press (2021). © William B. Rouse. DOI: 10.1093/oso/9780198870999.003.0003

Table 3.1 Consequences of failures of complex systems

Case study	Domain	Proximal consequences
Three Mile Island	Energy	Minor radiation leak, no deaths, confidence lost
Chernobyl	Energy	Major radiation leak, many deaths, confidence lost
Challenger	Space	Crew lost, confidence lost
Columbia	Space	Crew lost, confidence lost
Valdez	Ocean	Environment despoiled and economic consequences
Horizon	Ocean	Environment despoiled and economic consequences

I became heavily involved in the nuclear power industry in the 1980s when a variety of research initiatives were pursued following the Three Mile Island incident. We had several research contracts from the Nuclear Regulatory Commission and the Electric Power Research Institute, as well as consulting contracts with several electric utility companies. This research focused on the training and aiding of nuclear power plant operators, i.e., the crew of people in the control room.

Their jobs were challenging due to the fact that most of the time nothing happened. They just monitored the process flows, levels, temperatures, etc. Occasionally, however, hundreds of alarms went off and the crew had to determine the root cause of all these alarms. The training and decision support capabilities we addressed were intended to help in such situations.

Three Mile Island (1979)

This case study draws heavily upon the *Report of the President's Commission on the Accident at Three Mile Island* (TMI, 1979). The accident occurred at the Three Mile Island power plant near Harrisburg, PA on March 28, 1979 in TMI-2, one of the two nuclear reactors at the site.

Accident Timeline. At 04:00, TMI-2 feedwater pumps, condensate booster pumps, and condensate pumps shut down, causing a turbine trip. With the steam generators no longer receiving feedwater, heat and pressure increased in the reactor coolant system, causing the reactor to perform an emergency shutdown, inserting control rods into the core to halt the nuclear chain reaction. Steam was no longer being fed to the turbine. Consequently, heat was no longer being removed from the reactor's primary water loop.

Once the secondary feedwater pumps stopped, three auxiliary pumps activated automatically. However, because the valves had been closed for routine maintenance, the system was unable to pump any water. The closure of these valves was a violation of a key Nuclear Regulatory Commission (NRC) rule, according to which the reactor must be shut down if all auxiliary feed pumps are closed for maintenance. NRC officials later singled this out as a key failure.

The loss of heat removal from the primary loop and the failure of the auxiliary system to activate caused the primary loop pressure to increase, triggering the pilot-operated relief valve at the top of the pressure regulator tank to open automatically. The relief valve should have closed when the excess pressure had been released. However, while electric power to the solenoid controlling the valve was automatically cut, the relief valve stuck open because of a mechanical fault. The open valve permitted coolant water to escape from the primary system, and was the principal mechanical cause of the primary coolant system depressurization and partial core disintegration that followed.

Critical problems were revealed in the investigation of the reactor control system's user interface. Despite the valve being stuck open, a light on the control panel ostensibly indicated that the valve was closed. In fact the light did not indicate the position of the valve, only the status of the solenoid, thus giving false evidence of a closed valve. As a result, the operators did not correctly diagnose the problem for several hours.

The design of the pilot-operated relief valve indicator light was fundamentally flawed. The bulb was simply connected in parallel with the valve solenoid. This implied that the pilot-operated relief valve was shut when the light went dark, but did not verify the actual position of the valve. The unlighted lamp misled the operators and caused the operators considerable confusion, because the pressure, temperature, and coolant levels in the primary circuit, so far as they could observe them via their instruments, were not behaving as they would have if the pilot-operated relief valve were shut. This confusion contributed to the severity of the accident because the operators were unable to move beyond their assumptions that conflicted with what their instruments were telling them.

The operators had not been trained to understand the ambiguous nature of the pilot-operated relief valve indicator and to look for alternative confirmation that the main relief valve was closed. A downstream temperature indicator, the sensor for which was located in the tail pipe between the pilot-operated relief valve and the pressurizer relief tank, could have hinted at a stuck valve had operators noticed its higher-than-normal reading. It was not, however, part of the suite of indicators intended for use after an incident, and personnel had not been trained to use it. Its location on the back of the seven-foot-high instrument panel also meant that it was effectively out of sight.

As the pressure in the primary system continued to decrease, reactor coolant continued to flow, but it was boiling inside the core, leading to steam voids in coolant channels, blocking the flow of liquid coolant and greatly increasing the fuel cladding temperature. Operators judged the level of water in the core solely by the level in the pressurizer. Since it was high, they assumed that the core was properly covered with coolant, unaware that because of steam forming in the reactor vessel, the indicator provided misleading readings. Indications of high water levels contributed to their confusion about the state of the system. This was a key contributor to their failure to recognize the accident as a loss-of-coolant accident, and led them to turn off the emergency core cooling pumps, which had automatically started after core coolant loss began.

With the pilot-operated relief valve still open, the pressurizer relief tank that collected the discharge from the pilot-operated relief valve overfilled, resulting in the containment building sump filling and sounding an alarm. This alarm, along with higher than normal temperatures on the pilot-operated relief valve discharge line and unusually high containment building temperatures and pressures, were clear indications that there was an ongoing loss-of-coolant accident, but these indications were initially ignored by operators. The relief diaphragm of the pressurizer relief tank ruptured, and radioactive coolant began to leak out into the general containment building. This radioactive coolant was pumped from the containment-building sump to an auxiliary building, outside the main containment.

After almost 80 minutes of slow temperature rise, the primary loop's four main reactor coolant pumps began to cavitate as a steam bubble/water mixture, rather than water, passed through them. The pumps were shut down, and it was believed that natural circulation would continue the water movement. Steam in the system prevented flow through the core, and as the water stopped circulating it was converted to steam in increasing amounts. About 130 minutes after the first malfunction, the top of the reactor core was exposed and the intense heat caused a reaction to occur between the steam forming in the reactor core and the zircaloy nuclear fuel rod cladding. This reaction melted the nuclear fuel rod cladding and damaged the fuel pellets, which released radioactive isotopes to the reactor coolant, and produced hydrogen gas that is believed to have later caused a small explosion in the containment building.

At 06:00, there was a shift change in the control room. A new arrival noticed that the temperature in the pilot-operated relief valve tail pipe and the holding tanks was excessive and used a backup valve to shut off the coolant venting via the pilot-operated relief valve, but around 32,000 gallons of coolant had already leaked from the primary loop. It was not until 165 minutes after the start of the problem that radiation alarms activated as contaminated water reached detectors. By then, the radiation levels in the primary coolant water were around 300 times expected levels, and the general containment building was seriously contaminated.

Findings and Recommendations. The overall recommendation of the Commission was: "To prevent nuclear accidents as serious as Three Mile Island, fundamental changes will be necessary in the organization, procedures, and practices—and above all—in the attitudes of the Nuclear Regulatory Commission and, to the extent that the institutions we investigated are typical, of the nuclear industry."

This recommendation was based on several findings:

- "The fundamental problems are people-related problems, not equipment problems."
- "The equipment was sufficiently good that, except for human failures, the major accident at Three Mile Island would have been a minor incident."
- "We are disturbed both by the highly uneven quality of emergency plans and by the problems created by multiple jurisdictions in the case of radiation emergency."
- "The response to the emergency was dominated by an atmosphere of almost total confusion."
- "The major health effect of the accident was found to be mental stress."

Four more specific findings were:

- "Training of the TMI operators was greatly deficient."
- "Specific operating procedures are at the very least confusing and could be read in such a way as to lead the operators to take the incorrect actions they did."
- "The control room was lacking, with hundreds of alarms and some indicators placed in locations where the operators cannot see them."
- "Lessons from previous accidents did not result in new, clear instructions being passed on to the operators."

Multi-level Interpretation. These findings and conclusions can be framed in the multi-level framework discussed in Chapter 2, where the levels for this case study are personnel, plant, utility, and government:

- Government: Lack of oversight
- Utility: Production pressures; lack of incorporation of lessons learned
- Plant: Lack of consideration of complex failure scenarios
- Personnel: Serious design flaws—human factors, procedures, training

Chernobyl (1986)

This case study draws heavily upon the *Report of the Accident at the Chernobyl Nuclear Power Station* (NRC, 1987), as well as reports by the International Nuclear Safety Advisory Group (INSAG, 1986, 1992). The accident occurred on April 26, 1986 at the No. 4 nuclear reactor in the Chernobyl Nuclear Power Plant, near the city of Pripyat in the north of the Ukraine.

Timeline. The Chernobyl power plant had been in operation for two years without the ability to ride through the first 60–75 seconds of a total loss of electric power, and thus the plant lacked an important safety feature. A test was needed to assure the safety of the plant during a loss of electrical power. The test focused on the switching sequences of electrical supplies to the reactor. The test procedure was expected to begin with an automatic emergency shutdown. No detrimental effect on the safety of the reactor was anticipated, so the test program was not formally coordinated with either the chief designer of the reactor or the scientific manager. Instead, only the director of the plant approved it. Even this approval was not consistent with established procedures.

The thermal output of the reactor was to have been no lower than 700 MW at the start of the experiment. If prescribed test conditions had been maintained, the procedure would almost certainly have been carried out safely. The eventual disaster resulted from an operational misstep that had let the output fall below the approved level and attempts to increase the reactor output.

The station managers' desires to satisfy the safety requirement may explain why they continued the test even when serious problems arose, and why the requisite approval for the test had not been sought from the Soviet nuclear oversight regulator (even though there was a representative at the complex of four reactors).

The experimental procedure was intended to run as follows:

1. The reactor was to be running at a low power level, between 700 MW and 800 MW

2. The steam-turbine generator was to be run up to full speed
3. When these conditions were achieved, the steam supply for the turbine generator was to be closed off
4. Turbine generator performance was to be recorded to determine whether it could provide the bridging power for coolant pumps until the emergency diesel generators started to provide power to the cooling pumps automatically
5. After the emergency generators reached normal operating speed and voltage, the turbine generator would be allowed to continue to freewheel down.

At 01:23:04, the test began. Four of the main circulating pumps (MCP) were active (of the eight total, six were normally active under regular operation). The steam to the turbines was shut off, beginning a run-down of the turbine generator. The diesel generators started and sequentially picked up loads. The generators were to have completely picked up the power needs. In the interim, the power for the MCPs was to be supplied by the turbine generator as it coasted down. As the momentum of the turbine generator decreased, so did the power it produced for the pumps. The water flow rate decreased, leading to increased formation of steam voids in the coolant flowing up through the fuel pressure tubes.

Unlike Western light-water reactors, the Chernobyl reactor has a positive void coefficient of reactivity at low power level, meaning that when cooling water boils excessively in the fuel pressure tubes it produces large steam voids in the coolant rather than small bubbles. This intensifies the nuclear chain reaction, as it reduces the relative volume of cooling water available to absorb neutrons. The consequent power increase then produces more voids which further intensifies the chain reaction, and so on. Given this characteristic, reactor No. 4 was now at risk of a runaway increase in its core power with nothing to restrain it.

Throughout most of the experiment the local automatic control system successfully counteracted this positive feedback, by inserting control rods into the reactor core to limit the power rise. However, this system had control of only 12 rods, as the reactor operators had manually retracted nearly all the others.

A scram (emergency shutdown) of the reactor was initiated. The scram was started when the infamous AZ-5 button of the reactor emergency protection system was pressed. This engaged the drive mechanism on all control rods to fully insert them, including the manual control rods that had been withdrawn earlier. The reason why the button was pressed is not known, whether it was done as an emergency measure in response to rising temperatures, or simply as a routine method of shutting down the reactor upon completion of the experiment.

One view is that the scram may have been ordered as a response to the unexpected rapid power increase, although there is no recorded data showing this. It has been suggested that the button was not manually pressed, and that the scram signal was automatically produced by the emergency protection system, but the control system registered a manual scram signal. Despite this, the question as to when or even whether the AZ-5 button was pressed was the subject of debate. There were assertions that the manual scram was initiated due to the initial rapid power acceleration. Others suggested that the button was not pressed until the reactor began to self-destruct, while others believe that it happened earlier and under calm conditions.

When the AZ-5 button was pressed, the insertion of control rods into the reactor core began. The control rod insertion mechanism moved the rods at 0.4 meters per second, so that the rods took 18 to 20 seconds to travel the full 7-meter height of the core. A bigger problem was the design of the control rods, each of which had a graphite neutron moderator section attached to its end to boost reactor output by displacing water when the control rod section had been fully withdrawn from the reactor.

Consequently, injecting a control rod downward into the reactor in a scram initially displaced (neutron-absorbing) water in the lower portion of the reactor with (neutron-moderating) graphite. Thus, an emergency scram initially increased the reaction rate in the lower part of the core. This behavior had been discovered when the initial insertion of control rods in another reactor at Ignalina Nuclear Power Plant in 1983 induced a power spike. Procedural countermeasures were not implemented in response to Ignalina.

INSAG-7 (1992) later stated, "Apparently, there was a widespread view that the conditions under which the positive scram effect would be important would never occur. However, they did appear in almost every detail in the course of the actions leading to the (Chernobyl) accident."

A few seconds into the scram, a power spike did occur and the core overheated, causing some of the fuel rods to fracture, blocking the control rod columns and jamming the control rods at one-third insertion, with the graphite water-displacers still in the lower part of the core. Within three seconds the reactor output rose above 530 MW.

Instruments did not register the subsequent course of events. It was reconstructed through mathematical simulation. Per the simulation, the power spike would have caused an increase in fuel temperature and steam buildup, leading to a rapid increase in steam pressure. This would cause the fuel cladding to fail, releasing the fuel elements into the coolant, and rupturing the channels in which these elements were located.

As the scram was starting, the reactor output jumped to around 30,000 MW thermal, 10 times its normal operational output, the indicated last reading on the power meter on the control panel. It was not possible to reconstruct the precise sequence of the processes that led to the destruction of the reactor and the power unit building, but a steam explosion, like the explosion of a steam boiler from excess vapor pressure, appears to have been the next event. There is a general understanding that it was explosive steam pressure from the damaged fuel channels escaping into the reactor's exterior cooling structure that caused the explosion that destroyed the reactor casing, tearing off and blasting the upper plate through the roof of the reactor building. This was believed to be the first explosion that many heard.

This explosion ruptured further fuel channels, as well as severing most of the coolant lines feeding the reactor chamber, and as a result, the remaining coolant flashed to steam and escaped the reactor core. The total water loss in combination with a high positive void coefficient further increased the reactor's thermal power.

A second, more powerful explosion occurred about two or three seconds after the first; this explosion dispersed the damaged core and effectively terminated the nuclear chain reaction. This explosion also compromised more of the reactor containment vessel and ejected hot lumps of graphite moderator. The ejected graphite and the demolished channels still in the remains of the reactor vessel caught fire on exposure to air, greatly contributing to the spread of radioactive fallout and the contamination of outlying areas.

According to observers outside Unit 4, burning lumps of material and sparks shot into the air above the reactor. Some of them fell onto the roof of the machine hall and started a fire. About 25 percent of the red-hot graphite blocks and overheated material from the fuel channels was ejected. Parts of the graphite blocks and fuel channels were out of the reactor building. As a result of the damage to the building, an airflow through the core was established by the high temperature of the core. The air ignited the hot graphite and started a graphite fire.

After the larger explosion, a number of employees at the power station went outside to get a clearer view of the extent of the damage. One such survivor, Alexander Yuvchenko, recounts that once he stepped outside and looked up towards the reactor hall, he saw a "very beautiful" laser-like beam of blue light caused by the ionized-air glow that appeared to "flood up into infinity."

There were initially several hypotheses about the nature of the second explosion. One view was that the second explosion was caused by the combustion of hydrogen, which had been produced either by the overheated steam-zirconium reaction or by the reaction of red-hot graphite with steam that produced hydrogen and carbon monoxide. Another hypothesis was that the second explosion was a thermal explosion of the reactor as a result of the uncontrollable escape of fast neutrons caused by the complete water loss in the reactor core. A third hypothesis was that the second explosion was another steam explosion. According to this version, the first explosion was a more minor steam explosion in the circulating loop, causing a loss of coolant flow and pressure that in turn caused the water still in the core to flash to steam. This second explosion then caused the majority of the damage to the reactor and containment building.

Contributing Factors. The INSAG-1 (1986) and INSAG-7 (1992) reports both identified operator error as an issue of concern. INSAG-7 identified that there were numerous other issues that contributed to the incident. These contributing factors include (IAEA, 1992):

- The plant was not designed to safety standards in effect and incorporated unsafe features
- "Inadequate safety analysis" was performed
- There was "insufficient attention to independent safety review"
- "Operating procedures (were) not founded satisfactorily in safety analysis"
- Safety information not adequately and effectively communicated between operators, and between operators and designers
- The operators did not adequately understand safety aspects of the plant
- Operators did not sufficiently respect formal requirements of operational and test procedures
- The regulatory regime was insufficient to effectively counter pressures for production
- There was a general lack of safety culture in nuclear matters at the national level as well as locally.

Multi-level Interpretation. These findings and conclusions can be framed in the multi-level framework discussed in Chapter 2, where the levels for this case study are personnel, plant, utility, and government:

- Government: Lack of oversight, repression of communications
- Utility: Production pressures; lack of incorporation of lessons learned
- Plant: Lack of consideration of complex failure scenarios
- Personnel: Serious design flaws—human factors, procedures, training.

NASA Challenger and NASA Columbia

The space shuttle was a reusable low Earth orbital spacecraft system operated by the National Aeronautics and Space Administration from 1981 to 2011. Its official program name was Space Transportation System (STS). Five complete shuttle systems were built and used on a total of 135 missions, launched from the Kennedy Space Center in Florida.

There were three main parts of the space shuttle. The orbiter was the part that looked like an airplane. The orbiter flew around Earth. The astronauts rode and lived in this part. The external tank was a large orange fuel tank. The solid rocket boosters were two thin rockets on either side of the orbiter. These boosters provided the lift from Earth's gravity.

I was heavily involved with NASA throughout the 1980s and 1990s. During 1986–1993, I served on the Aerospace Research and Technology Subcommittee of the Space Systems and Technology Advisory Committee (SSTAC/ARTS). I served on several other ad hoc advisory committees, both for aeronautics and space; a particularly memorable committee addressed the mission to Mars. I also had contractual relationships with the Ames, Glenn, and Langley research centers. The focus of these activities included mission planning, technology development, and training and aiding of personnel.

NASA Challenger (1986)

This case study draws heavily upon the *Report of the President's Commission on the Space Shuttle Challenger Accident* (NASA, 1986). On January 28, 1986, the NASA Space Shuttle orbiter on the tenth flight of Space Shuttle Challenger broke apart 73 seconds into its flight, killing all seven crew members: five NASA astronauts, one payload specialist, and a civilian school teacher.

Timeline. The disintegration of the vehicle began after a joint in its right solid rocket booster (SRB) failed at liftoff. The failure was caused by the failure of O-ring seals used in the joint that were not designed to handle the unusually cold conditions that existed at this launch. The seals' failure caused a breach in the SRB joint, allowing pressurized burning gas from within the solid rocket motor to reach the outside and impinge upon the adjacent SRB and external fuel tank. This led to the separation of the right-hand SRB and the structural failure of the external tank. Aerodynamic forces broke up the orbiter.

The Rogers Commission (NASA, 1986) found NASA's organizational culture and decision-making processes had been key contributing factors to the accident, with the agency violating its own safety rules. NASA managers had long known that the design of the SRBs contained a potentially catastrophic flaw in the O-rings, but they had failed to address this problem properly. NASA managers also disregarded warnings from engineers about the dangers of launching posed by the low temperatures of that morning, and failed to adequately report these technical concerns to their superiors.

Each of the Space Shuttle's two Solid Rocket Boosters was constructed of seven sections, six of which were permanently joined in pairs at the factory. For each flight, the four resulting segments were then assembled in the Vehicle Assembly Building at Kennedy Space Center, with three field joints. The factory joints were sealed with asbestos-silica insulation applied over the joint, while each field joint was sealed with two rubber O-rings. After the destruction of Challenger, the number of O-rings per field joint was increased to three. The seals of all of the SRB joints were required to contain the hot, high-pressure gases produced by the burning solid propellant inside, thus forcing them out of the nozzle at the aft end of each rocket.

Evidence of serious O-ring erosion was present as early as the second space shuttle mission, STS-2, which was flown by Columbia. Contrary to NASA regulations, the Marshall Center did not report this problem to senior management at NASA, but opted to keep the problem within their reporting channels with Thiokol. Even after the O-rings were redesignated as "Criticality 1"—meaning that their failure would result in the destruction of the Orbiter—no one at Marshall suggested that the shuttles be grounded until the flaw could be fixed.

By 1985, with seven of nine shuttle launches that year using boosters displaying O-ring erosion or hot gas blow-by, NASA realized that they had a potentially catastrophic problem on their hands. Perhaps most concerning was the launch of STS-51-B in April 1985, flown by Challenger, in which the worst O-ring damage to date was discovered in post-flight analysis. The primary O-ring of the left nozzle had been eroded so extensively that it had failed to seal, and for the first time hot gases had eroded the secondary O-ring. They began the process of redesigning the joint with 3 inches (76 mm) of additional steel around the tang. This tang would grip the inner face of the joint and prevent it from rotating. They did not call for a halt to shuttle flights until the joints could be redesigned, but rather treated the problem as an acceptable flight risk.

Later review of launch film showed that strong puffs of dark gray smoke were emitted from the right-hand SRB near the aft strut that attached the booster to the ET. It was later determined that these smoke puffs were caused by the opening and closing of the aft field joint of the right-hand SRB. The booster's casing had ballooned under the stress of ignition. As a result of this ballooning, the metal parts of the casing bent away from each other, opening a gap through which hot gases leaked. This had occurred in previous launches, but each time the primary O-ring had shifted out of its groove and formed a seal. Although the SRB was not designed to function this way, it appeared to work well enough.

While this extrusion was taking place, hot gases leaked past (a process called "blow-by"), damaging the O-rings until a seal was made. Investigations determined that the amount of damage to the O-rings was directly related to the time it took for extrusion to occur, and that cold weather, by causing the O-rings to harden, lengthened the time of extrusion. The redesigned SRB field joint used subsequent to the Challenger accident used an additional interlocking mortise and tang with a third O-ring, mitigating blow-by.

On the morning of the disaster, the primary O-ring had become so hard due to the cold that it could not seal in time. The temperature had dropped below the glass transition temperature of the

O-rings. Above the glass transition temperature, the O-rings display properties of elasticity and flexibility, while below the glass transition temperature, they become rigid and brittle. The secondary O-ring was not in its seated position due to the metal bending. There was now no barrier to the gases, and both O-rings were vaporized.

As the vehicle cleared the tower, the main engines (SSMEs) were operating at 104 percent of their rated maximum thrust, and control switched from the Launch Control Center (LCC) at Kennedy to the Mission Control Center (MCC) at Johnson Space Center in Houston, Texas. To prevent aerodynamic forces from structurally overloading the orbiter, the SSMEs began throttling down to limit the velocity of the shuttle in the dense lower atmosphere, per normal operating procedure. Seconds later, at about 19,000 feet, Challenger passed through Mach 1 and the SSMEs began throttling back up to 104 percent as the vehicle passed beyond the period of maximum aerodynamic pressure on the vehicle.

Soon after, the shuttle experienced a series of wind shear events that were stronger than on any previous flight. A tracking film camera captured the beginnings of a plume near the right SRB. Unknown to those on Challenger or in Houston, hot gas had begun to leak through a growing hole in one of the right-hand SRB joints. The force of the wind shear shattered the temporary oxide seal that had taken the place of the damaged O-rings, removing the last barrier to flame passing through the joint. Had it not been for the wind shear, the fortuitous oxide seal might have held through booster burnout.

Within a second, the plume became well defined and intense. Internal pressure in the right SRB began to drop because of the rapidly enlarging hole in the failed joint, and there was soon visual evidence of flame burning through the joint and impinging on the external tank. Soon after, the plume suddenly changed shape, indicating that a leak had begun in the liquid hydrogen tank, located in the aft portion of the external tank. The nozzles of the main engines pivoted under computer control to compensate for the unbalanced thrust produced by the booster burn-through.

At this stage the situation still seemed normal both to the crew and to flight controllers. Richard O. Covey informed the crew that they were "go at throttle up", and Commander Dick Scobee confirmed, "Roger, go at throttle up." This was the last communication from Challenger on the air-to-ground loop.

A tracking camera located north of the pad captured the SRB plume as it burned through the external tank. The damaged SRB was seen exiting the vapor cloud with clear signs of O-ring failure on one of its segments. The right SRB pulled away from the aft strut attaching it to the external tank. Later analysis of telemetry data showed a sudden lateral acceleration to the right, which may have been felt by the crew. The last statement captured by the crew cabin recorder came just half a second after this acceleration, when pilot Michael J. Smith said, "Uh-oh." Smith may also have been responding to onboard indications of main engine performance, or to falling pressures in the external fuel tank.

The aft dome of the liquid hydrogen tank failed, producing a propulsive force that rammed the hydrogen tank into the LOX tank. At the same time, the right SRB rotated about the forward attach strut, and struck the intertank structure. The external tank at this point suffered a complete structural failure, the LH2 and LOX tanks rupturing, mixing, and igniting, creating a fireball that enveloped the whole stack.

The breakup of the vehicle began at an altitude of 48,000 feet. With the external tank disintegrating (and with the semi-detached right SRB contributing its thrust on an anomalous vector), Challenger veered from its correct attitude with respect to the local airflow and was quickly ripped apart by abnormal aerodynamic forces. The two SRBs, which could withstand greater aerodynamic loads, separated and continued in uncontrolled powered flight.

The more robustly constructed crew cabin also survived the breakup of the launch vehicle. The detached cabin continued along a ballistic trajectory and was observed exiting the cloud of gases 25 seconds after the breakup of the vehicle. The altitude of the crew compartment peaked at a height of 65,000 feet. It is likely that crew members lost consciousness due to loss of cabin pressure and probably quickly died due to oxygen deficiency.

Multi-level Interpretation. These findings and conclusions can be framed in the multi-level framework discussed in Chapter 2, where the levels for this case study are vehicle, mission, program, and government:

- Government: Focus on delivering missions rather than safety
- Program: Schedule driven; lack of incorporation of lessons learned
- Mission: Flawed launch procedures
- Vehicle: Serious design flaws, O-rings.

NASA Columbia (2003)

This case study draws heavily upon the *Report of the Columbia Accident Investigation Board* (NASA, 2003). On February 1, 2003, the Space Shuttle Columbia disintegrated during atmospheric entry, killing all seven members of the crew. During the launch, a piece of foam insulation broke off from the Space Shuttle external tank and struck the left wing of the orbiter. When Columbia re-entered the atmosphere of Earth, the damage allowed hot atmospheric gases to penetrate the heat shield and destroy the internal wing structure, which caused the spacecraft to become unstable and break apart.

Timeline. A few previous shuttle launches had seen damage ranging from minor to nearly catastrophic from foam shedding, but some engineers suspected that the damage to Columbia was more serious. NASA managers limited the investigation, reasoning that the crew could not have fixed the problem if it had been confirmed.

After the disaster, Space Shuttle flight operations were suspended for more than two years, as they had been after the Challenger disaster. Construction of the International Space Station (ISS) was put on hold. The station relied entirely on the Russian Roscosmos State Space Corporation for resupply for 29 months, until Shuttle flights resumed with STS-114, and 41 months for crew rotation until STS-121.

Several technical and organizational changes were made, including adding a thorough on-orbit inspection to determine how well the shuttle's thermal protection system had endured the ascent, and keeping a designated rescue mission ready in case irreparable damage was found. Except for one final mission to repair the Hubble Space Telescope, subsequent shuttle missions were flown only to the ISS so that the crew could use it as a haven in case damage to the orbiter prevented safe re-entry.

Roughly 80 seconds after launch from Kennedy Space Center, a suitcase-sized piece of foam broke off from the external tank, striking Columbia's left wing reinforced carbon-carbon panels. As demonstrated by ground experiments conducted by the Columbia Accident Investigation Board, this likely created a 6-to-10-inch-diameter hole, allowing hot gases to enter the wing when Columbia later re-entered the atmosphere.

Ramp insulation had been observed falling off, in whole or in part, on four previous flights, and most recently just two launches before STS-107. All affected shuttle missions completed successfully. NASA management came to refer to this phenomenon as "foam shedding". As with the O-ring erosion problems that ultimately doomed the Space Shuttle Challenger, NASA management became accustomed to these phenomena when no serious consequences resulted from these earlier episodes. This phenomenon was termed "normalization of deviance" by sociologist Diane Vaughan in her book on the Challenger launch decision process (Vaughan, 1997).

STS-112 was the first flight with the "ET cam", a video feed mounted on the external tank for the purpose of giving greater insight to the foam shedding problem. During that launch a chunk of foam broke away from the ET bipod ramp and hit the SRB-ET attach ring near the bottom of the left solid rocket booster (SRB) causing a dent 4 inches wide and 3 inches deep in it. After STS-112, NASA leaders analyzed the situation and decided to press ahead under the justification that "the ET is safe to fly with no new concerns (and no added risk)" of further foam strikes.

Video taken during lift-off of STS-107 was routinely reviewed two hours later and revealed nothing unusual. The following day, higher-resolution film that had been processed overnight revealed the foam debris striking the left wing, potentially damaging the thermal protection on the Space Shuttle. At the time, the exact location where the foam struck the wing could not be determined due to the low resolution of the tracking camera footage.

Post-disaster analysis revealed that two previous shuttle launches also had bipod ramp foam loss that went undetected. In addition, protuberance air load ramp foam had also shed pieces, and there were also spot losses from large-area foams.

In a risk-management scenario similar to the Challenger disaster, NASA management failed to recognize the relevance of engineering concerns for safety and suggestions for imaging to inspect possible damage, and failed to respond to engineers' requests about the status of astronaut inspection of the left wing. Engineers made three separate requests for Department of Defense (DOD) imaging of the shuttle in orbit to determine damage more precisely. While the images were not guaranteed to show the damage, the capability existed for imaging of sufficient resolution to provide meaningful examination. NASA management did not honor the requests and in some cases intervened to stop the DOD from assisting.

Throughout the risk assessment process, senior NASA managers were influenced by their belief that nothing could be done even if damage were detected. This affected their stance on investigation urgency, thoroughness, and possible contingency actions. They decided to conduct a parametric "what-if" scenario study more suited to determine risk probabilities of future events, instead of inspecting and assessing the actual damage.

Much of the risk assessment hinged on damage predictions to the thermal protection system. These fall into two categories: damage to the silica tile on the wing lower surface, and damage to the reinforced carbon-carbon leading-edge panels. The thermal protection system includes a third category of components, thermal-insulating blankets, but damage predictions are not typically performed on them. Damage assessments on the thermal blankets can be performed after an anomaly has been observed, and this was done at least once after the return to flight following Columbia's loss.

Before the flight NASA believed that the reinforced carbon-carbon leading-edge panels were very durable. Damage-prediction software was used to evaluate possible tile and panel damage. The software predicted severe penetration of multiple tiles by the impact if it struck the thermal protection system tile area, but NASA engineers downplayed this. It had been shown that the model overstated damage from small projectiles, and engineers believed that the model would also overstate damage from larger foam impacts.

Despite engineering concerns about the energy imparted by the foam material, NASA managers ultimately accepted the rationale to reduce predicted damage of the panels from possible complete penetration to slight damage to the panel's thin coating. Ultimately the NASA Mission Management Team felt there was insufficient evidence to indicate that the strike was an unsafe situation, so they declared the debris strike a "turnaround" issue (not of highest importance) and denied the requests for the Department of Defense images.

On January 23, flight director Steve Stich sent an e-mail to Columbia, informing commander Husband and pilot McCool of the foam strike while unequivocally dismissing any concerns about entry safety. Photo analysis shows that some debris came loose and subsequently impacted the orbiter left wing, creating a shower of smaller particles. The impact appears to be totally on the lower surface and no particles are seen to traverse over the upper surface of the wing. Experts concluded that they had seen this same phenomenon on several other flights and there was absolutely no concern for entry.

Edward Tufte (1997), an expert in information design and presentation, remarked on poor modes of communication during the assessment made on the ground, before Columbia's re-entry. NASA and Boeing favored Microsoft PowerPoint for conveying information. PowerPoint uses multi-level bullet points and is oriented towards single-page-of-information groupings. This is not ideal for complex scientific and engineering reports and may have caused recipients to draw incorrect conclusions. In particular, the slide format may have emphasized optimistic options and glossed over the more accurate pessimistic viewpoints.

Multi-level Interpretation. These findings and conclusions can be framed in the multi-level framework discussed in Chapter 2, where the levels for this case study are vehicle, mission, program, and government:

- Government: Focus on delivering missions rather than safety
- Program: Schedule driven; lack of incorporation of lessons learned
- Mission: Flawed launch and re-entry procedures
- Vehicle: Serious design flaws, e.g., foam.

The focus on delivering missions indicated for both the Challenger and Columbia accidents warrants some elaboration. Over half of the missions of the space shuttle from 1998 through 2011 included carrying large payloads to the International Space Station (ISS) and providing crew rotation for ISS. The shuttle also performed service missions to the Hubble Space Telescope. Following the termination of the Space Shuttle program in 2011, transportation to the ISS has been provided by Russia. There was intense pressure at NASA to get the ISS completed and serviced.

Exxon Valdez and BP Deepwater Horizon

The two case studies in this section consider the ocean transport of oil and undersea extraction of oil. There are over 4,000 oil tankers in the world. Very large crude carriers are rated at 160,000 to 320,000 tons, and comprise roughly 10 percent of all tankers. Ultra large crude carriers are rated at 320,000 to 550,000 tons. There are fewer than 10 ULCCs. The capacity of the Exxon Valdez was rated at 215,000 tons.

There are roughly 900 oil and gas platforms worldwide. The five largest platforms include Berkut in the Sakhalin oil field off the Russian Pacific Coast, Perdido and Olympus in the Gulf of Mexico, Hibernia in the North Atlantic, east of Newfoundland, Canada, and Petronius in the Gulf of Mexico. At a bit over 50,000 tons, Deepwater Horizon was on the smaller end of the range. It was a dynamically positioned, column-stabilized, semi-submersible mobile offshore unit, designed for oil exploration and production.

My maritime experiences throughout the 1980s focused on training supertanker engineering officers, with emphasis on keeping the propulsion system operating smoothly, including detecting, diagnosing, and compensating for failures. Projects at the Netherlands Organization for Applied Scientific Research (TNO) and Marine Safety International involved developing and evaluating training simulators for these personnel. It was quite common for there to only be one engineer on duty and failure situations could be quite challenging.

Exxon Valdez (1989)

This case study draws heavily upon the report *Marine Accident Report: Grounding of the US Tankship Exxon Valdez on Bligh Reef, Prince William Sound, Near Valdez Alaska, March 24, 1989* (NTSB, 1990). The Exxon Valdez oil spill occurred in Prince William Sound, Alaska, on March 24, 1989, when Exxon Valdez, an oil tanker owned by Exxon Shipping Company, bound for Long Beach, California, struck Prince William Sound's Bligh Reef, 1.5 mi west of Tatitlek, Alaska, at 12:04 local time and spilled 10.8 million gallons of crude oil over the next few days.

Timeline. The Valdez spill is the second largest in US waters, after the 2010 Deepwater Horizon oil spill, in terms of volume released. Prince William Sound's remote location, accessible only by helicopter, plane, or boat, made government and industry response efforts difficult and severely taxed existing response plans. The region is a habitat for salmon, sea otters, seals, and seabirds. The oil, originally extracted at the Prudhoe Bay Oil Field, eventually affected 1,300 miles of coastline, of which 200 miles were heavily or moderately oiled. The ship was carrying 53.1 million US gallons of oil.

Multiple factors have been identified as contributing to the incident:

- Exxon Shipping Company failed to supervise the master and provide a rested and sufficient crew for Exxon Valdez. The NTSB found this was widespread throughout the industry, prompting a safety recommendation to Exxon and to the industry.

- The third mate failed to properly maneuver the vessel, possibly due to fatigue or excessive workload.
- Exxon Shipping Company failed to properly maintain the Raytheon Collision Avoidance System radar, which, if functional, would have indicated to the third mate an impending collision with the Bligh Reef by detecting the "radar reflector," placed on the next rock inland from Bligh Reef for the purpose of keeping ships on course. This cause was later unearthed by Greg Palast and is not present in the official accident report (Palast, 1999).

Captain Joseph Hazelwood, who was widely reported to have been drinking heavily that night, was not at the controls when the ship struck the reef. Exxon blamed Captain Hazelwood for the grounding of the tanker, but Hazelwood accused the corporation of making him a scapegoat. As the senior officer in command of the ship, he was accused of being intoxicated and thereby contributing to the disaster, but he was cleared of this charge at his 1990 trial after witnesses testified that he was sober around the time of the accident.

At the helm, the third mate may never have collided with Bligh Reef had he looked at his Raytheon radar. "But the radar was not turned on. In fact, the tanker's radar was left broken and disabled for more than a year before the disaster, and Exxon management knew it. It was just too expensive to fix and operate."

Leveson (2005) reports other factors involved:

- Ships were not informed that the previous practice of the Coast Guard tracking ships out to Bligh Reef had ceased.
- The oil industry promised, but never installed, state-of-the-art iceberg monitoring equipment.
- Exxon Valdez was sailing outside the normal sea lane to avoid small icebergs thought to be in the area.
- The 1989 tanker crew was half the size of the 1977 crew, worked 12- to 14-hour shifts, plus overtime. The crew was rushing to leave Valdez with a load of oil.

- Coast Guard vessel inspections in Valdez were not performed, and the number of staff was reduced.
- Lack of available equipment and personnel hampered the spill cleanup.

This disaster resulted in the International Maritime Organization introducing comprehensive marine pollution prevention rules (MARPOL) through various conventions. The rules were ratified by member countries and, under International Ship Management rules, ships are being operated with a common objective of "safer ships and cleaner oceans."

Multi-level Interpretation. These findings and conclusions can be framed in the multi-level framework discussed in Chapter 2, where for this case study the levels are platform, company, industry, and government:

- Government: Lack of inspections, communications about practices
- Industry: Driven by economics, not safety, e.g., no iceberg detection
- Company: Crew size halved, production driven
- Platform: Inoperable detection system; not repaired after a year.

BP Deepwater Horizon (2010)

This case study draws heavily upon the report *Explosion and Fire at Macondo Well: Volume 1* (CSB, 2014), as well as other reports (Berman, 2010; Williams, 2010). The process of temporarily abandoning the Macondo well had begun on April 19, 2010. Temporary abandonment, a common practice, involved using cement to secure the annulus between the 7-inch production casing and 9 7/8-inch protection casing. Abandonment caps are secured over the production casing. These are devices that enable later reengagement with the well.

The pumping sequence of cement slurries and other fluids used for cementing the Macondo well subjected the volume of the cement slurry to contamination by the spacer or mud that was placed ahead of it. If the slurry became heavily contaminated, it would not establish a cement cap with the compressive strength of uncontaminated cement. Test data on the status of the cement was being communicated but not reviewed by BP onshore management or a regulatory agency.

Timeline. The Deepwater Horizon oil spill began on April 20, 2010, in the Gulf of Mexico at the BP-operated Macondo well. The Deepwater Horizon was a semi-submersible, mobile, floating, dynamically positioned drilling rig. The Macondo well had reached a depth of 13,293 feet below the sea floor. As noted above, the final production casing from the wellhead at the sea floor to total depth had been put in the hole, and cemented in place on April 19, 2010.

At approximately 19:45 CDT, on April 20, 2010, high-pressure methane gas from the well expanded into the marine riser and rose to the drilling rig, where it ignited and exploded, engulfing the platform. One hundred and twenty-six crew members were on board: eleven missing workers were never found. Most crew members were rescued by lifeboat or helicopter. The Deepwater Horizon sank on the morning of April 22, 2010. It resulted in the largest marine oil spill in the history of the petroleum industry.

The US Government report, published in September 2011, pointed to defective cement in the well, faulting mostly BP, but also rig operator Transocean and contractor Halliburton. Earlier in 2011, a White House commission also blamed BP and its partners for a series of cost-cutting decisions and an inadequate safety system, but also concluded that the spill resulted from systemic root causes and "absent significant reform in both industry practices and government policies, might well recur."

Berman (2010) outlines the series of events associated with the Deepwater Horizon disaster:

- The well had reached a depth of 13,293 feet below the sea floor. The final string of production casing from the wellhead at the sea floor to total depth had been put in the hole, and cemented in place on April 19, 2010.

- Only 51 barrels of cement were used according to the well plan. This was not sufficient to ensure a seal between the 7-inch production casing and the previously cemented 9 7/8-inch protection casing
- Mud had been lost to the reservoir while drilling the bottom portion of the well, possibly resulting in difficulty creating a good cement seal between the casing and the formation.
- It also would have been impossible to ensure the effectiveness of the cement seal without running a cement-bond log, and this was not done.
- The cement contained a nitrogen additive to make it lighter so that it would flow more easily and better fill the area of the annulus, possibly further decreasing its sealing effectiveness.
- While waiting approximately 20 hours for the cement to dry on April 20, the crew began displacing the mud in the wellbore and riser with sea water before setting a cement plug and moving off location. This mud was pumped into tanks at the surface.
- Sea water is much lighter than drilling mud so there was less downward force in the wellbore to balance the flow of gas. Supervisors knew that there was gas in the drilling fluid because a gas flare can be seen in photos probably coming from a diverter line in the riser.
- The riser and upper 3,000 feet of the wellbore were fully displaced with seawater by 20:00 on April 20. Beginning 10 minutes later, the mud pit volume began to increase, probably because of gas influx. The volume increased so much that the recorder re-zeroed four times.
- Standpipe pressure increased and decreased twice over the next 12 minutes, suggesting that surges of gas were entering the drilling fluid from a gas column below the wellhead, and outside of the 7-inch production casing.
- Gas had probably channeled past the inadequate cement job near the bottom of the well and, by now, had reached the seals and pack-offs separating it from the riser at the sea floor.
- At 21:47, the rate of standpipe pressure and mud pit volume went off scale, and water flow was measured at the surface. The blowout had begun.

- Between 21:47 and 21:49 the gas behind the 7-inch production casing apparently overcame the wellhead seals and pack-offs that separated the wellbore from the riser.
- Almost instantaneously, the gas shot the water out of the riser and above the crown of the derrick. Then, the gas ignited and exploded.

"A flawed, risky well plan for the Macondo well was approved by the Minerals Management Service, a division within the Interior Department, and BP, Anadarko, and Mitsui management. Similar or identical plans were undoubtedly approved and used by many operators on other wells drilled in the Gulf of Mexico. Lack of blowouts on previous wells does not justify the approval and use of an unsafe plan" (Berman, 2010).

The CSB commission (2014) concluded, "Halliburton may not have had—and BP did not have—the results of that test before the evening of April 19, meaning that the cement job may have been pumped without any lab results indicating that the foam cement slurry would be stable." Further, the panel found, "Halliburton and BP both had results in March showing that a very similar foam slurry design to the one actually pumped at the Macondo well would be unstable, but neither acted upon that data."

Williams (2010) outlines the concatenation of failures that cause this accident. First, of course, is the inadequate cement. Then, the valves designed to stop flow of oil and gas had failed. The pressure test was misinterpreted. The gas leak was not spotted until quite late. Then, a valve in the blowout preventer failed and the mud–gas separator was overwhelmed. Finally, the blowout preventer safety mechanism failed due to a dead battery and a defective switch.

Multi-level Interpretation. These findings and conclusions can be framed in the multi-level framework discussed in Chapter 2, where for this case study the levels are platform, company, industry, and government:

- Government: Lack of oversight
- Industry: Failure to incorporate lessons learned

- Company: Focus on production, ignoring tests and results
- Platform: Concatenation of malfunctions; inadequate procedures and training.

Comparison across Case Studies

Table 3.2 provides a multi-level comparison of the six case studies of failures of complex systems. At the lowest level—personnel, platform, or vehicle—all six cases involved physical malfunctions. However, these malfunctions only constituted the proximate causes of these accidents.

At the next level—plant, mission, or company—poor decisions exacerbated the consequences of the physical malfunctions. Design of controls, displays, procedures, and training were inadequate for appropriately responding to the consequences as these accidents evolved.

At the next level—program, utility, or industry—operational goals dominated safety considerations. Production and scheduling goals were prioritized. Lessons learned from other experiences were either ignored or shelved.

Finally, at the level of government, there was a lack of appropriate oversight and inspections, exacerbated by oversight personnel becoming, in effect, members of the operational teams. Communications were limited and, in one case, actively repressed.

Were the only deficiencies in the bottom row of Table 3.2, these six cases would likely have been handled routinely, preventing the accidents and consequences that ensued due to the deficiencies in the higher rows of Table 3.2. As later chapters will address, things can go wrong without becoming disastrous.

Anticipating Failures

It is useful to consider how industry currently addresses the types of safety risks illustrated by the six case studies. The physical malfunctions exemplified by these case studies were discounted, but they were not ignored. The three analytic techniques reviewed here are representative of how such safety issues are often addressed.

Table 3.2 Multi-level analysis of failures of six complex systems

Level of analysis	Energy		Space		Ocean	
	Three Mile Island	Chernobyl	NASA Challenger	NASA Columbia	Exxon Valdez	BP Deepwater Horizon
Government	Lack of oversight	Lack of oversight, repression of communications	Focus on delivering missions rather than safety	Focus on delivering missions rather than safety	Lack of inspections, communications about practices	Lack of oversight
Program, utility, industry	Production pressures; lack of incorporation of lessons learned	Production pressures; lack of incorporation of lessons learned	Schedule driven; lack of incorporation of lessons learned	Schedule driven; lack of incorporation of lessons learned	Driven by economics, not safety, e.g., no iceberg detection	Failure to incorporate lessons learned
Plant, mission, company	Lack of consideration of complex failure scenarios	Lack of consideration of complex failure scenarios	Flawed launch procedures	Flawed launch and re-entry procedures	Crew size halved, production driven	Focus on production, ignoring tests and results
Personnel, platform, vehicle	Serious design flaws—human factors, procedures, training	Serious design flaws—human factors, procedures, training	Serious design flaws, O-rings	Serious design flaws, e.g., foam	Inoperable detection system; not repaired after a year	Concatenation of malfunctions; inadequate procedures and training

Hazard Analysis

A hazard analysis is used as the first step in a process of assessing risks. The result of a hazard analysis is the identification of different types of hazards. A hazard is a potential condition that may exist singly or in combination with other hazards and conditions. Hazards are mapped to sequences or scenarios. A scenario has a probability of occurrence. Often a system has many potential failure scenarios. It also is assigned a classification, based on the worst-case severity of the end condition. Risk is the combination of probability and severity. Preliminary risk levels can be provided in the hazard analysis. The validation and acceptance of risks are determined via risk analysis. The goal is to identify the best means of controlling or eliminating risks (Ericson, 2015).

Failure Modes and Effects Analysis

This is a process of reviewing as many components, assemblies, and subsystems as possible to identify potential failure modes in a system and their likely causes and effects. For each component, the failure modes and their resulting effects on the rest of the system are recorded in worksheets. There are numerous variations of such worksheets. Analysis can be qualitative (Rousand and Hoylan, 2004) but may also be put on a quantitative basis when mathematical failure rate models are combined with a statistical failure mode databases (Tay and Lim, 2008). This was one of the first highly structured, systematic techniques for failure analysis and has been generalized over the years (Edsel, 2015).

Systems Theoretic Process Analysis

This approach involves four overall steps: 1) define purpose of analysis; 2) model the control structure; 3) identify unsafe control actions; and 4) identify loss scenarios. The control structure is central to understanding functional relationships and interactions.

Analyzing control actions in the control structure involves examining how they could lead to losses as defined by the purpose of analysis. The last step involves examining how unsafe control actions might occur in the system (Leveson, 2012; Leveson and Thomas, 2018).

Safety Science

These methods and tools fit within the broad multidisciplinary field of safety science, which emphasizes evidence-based approaches to assuring safety in industry, transportation, and other domains. This field has been developing for decades (Kuhlmann, 1986) and there is a wealth of recent books on the topic (Möller et al., 2018; Dekker, 2019; Le Coze, 2019). The leading journals include the *Journal of Safety Research* and *Safety Science*, both published by Elsevier, *Workplace Health and Safety*, published by Sage, and *International Journal of Occupational Safety and Ergonomics*, published by Taylor and Francis.

Summary

These techniques are useful for addressing the types of physical malfunctions that occurred in the six case studies considered in this chapter. The emphasis on control structure also enables analysis of operational processes that act on the physical infrastructure. These techniques are less useful for addressing management decisions that affected system design and decisions for addressing the consequences of failures, for example, disregarding risks to focus on operational or production goals.

In later chapters, I discuss approaches to predictive surveillance and control as proactive means of failure management. Analytic techniques employed during system design are important, but failure management is also needed during system operations. Design cannot eliminate all failures, especially at higher levels of management and government. Failures will happen during operations and means are needed to manage these failures.

Higher-Order Consequences

Failures of the types discussed in this chapter can have consequences far beyond the immediate platform, company, or industry. The Fukushima earthquake and tsunami provides a compelling example. This event on March 11, 2011 resulted in the destruction of the Fukushima-Daiichi nuclear power station.

Boudette and Bennett (2011) report that this event resulted in a shortage of a type of shiny pigment, Xirallic, which is used in automobile paints. Users of this pigment include Chrysler, Ford, General Motors, and Toyota. Xirallic is only produced at an Onahama plant near the Fukushima-Daiichi plant. Operated by the German chemical company Merck, this plant had been evacuated and the company did not know when it would be permitted to reopen. Thus, the Fukushima accident disrupted the automobile industry.

Major accidents as typified by the six case studies in this chapter are rarely isolated events. They can affect companies, industries, and regions. As the recent *Chernobyl* series on HBO depicted, there was a point at which people were concerned that the accident would poison the water supply of all of Western Europe. Fortunately, this scenario was avoided.

Who should be responsible for surveillance of such possibilities? I will outline approaches to answering this question when we consider failures of complex ecosystems in Chapter 5. Integrated oversight capabilities are key and emerging technologies can enable such capabilities. The biggest challenge may be the needed alignment of stakeholders.

Conclusions

In all six cases, there was a physical failure of some sort; other operational factors often complicated things. Design flaws of the human–machine interface, as well as procedures and training played a major role. Human errors often resulted, but these can usually be attributed to design decisions that created an unforgiving environment.

Management decision making, both for design and operational decisions, played a major role. In retrospect, these accidents were not inevitable, but the above higher-order factors often converged to precipitate the unfortunate consequences. The physical failures were usually difficult to preempt, but management of these failures could have averted the extreme consequences that resulted.

Approaches to surveillance and control of possible failures are addressed in later chapters. The emphasis is on all levels of the enterprise, ranging from technologies, to organizations, to societal interests. Proactive, predictive surveillance and control is the overall goal. I next consider the failure of complex enterprises.

References

Berman, A.E. (2010). What caused the Deepwater Horizon disaster? *The Oil Drum*, May 22.

Boudette, N.E., and Bennett, J. (2011). Pigment shortage hits auto makers. *Wall Street Journal*, March 26.

CSB (2014). *Explosion and Fire at Macondo Well: Volume 1*. Washington, DC: US Chemical Safety and Hazard Investigation Board.

Dekker, S. (2019). *Foundations of Safety Science*. Abingdon, UK: Routledge.

Edsel, A. (2015). *Breaking Failure: How to Break the Cycle of Business Failure and Underperformance Using Root Cause, Failure Mode, and Effects Analysis, and an Early Warning System*. New York: Pearson.

Ericson, C.A. (2015). *Hazard Analysis Techniques for System Safety* (2nd edition). New York: Wiley.

IAEA (1992). *INSAG-7, The Chernobyl Accident: Updating of INSAG-1*. Vienna, Austria: International Atomic Energy Agency.

INSAG (1986). *International Nuclear Safety Advisory Group's Summary Report on the Post-Accident Review Meeting on the Chernobyl Accident (INSAG-1)*. Vienna: International Nuclear Safety Advisory Group.

INSAG (1992). *INSAG-7, The Chernobyl Accident, Updating of INSAG-1: A Report by the International Nuclear Safety Advisory Group*. Vienna: International Nuclear Safety Advisory Group.

Kuhlmann, A. (1986). *Introduction to Safety Science*. Berlin: Springer.

Le Coze, J-C. (ed.) (2019). *Safety Science Research: Evolution, Challenges, and New Directions*. Boca Raton, FL: CRC Press.

Leveson, N.G. (2005). *Software System Safety*. Cambridge, MA: Massachusetts Institute of Technology.

Leveson, N.G. (2012). *Engineering a Safer World: Systems Thinking Applied to Safety*. Cambridge, MA: MIT Press.

Leveson, N.G., and Thomas, J.P. (2018). *STPA Handbook*. Cambridge, MA: Massachusetts Institute of Technology.

Möller, N., Hansson, S.O., Holmberg, J.-E., and Rollenhagen, C. (eds) (2018). *Handbook of Safety Principles*. New York: Wiley.

NASA (1986). *Report of the President's Commission on the Space Shuttle Challenger Accident*. Washington, DC: Government Printing Office.

NASA (2003). *Report of the Columbia Accident Investigation Board*. Washington, DC: Government Printing Office.

NRC (1987). *Report of the Accident at the Chernobyl Nuclear Power Station*. Washington, DC: US Nuclear Regulatory Commission.

NTSB (1990). *Marine Accident Report: Grounding of the US Tankship Exxon Valdez on Bligh Reef, Prince William Sound, Near Valdez Alaska, March 24, 1989*. Washington, DC: National Transportation Safety Board.

Palast, G. (1999). Ten Years after But Who Was to Blame? *Observer/Guardian*, March 21.

Rausand, M., and Hoylan, A. (2004). *System Reliability Theory: Models, Statistical Methods, and Applications*. New York: Wiley.

Rouse, W.B. (2015). *Modeling and Visualization of Complex Systems and Enterprises: Explorations of Physical, Human, Economic, and Social Phenomena*. New York: Wiley.

Rouse, W.B. (2019). *Computing Possible Futures: Model-Based Explorations of "What if?"* Oxford: Oxford University Press.

Tay, K.M., and Lim, C.P. (2008). On the use of fuzzy inference techniques in assessment models: Part II: industrial applications. *Fuzzy Optimization and Decision Making*, 7 (3), 283–302.

TMI (1979). *Report of the President's Commission on the Accident at Three Mile Island*. Washington, DC: Government Printing Office.

Tufte, E.R. (1997). *Visual Explanations: Images and Quantities, Evidence and Narrative*. Cheshire, CT: Graphics Press.

Vaughan, D. (1997). *The Challenger Launch Decision: Risky Technology, Culture, and Deviance at NASA*. Chicago: University of Chicago Press.

Williams, J. (2010). The eight failures that caused the Gulf Oil spill. *New Scientist*, September 8.

4

Failures of Complex Organizations

Introduction

The average age of a company in the S&P 500 has decreased to less than 20 years, down from 60 years in the 1950s (Sheetz, 2017). The average tenure of companies in the S&P 500 was 33 years in 1964, 24 years by 2016 and forecasted to shrink to just 12 years by 2027 (Anthony et al., 2018). Failures of large enterprises is, perhaps surprisingly, quite common.

Technology is often the driving force behind this phenomenon. This chapter considers six companies that succumbed to this force over the past three decades. More recently, the "platform" companies (McAfee and Brynjolfsson, 2017) have disrupted traditional companies in retail and entertainment, for example. Amazon, Netflix, Walmart, and Wayfair, to name a few, sell the same things as traditional companies, but sell them quite differently.

These companies are leaders in the ongoing digital transformation of corporations (Siebel, 2019). Infusions of cloud computing, big data, artificial intelligence, and the Internet of Things are enabling business models that are much more efficient and better serve consumers. Siebel argues that digital transformation is key to surviving the competition. It is an imperative rather than an option.

Table 4.1 summarizes the six organizational failures discussed in this chapter. These six technology companies—in photography, computing, and communications—hesitated in the face of fundamental technology changes. These companies no longer exist or are mere shadows of their former selves.

These case studies differ substantially in terms of the nature of technology disruptions. However, they are similar relative to how management addressed needs for change. There were similar

Failure Management: Malfunctions of Technologies, Organizations, and Society. William B. Rouse, Oxford University Press (2021). © William B. Rouse. DOI: 10.1093/oso/9780198870999.003.0004

Table 4.1 Consequences of failures of complex enterprises

Case study	Domain	Proximal consequences
Kodak	Photography	Failed to transition from sales of photographic film to digital photography, despite having invented the first digital camera.
Polaroid	Photography	Failed to compete with rapid film processing, single-use cameras, videotape camcorders, and digital cameras.
Digital	Computing	Fortunes declined after failing to pursue critical market changes, particularly the personal computer.
Xerox	Computing	Failed to leverage their investments in personal computing, such as the desktop metaphor, GUI, computer mouse, and desktop computing.
Motorola	Communications	Failed to transition quickly from analog to digital cell phone technology, despite having invented a digital cell phone.
Nokia	Communications	Focused on low-priced cell phones and was surprised by the quickly growing popularity of high-priced smartphones.

delusions, delays, and dissipations of resources, resulting in "too little, too late."

The multi-level framework from Chapter 2 is used to organize the findings from these case studies, contrast phenomena at multiple levels, and provide cross-cutting interpretations. This sets the stage for discussions of alternative approaches to anticipating failures of complex organizations. Anticipation is completely feasible, assuming that enterprise leaders are willing to entertain futures beyond just projections of the status quo.

Kodak and Polaroid

Eastman Kodak pioneered the film-based photography market in the United States, dominating the industry through the 1970s. At its height, Kodak had an 80 percent market share in the United States. Polaroid introduced the instant camera in 1947 with film that included all the chemicals needed to develop the film. By the 1970s, Polaroid had two thirds of the instant camera market.

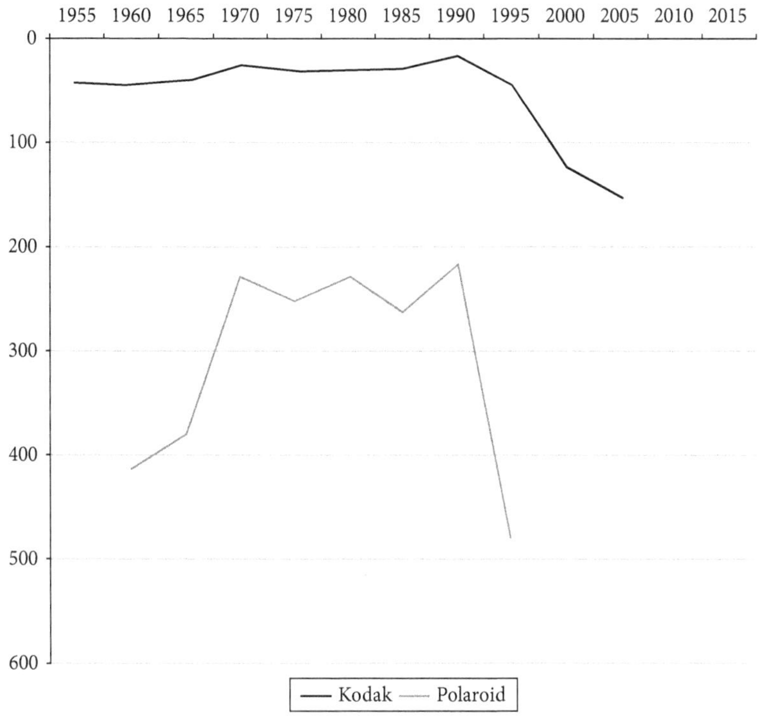

Figure 4.1 Fortune 500 rankings of Kodak and Polaroid

Film-based photography eventually lost to digital photography. The fortunes of Kodak and Polaroid faded with this change. Figure 4.1 shows the Fortune 500 rankings of the two companies for the years that they were in the Fortune 500. The data clearly reflect the failures of these once-innovative enterprises.

Kodak (1888–2012)

George Eastman and Henry A. Strong founded the Eastman Kodak Company on September 4, 1888. During most of the twentieth century, Kodak held a dominant position in photographic film. The company's ubiquity was such that its "Kodak moment" tagline was commonly used to describe any personal event that demanded to be recorded for posterity.

Kodak adopted Gillette's razor and blades strategy of selling inexpensive cameras and making large margins from consumables—film, chemicals, and paper. As late as 1976, Kodak commanded 90 percent of film sales and 85 percent of camera sales in the United States. From the 1970s, however, Kodak and its archrival Fuji, both recognized the upcoming threat of digital photography, and although both sought diversification as a mitigation strategy, Fuji was more successful at diversification (*Economist*, 2012).

Kodak began to struggle financially in the late 1990s, as a result of the decline in sales of photographic film and its slowness in transitioning to digital photography, despite Steve Sasson, a Kodak engineer, having invented the digital camera in 1975. As a part of a turnaround strategy, Kodak began to focus on digital photography and digital printing, and attempted to generate revenues through aggressive patent litigation (Hiltzik, 2011).

> The right lessons from Kodak are subtle. Companies often see the disruptive forces affecting their industry. They frequently divert sufficient resources to participate in emerging markets. Their failure is usually an inability to truly embrace the new business models the disruptive change opens up. Kodak created a digital camera, invested in the technology, and even understood that photos would be shared online. Where they failed was in realizing that online photo sharing *was* the new business, not just a way to expand the printing business. (Anthony, 2016)

Snyder (2013) describes how corporate hubris caused the downfall of America's largest photography company. He provides meticulously documented history of Eastman Kodak Company's financial implosion. Enormous financial and human resources were wasted in investments in obsolete capacities.

Multi-level Interpretation. These findings and conclusions can be framed in the multi-level framework discussed in Chapter 2, where the levels for this case study are products, processes, company, and industry:

- Industry: All film producers—Kodak, Fuji, and Polaroid—faced serious market threats, possibly much more so than they realized

- Company: Kodak was reluctant to cannibalize its massive film business, assumed photo printing would continue, and invested accordingly
- Processes: Business processes for printing film-based photos had been refined and optimized over many decades, but were no longer relevant
- Products: Digital technology increasingly displaced film-based photography, as did consumers' preferences for photo management.

Polaroid (1937–2001)

Edwin H. Land founded Polaroid in 1937. His vision was to exploit the use of its polarizing polymer. Land ran the company until 1981. Its peak employment was 21,000 in 1978, and its peak revenue was $3 billion in 1991. It is best known for its Polaroid instant film and cameras. Recognized by most as the father of instant photography, Land included all the operations of a darkroom inside the film itself. He was pictured on the cover of *Life* magazine in 1972 with the inscription, "A Genius and his Magic Camera"

Bonanos (2012) chronicles the story of Polaroid:

> During the 1960s and '70s, Polaroid was the coolest technology company on earth. Like Apple, it was an innovation machine that cranked out one must-have product after another. Led by its own visionary genius founder, Edwin Land, Polaroid grew from a 1937 garage start-up into a billion-dollar pop-culture phenomenon.

Bonanos chronicles Land's one-of-a-kind invention from Polaroid's first instant camera to hit the market in 1948, to its meteoric rise in popularity and adoption by artists, to the company's dramatic decline into bankruptcy in the late 1990s and its brief resurrection in the digital age. He contrasts American ingenuity with the perils of companies that lose their creative edge.

Reeves and Harnoss (2015) discuss how Polaroid got trapped by success. They argue that: "Leaders of large, established companies need more than ever to run and reinvent the business at the same time." The key is balancing exploitation of existing capabilities and exploration of potential new capabilities. Polaroid failed to do this.

Multi-level Interpretation. These findings and conclusions can be framed in the multi-level framework discussed in Chapter 2, where the levels for this case study are products, processes, company, and industry:

- Industry: All film producers—Kodak, Fuji, and Polaroid—faced serious market threats, possibly much more so than they realized
- Company: Polaroid assumed that its success with instant photography could be sustained, ignoring initially the instant nature of digital photography
- Processes: Business processes for instant film-based photography had been refined and optimized over many decades, but were no longer relevant
- Products: Digital technology increasingly displaced film-based photography, as did consumers' preferences for photo management.

Digital and Xerox

During the latter half of the nineteenth century and first half of the twentieth century, IBM, NCR, Burroughs, Remington Rand, and other companies became dominant in the business equipment industry with tabulators (IBM), cash registers (NCR), calculators (Burroughs), and typewriters (Remington). The dominance of these companies in their respective domains set the stage for their becoming primary players in the computer market.

IBM understood the tremendous potential of computers and how they had to be marketed. Fairly quickly, although not immediately, IBM recognized what was likely to happen in the business machines industry. They responded to long-term market trends by developing a customer-oriented strategy that helped their customers to deal successfully with trends that were affecting them.

In the late 1950s and early 1960s, a whole new segment of the computer market emerged—interactive rather than centralized computing. IBM dismissed and then ignored this segment. They apparently could not imagine that customers would want to do their own computing rather than have IBM support and possibly staff a centralized computing function. Later IBM tried to catch up, but did so poorly. By the late 1960s, Digital Equipment Corporation (DEC) dominated interactive computing with their minicomputers.

By the late 1970s, Apple was putting the finishing touches on the first microcomputer, which would spark a new industry. DEC, in a classic business oversight described below, failed to take interactive computing to its next logical step—personal computing. Apple built on pioneering inventions at Xerox, which Xerox failed to leverage for business success, as outlined below. Apple created the Macintosh in the mid 1980s, which became the industry standard in the sense that its features and benefits were adopted throughout the personal computer industry.

The failures of DEC and Xerox to exploit their inherent advantages in personal computing contributed to their eventual demise as reflected in Figure 4.2. DEC faded quickly as computers were their core business. Xerox faded more slowly as computing was a business they entertained but chose not to leverage in their document-oriented business.

Digital (1957–1998)

Ken Olsen and Harlan Anderson founded the Digital Equipment Corporation in 1957. DEC was a leading vendor of computer systems, including computers, software, and peripherals. Their PDP and successor VAX products were the most successful of all minicomputers in terms of sales. The company grew to become the number two computer maker behind IBM.

When a DEC research group demonstrated two prototype microcomputers in 1974. Olsen chose to not proceed with the project. The company similarly rejected another personal computer proposal

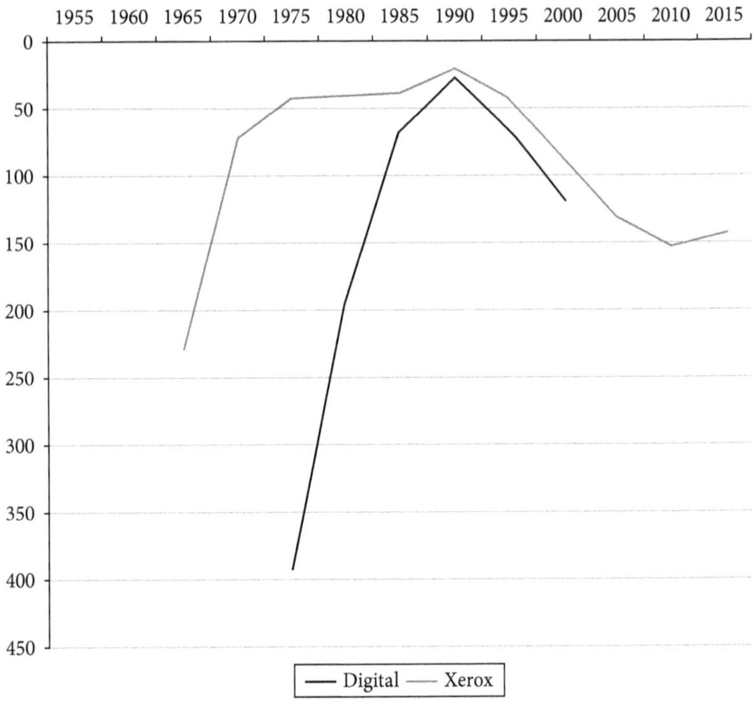

Figure 4.2 Fortune 500 rankings of DEC and Xerox

in 1977. At the time these systems were of limited utility, and Olsen famously derided them in 1977, stating: "There is no reason for any individual to have a computer in his home."

The rapid rise of the microcomputer, or personal computer, in the late 1980s, and especially the introduction of powerful 32-bit systems in the 1990s, quickly eroded the value of DEC's systems. DEC's last major attempt to find a space in the rapidly changing market was the 64-bit Alpha. DEC saw the Alpha as a way to re-implement their VAX series, but also employed it in a range of high-performance workstations. The Alpha processor family, for most of its lifetime, was the fastest processor family on the market. However, high Alpha prices could not compete with lower priced x86 chips from Intel and AMD.

I was heavily involved with DEC in the 1990s helping them plan several new generations of Alpha chip using our Product Planning Advisor toolkit. One strongly stated objective for each generation was that it retain its *Guinness Book of Records* status as the fastest processor in the world. This objective dominated even when processing speed provided users with minimal benefits. Technical excellence was highly valued at DEC.

Management thought leader Edgar Schein and colleagues wrote a requiem for the company—*DEC Is Dead, Long Live DEC: The Lasting Legacy of Digital Equipment Corporation* (Schein et al., 2004). The Digital Equipment Corporation created the minicomputer, networking, the concept of distributed computing, speech recognition, and other major innovations. Yet it ultimately failed as a business. What happened?

Schein shows how the unique organizational culture established by DEC's founder, Ken Olsen, gave the company important competitive advantages in its early years, but later became a hindrance and ultimately led to the company's downfall. The authors explain how a culture can become so embedded that an organization is unable to adapt to changing circumstances even though it sees the need very clearly.

They conclude: "Even a culture of innovation can become dysfunctional as markets change. A corporation's founding values, if they lead to success, tend to ossify as a set of tacit assumptions about successful strategy."

Beyond Olsen dismissing personal computing, other hurdles kept DEC from competing. Computer companies had traditionally developed the whole computer system themselves. This included both hardware and proprietary software. However, the personal computing market quickly evolved to wanting one operating system, primarily Microsoft's DOS, to operate on all platforms. Consumers also wanted third-party software, initially Lotus 1-2-3, to be usable on all platforms. DEC was not prepared to play in this game.

In contrast, IBM gained a prominent position in the personal computing market by adapting to the changing game:

> In sum, the development team broke all the rules. They went outside the traditional boundaries of product development within IBM. They went to outside vendors for most of the parts, went to outside software developers for the operating system (Microsoft) and application software, and

> acted as an independent business unit. Those tactics enabled them to develop and announce the IBM PC in 12 months—at that time faster than any other hardware product in IBM's history. (IBM, 2019)

MIT (2011) discusses lessons from Ken Olsen and DEC. From 1957, the company grew to $14 billion in sales and 130,000 employees. In 1998, the computing part of DEC was sold to Compaq and semiconductor operations were sold to Intel. Hewlett Packard later acquired Compaq. Intel recently closed the Massachusetts semiconductor operations. Similar to the observations of Schein and his colleagues, MIT suggests three lessons:

- "Watch out for disruptive innovations that make formerly complicated, expensive, and inaccessible affordable and accessible.
- Even a culture of innovation can become dysfunctional as markets change.
- In an age when companies come and go, one of an executive's most lasting legacies may be how he (or she) treats people."
- The third observation explains why so many former DEC employees look back at their time with DEC so fondly.

Multi-level Interpretation. These findings and conclusions can be framed in the multi-level framework discussed in Chapter 2, where the levels for this case study are products, processes, company, and industry:

- Industry: Business models in the computing industry were changing. IBM adapted. DEC did not.
- Company: DEC leadership dismissed the concept of personal computing; when they finally invested, it was too little too late
- Processes: Hardware and software design practices were not adaptable to where the industry was headed; they took too long and cost too much
- Products: Personal computing quickly became dominant, beginning the path to contemporary, ubiquitous personal digital devices.

Xerox (1906–2018)

Xerox was founded in 1906 in Rochester as The Haloid Photographic Company, which originally manufactured photographic paper and equipment. Joseph C. Wilson, credited as the "founder of Xerox", took over Haloid from his father, Joseph R. Wilson in 1946.

In 1938 Chester Carlson invented a process for printing images using an electrically charged photoconductor-coated metal plate and dry powder "toner." It would take more than 20 years of refinement before the first automated machine to make copies was commercialized.

Wilson saw the promise of Carlson's invention and, in 1946, signed an agreement to develop it as a commercial product. Wilson remained as president/CEO of Xerox until 1967 and served as chairman until his death in 1971. Haloid subsequently changed its name to Haloid Xerox in 1958 and then Xerox Corporation in 1961.

Charles Ellis (2006) provides a portrait of Joseph Wilson and his understanding of the commercial need and usefulness of imaging technology. Xerox and xerography became not only a part of our vocabulary, but part of our everyday life. Ellis provides an in-depth understanding of the critical business decisions, and vision of Wilson and his team.

The Xerox Palo Research Center was formed in 1970 with a mandate to create computer technology-related products and hardware systems. PARC introduced the Xerox Alto in 1973, with an operating system based on a graphical user interface (GUI). In 1981, a much-changed version of the Alto was brought to market at the Xerox Star for $17,000 per workstation. I briefly consulted with Xerox PARC in the 1980s and saw various demonstrations of these platforms. The GUI displays were impressive, but the workstations seemed rather expensive.

Steve Jobs saw these demonstrations in 1979. He saw the future of computing. In Walter Isaacson's biography of him (Isaacson, 2011), Jobs said of Xerox management: "They were copier heads who had no clue about what a computer could do. They could have owned the entire industry."

Smith and Alexander (1988) discuss how Xerox "fumbled the future." They observe: "Fifteen years after it invented personal computing, Xerox still means copy." They chronicle how innovation can succeed or fail within large corporate structures. They assert that this chronicle is a "tale of human beings whose talents, hopes, fears, habits, and prejudices determine the fate of our largest organizations and of our best ideas."

More recently, Press (2018) has outlined a range of corporate fumbles. He argues that IBM and AT&T "had the visions but not the right sense of how to get there. They assumed the business market would lead the consumer market." They were aware of the Internet but did not envision the convergence.

Apple did not get it right at first. Lisa failed in 1983, but they got the package right with Macintosh in 1984, the first mass-market personal computer that featured a graphical user interface, built-in screen, and mouse. Press argues that Apple finally had the compelling vision with *Knowledge Navigator* in 1987, a video that portrayed the types of capabilities we have come to enjoy.

My team soon embraced the *Knowledge Navigator* concept. We were developing a decision support system for designers of aircraft cockpits. We shot our own video of the *Designer's Associate* as a means of reaching consensus with sponsors on the objectives of this system. We still employ this approach to envision user experiences and user interfaces, now for clinicians, as well as disabled and older adults.

Multi-level Interpretation. These findings and conclusions can be framed in the multi-level framework discussed in Chapter 2, where the levels for this case study are products, processes, company, and industry:

- Industry: Xerox was not mainstream in computing, and the computing industry was quickly morphing to outsourcing for hardware and software
- Company: Xerox was a document technology company and saw computing through the lens of how it could support document management

- Processes: Hardware and software design practices were not adaptable to where the industry was headed; they took too long and cost too much
- Products: Personal computing quickly became dominant, beginning the path to contemporary, ubiquitous personal digital devices.

Motorola and Nokia

Alexander Graham Bell was granted a US patent for the telephone in 1876. Almost a century later, Motorola's DynaTAC mobile phone was demonstrated in 1973. The DynaTAC 8000X became the first mobile phone in the market in 1983. With a price of almost $4,000, sales were limited to corporate applications. The consumer market started to emerge in the 1990s and the market became increasingly competitive.

Motorola's dominance in the market waned as it clung to analog technology. Nokia came to dominate but failed to appreciate the game-changing nature of smartphones. These two strategy failures are outlined below. Figure 4.3 reflects the consequences of these failures. Apple and Samsung have replaced Motorola and Nokia.

Motorola (1928–2012)

Brothers Paul V. and Joseph E. Galvin founded Motorola, Inc. as the Galvin Manufacturing Corporation in 1928 in Schaumburg, Illinois. They began selling Motorola car-radio receivers to police departments and municipalities in late 1930s. Motorola's DynaTAC 8000X became the first mobile phone in the market on 1983 and they led the market until 1998, when Nokia's digital offering took over the market.

Forbes reported in 2004 that Motorola had been number two behind Nokia for several years, with a brief resurgence with the release of the Razr flip phone in 2005. Motorola led in phones based

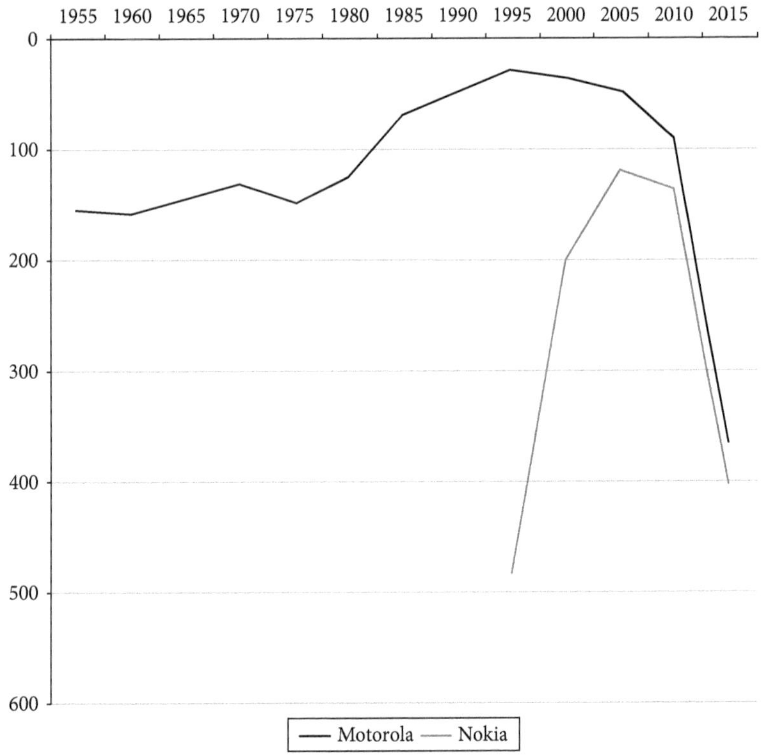

Figure 4.3 Fortune 500 rankings of Motorola and Nokia

on CDMA while Nokia led in GSM-based phones, but Samsung was catching up and no one was thinking about Apple (Hessledahl, 2004).

Linge (2016) notes that Motorola was a hardware company but, from the mid 2000s, software drove innovation. Rockman (2012) argues that Motorola's dismal software competencies led to their demise. He chronicles a long stream of hardware successes, concluding that Motorola succeeded by hardware and failed by software. They tried to build a new version of the OS for each generation of phones. Frustrated product managers began to use suppliers' software. There were endless meetings. He chronicles many starts and restarts, poor management, and unfortunate outcomes.

Fishman (2014) observes that networks and handsets were virtually two separate companies within Motorola. This, in part, impeded the handset folks' move from analog to digital. The networks folks ended up using digital phones by Qualcomm, a bitter rival of the handset side of Motorola.

I worked with Motorola extensively in the 1990s. We used the Product Planning Advisor to explore new products and plans to manufacture them. We used the Technology Investment Advisor to consider alternative investments in technologies to support business units' planned product lines. I cannot recall any project where we explored software, which supports the above observations.

In the meantime, Motorola poured $2.6 billion into Iridium, a satellite-based mobile phone system that eventually offered $3,000 phones and $7/minute usage charges. This subsidiary declared bankruptcy in 1999 and sold off the bits and pieces for $25 million (Collins, 2018).

Fishman (2014) summarizes the demise of Motorola. After having lost $4.3 billion from 2007 to 2009, Motorola was divided into two independent public companies, Motorola Mobility and Motorola Solutions in 2011. Motorola Solutions is generally considered to be the direct successor to Motorola, as the reorganization was structured with Motorola Mobility being sold to Google in 2012 and acquired by Lenovo in 2014.

Dautovic (2019) provides a sketch of the smartphone market in the past, present, and future:

- 1980s: Motorola's analog phones dominate
- 1990s: Nokia takes lead with digital phones
- 2000s: Smartphones emerge; software comes to dominate; Apple leads
- 2010s: Chinese manufacturing dominates
- 2019: Apple and Samsung own the smartphone market.

Multi-level Interpretation. These findings and conclusions can be framed in the multi-level framework discussed in Chapter 2, where the levels for this case study are products, processes, company, and industry:

- Industry: Constant innovation and change in terms of both technology and consumers' desires and expectations

- Company: Tried to milk analog technology too long, despite knowing digital was the future; recognized smartphone market later than others
- Processes: Hardware processes were mature, but software processes were deeply flawed; realization of this was substantially delayed
- Products: Digital supplanted analog; software came to dominate hardware; smartphones emerged as digital devices, not just phones.

Nokia (1865–2014)

Nokia was founded in 1865 near Helsinki, Finland. It was founded as a pulp mill and was long associated with rubber and cables. Nokia started producing commercial and military mobile radio telephones in the 1960s.The Nokia DX 200, a digital switch for telephone exchanges, introduced in the 1970s, became the workhorse of the network equipment division. By the 1980s, Nokia was in the cellular phone business.

Beginning in the 1990s, Nokia focused on large-scale telecommunications infrastructures and technology development. Nokia was a major contributor to the mobile telephony industry, having assisted in the development of the GSM, 3G, and LTE standards, and was once the largest worldwide vendor of mobile phones and smartphones.

By 1999 Nokia had surged past Motorola to become the market leader (CNN, 1999). Worldwide sales of cell phones had increased by 51 percent during the past year. Motorola retained leadership in analog cell phones, but Nokia's growing hold on digital phones was the key to its success.

Doz and Wilson (2018) explore the rise and fall of Nokia in mobile phones. Nokia led the mobile phone revolution. It grew to have one of the most recognizable and valuable brands in the world and then fell into decline, leading to the sale of its mobile phone business to Microsoft.

The authors address why things fell apart and the extent to which mistakes made were avoidable. They consider whether the world around Nokia changed too fast for it to adapt, as well as whether Nokia's success contained the seeds of its failure?

CNET (2014) provides another chronicle of the rise and fall of Nokia. As this report was published, Nokia had just completed the sale of its entire devices and services business to Microsoft. Next to Motorola, who invented the mobile handset, there was no bigger name in the business than Nokia.

CNET observes that the company's obstinate attitude and vulnerability was exposed by Motorola's Razr and then more fully by Apple's iPhone. They conclude that the "Nokia DNA" limited design options. Motorola led a comeback of its own with the Razr, the first flip phone. It was the top seller for three years. Nokia executive dismissed the flip phone as a fad. Nokia then abandoned the US market.

While Nokia was a leader in smartphone offerings, the iPhone leapfrogged expectations and focused on consumers rather than business. RIM had toyed with the idea of the consumer market as well with the Blackberry Pearl. However, Apple's App Store cemented consumers' loyalty to iPhones.

CNET reported that Nokia executives said that their avoiding change was not arrogance, but an inability to take risks. There was also no sense of urgency. Their OS, Symbian, was also holding them back. Nokia finally countered with the Lumia smartphone but consumers were now focused on Apple and Samsung.

Multi-level Interpretation. These findings and conclusions can be framed in the multi-level framework discussed in Chapter 2, where the levels for this case study are products, processes, company, and industry:

- Industry: Constant innovation and change in terms of both technology and consumers' desires and expectations
- Company: Embraced digital as the future; focused on low-priced offerings; recognized smartphone market later than others

- Processes: Hardware processes were very constrained by precedent and software processes were deeply flawed; realization of this was delayed
- Products: Their digital offering supplanted analog; software came to dominate hardware; smartphones emerged as digital devices, not just phones.

Comparison Across Case Studies

Table 4.2 provides a multi-level comparison of the six case studies of failures of complex enterprises. At the lowest level—products and technologies—all six cases involved fundamental market challenges. However, these challenges only constituted the proximate causes of the failures of these organizations.

Contributing causes included business processes ill-matched to new markets, where outsourcing was central to time to market and software processes needed to enable migration of operating systems and apps across hardware platforms. The ultimate causes were the companies' inabilities to commit to the transformation of their businesses to exploit technology trends and market opportunities. They all worked to play the game better; Apple changed the game.

Anticipating Failures

All six companies knew technological changes were coming. Indeed, a few of them were leading such changes, in R&D at least if not in their product lines. They wanted to milk the incumbent business as long as possible. Their emerging competitors did not have this option. They had to innovate to get into the game and they did.

How might companies avoid the fates of these six companies? First of all, they need to be vigilant of market and technology trends. As indicated in the introduction to this chapter, technology is often the driving force behind change. Infusions of cloud computing, big data, artificial intelligence, and the Internet of Things are enabling business models that are much more efficient and better serve consumers.

Table 4.2 Multi-level analysis of failures of six complex organizations

Level of analysis	Photography		Computing		Communications	
	Kodak	**Polaroid**	**Digital**	**Xerox**	**Motorola**	**Nokia**
Industry	Photography transitioned from cameras to digital devices	Photography transitioned from cameras to digital devices	Steady transitions between computing generations	Steady transitions between computing generations	Transition between cell phone generations happened quickly	Transition between cell phone generations happened quickly
Management	Kept digital camera on shelf to sustain sales of photographic film	Failed to compete with new photographic technologies and products	Dismissed PC market; tried to catch up but lacked needed business processes	Failed to capitalize on desktop technology investment	Failed to transition quickly from analog to digital cell phone technology	Focused on low-priced cell phones; surprised by the quickly growing popularity of smartphones
Processes	Business process improvement was inadequate for the challenge faced	Business process improvement was inadequate for the challenge faced	Business processes did not support outsourcing	Computing was an orphan to document management	Inadequate software development process	Inadequate software development process
Products	Invented digital camera, but film-based photography dominated	Invented instant camera; digital photography is inherently instant	Dominated minicomputer market; PC market seemed obvious next step	Desktop metaphor, GUI, computer mouse, and desktop computing	Developed analog cell phone and later digital cell phone; late to smartphones	Initial digital cell phones led market; smartphones were too late and limited

McAfee and Brynjolfsson (2017) have outlined the ways in which the "platform" companies have disrupted traditional companies in how they sell products and services. These companies are leaders in the ongoing digital transformation of corporations (Siebel, 2019). He argues that digital transformation is key to surviving the competition. It is an imperative rather than an option.

Impedances to Change

Despite these driving forces, there are substantial impedances to change. First, companies often fail to correctly assess their market situation. Table 4.3 summarizes 10 archetypal market situations and the sentiment associated with them (Rouse, 1996). The six companies in this chapter experienced the first four situations in their paths to success—Steady Growth. However, they failed to anticipate their possible transitions to Consolidation, Silent War, or Paradigm Lost, particularly silent wars with new technologies and software innovations.

We developed a Situation Assessment Advisor that employed a large number of business metrics to assess where a company is and where it is headed. This expert system-based tool was used by a variety of companies to assess their current and emerging situations. We found that users very much valued historical cases of companies that faced their situations, e.g., currently in Steady

Table 4.3 Ten archetypal market situations

Situation	Sentiment
Vision Quest	No Matter What!
Evolution	Not Yet
Crossover	A Few Good Things
Crossing the Chasm	Beyond Friends
Steady Growth	Life Is Sweet
Consolidation	Too Many Players
Silent War	Unexpected Alternatives
Paradigm Lost	No Longer a Player
Commodity Trap	Differentiation Disappears
Process	Better Rather Than Different

Growth and headed to Silent War. They would consider what other companies did, whether they succeeded, and how these strategies applied to them.

Accurately assessing where you are is an important starting point. The next impedance to change is the prevalence of strategic delusions that undermine strategic thinking (Rouse, 1998). Table 4.4 summarizes 13 strategic delusions that we identified, both from our working with over 100 companies and the relevant literature, as well as possible remedies.

The top three delusions in this table are hallmarks of highly successful companies that are reluctant to address change. Combining these three with 1) We Have to Make the Numbers, and 2) We Just Have to Execute engenders a strong cultural bias against fundamental change. I have asked many corporate executives about this tendency. The various responses can be summarized as: "I am having great difficulty balancing investments in the company I have versus investing in the company I want." Quarterly pressures on revenues and profits, and hence share price, are relentless.

We developed a software tool that accompanied *Don't Jump to Solutions* (Rouse, 1998) that involved using answers to a structured set of questions to assess the extent to which each of the 13 delusions was likely impeding a company from insightfully addressing change. The book and software tool were selected as the Doubleday

Table 4.4 Strategic delusions

Delusion	Remedy
We have a great plan	Compare visions and realities
We are number one	Let go of the world class myth
We own the market	Assess relationships with markets
We have already changed	Move beyond the status quo
We know the right way	Overcome the myth of professional objectivity
We just need one big win	Avoid chasing purple rhinos
We have consensus	Manage conflicts of values and priorities
We have to make the numbers	Balance short term and long term
We have the ducks lined up	Navigate tangled webs of relationships
We have the necessary processes	Avoid institutionalized conflicts
We just have to execute	Maintain commitment and action
We found it was easy	Make sure you don't skip the hard part
We succeeded as we planned	Place yourself in the path of serendipity

Executive Book Club book of the month and later judged to be one of the top 20 business publications in the world that year.

Enterprise Transformation

Once a company has accurately assessed its market situation and understands the delusions that may hinder its addressing change, they may be ready to consider enterprise transformation (Rouse, 2005, 2006, 2019). They may be ready to entertain fundamental change as elaborated below.

Enterprise transformation goes far beyond business process improvement. Just getting better and better at what you are already doing is not enough. Motorola pioneered a version of Total Quality Management termed Six Sigma—a product or process that has just 3.4 defects per million units or opportunities. Six Sigma was not sufficient to overcome products that were no longer attractive to customers.

It is very difficult to successfully innovate when new offerings make your current offerings obsolete. It can require transformation of your enterprise. However, it has been suggested that transforming an enterprise is akin to rewiring a building while the power is on. How can we design and develop a transformed enterprise while also avoiding operational disruptions and unintended consequences in the process? To address this question, we need a deeper understanding of the notion of enterprise transformation.

Our earlier studies (Rouse, 2005, 2006) have led us to formulate a qualitative theory:

> Enterprise transformation is driven by experienced and/or anticipated value deficiencies that result in significantly redesigned and/or new work processes as determined by management's decision making abilities, limitations, and inclinations, all in the context of the social networks of management in particular and the enterprise in general.

Context of Transformation. Enterprise transformation occurs in—and is at least partially driven by—the external context of the economy and markets. As shown in Figure 4.4, the economy affects markets that, in turn, affect enterprises. Of course, it is not quite as crisply hierarchical as indicated in that the economy can directly affect enterprises, e.g., via regulation and taxation. The key point is that the nature and extent of transformation are context dependent.

There is also an internal context of transformation—the "intraprise" in Figure 4.4. Work assignments are pursued via work processes and yield work products, incurring costs. Values and culture, reward and recognition systems, individual and team competencies, and leadership are woven throughout the intraprise. These factors usually have strong impacts on an enterprise's inclinations and abilities to pursue transformation.

Qualitative Theory. Succinctly, experienced or expected value deficiencies drive enterprise transformation initiatives. Deficiencies are defined relative to both current enterprise states and expected states. Expectations may be based on extrapolation of past enterprise states. They may also be based on perceived opportunities to pursue expanded markets, new constituencies, technologies, etc. Thus, deficiencies may be perceived for both reactive and proactive reasons.

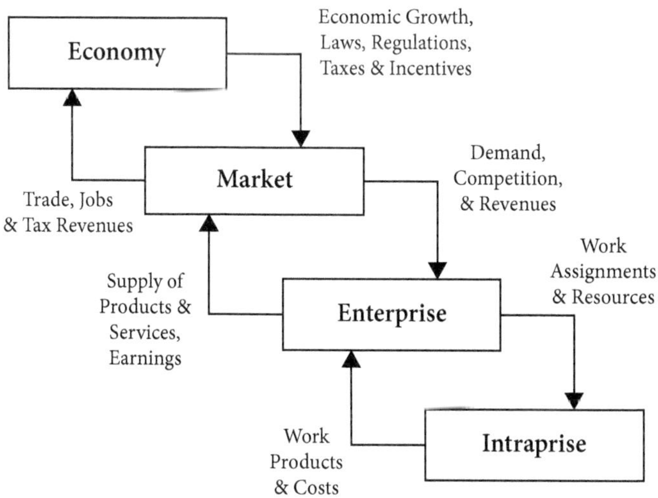

Figure 4.4 Context of enterprise transformation

Transformation initiatives involve addressing what work is undertaken by the enterprise and how this work is accomplished. The work of the enterprise ultimately affects the state of the enterprise, which is reflected, in part, in the enterprise's financial statements, Balanced Scorecard assessment, or the equivalent. Other important elements of the enterprise state might include market advantage, brand image, employee and customer satisfaction, and so on.

Ends, Means, and Scope of Transformation. There is a wide range of ways to pursue transformation. Figure 4.5 summarizes conclusions drawn from numerous case studies. The ends of transformation can range from greater cost efficiencies, to enhanced market perceptions, to new product and service offerings, to fundamental changes of markets. The means can range from upgrading people's skills, to redesigning business practices, to significant infusions of technology, to fundamental changes of strategy. The scope of transformation

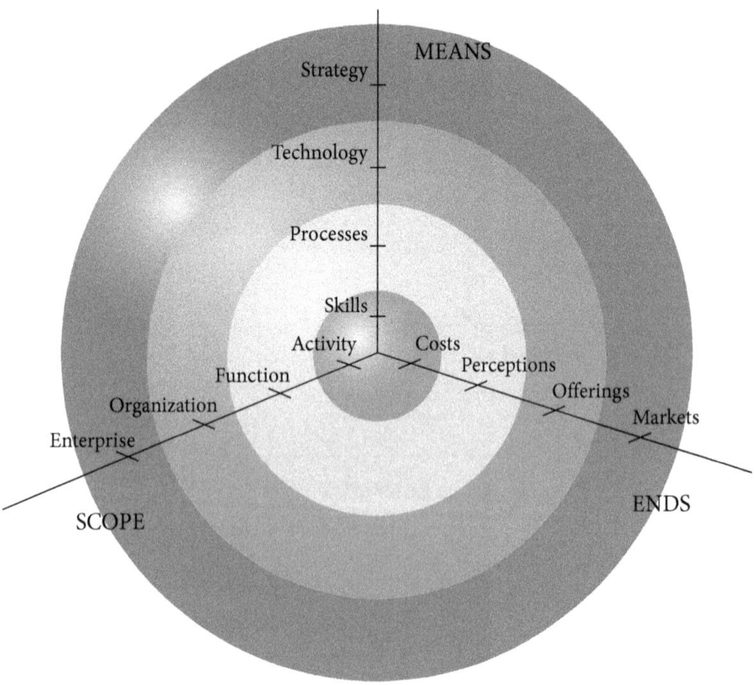

Figure 4.5 Transformation framework

can range from work activities, to business functions, to overall organizations, to the enterprise as a whole.

The framework in Figure 4.5 has provided a useful categorization of a broad range of case studies of enterprise transformation. Considering transformation of markets, Amazon leveraged IT to redefine book buying, while Wal-Mart leveraged IT to redefine the retail industry. In these two instances at least, it can be argued that Amazon and Wal-Mart just grew; they did not transform. Nevertheless, their markets were transformed and competitors were forced to adapt.

Illustrations of transformation of offerings include UPS moving from being a package delivery company to a global supply chain management provider, IBM's transition from manufacturing to services, Motorola moving from battery eliminators to radios to cell phones, and CNN redefining news delivery. Examples of transformation of perceptions include Dell repositioning computer buying, Starbucks repositioning coffee purchases, and Victoria's Secret repositioning lingerie buying. The many instances of transforming business operations include Lockheed Martin merging three aircraft companies, Newell Rubbermaid resuscitating numerous home products companies, and Interface adopting green business practices.

The costs and risks of transformation increase as the endeavor moves farther from the center in Figure 4.5. Initiatives focused on the center will typically involve well-known and mature methods and tools from industrial engineering and operations management. In contrast, initiatives towards the perimeter will often require substantial changes of products, services, channels, etc., as well as associated large investments.

It is important to note that successful transformations in the outer band of Figure 4.5 are likely to require significant investments in the inner bands also. In general, any level of transformation requires consideration of all subordinate levels. Thus, for example, successfully changing the market's perceptions of an enterprise's offerings is likely to also require enhanced operational excellence to underpin the new image being sought. As another illustration, significant changes of strategies often require new processes for decision making, e.g., for R&D investments.

I hasten to note that, at this point, I am only addressing what is likely to have to change, not how the changes can be accomplished. In particular, the success of transformation initiatives depends on gaining the support of stakeholders, managing their perceptions and expectations, and sustaining fundamental change (Rouse, 2001, 2006, 2007). Leading initiatives where these factors play major roles requires competencies in vision, leadership, strategy, planning, culture, collaboration, and teamwork (Rouse, 2011). I will return to these issues in Chapter 8.

Demographics of Change

We have discussed impedances to fundamental change and a framework for addressing change. How can a company assess the likelihood that needs for change are emerging? Declining revenues, profits, and rankings are good indicators that change should have been addressed earlier, perhaps several years earlier.

How might a company have seen these declines coming? We have found that current revenues and profits are not good predictors of future revenues and profits. This led us to the idea that the "story" playing out in a company may be a harbinger of future performance. In particular, we were interested in the extent to which this story, despite current strong financial performance, could predict future performance declines (Yu, Serban, and Rouse, 2013).

Sources of this story were 10+ years of press releases, news coverage, and other publications. There were typically over 10,000 documents per company. We developed an Enterprise Transformation Taxonomy Library using Northern Light's text-mining platform on their research portal Single Point (Seuss, 2011). First, we defined normalized concepts for types of business event including:

- Business expansion
- Downsizing
- Executive turnover
- Lawsuits and legal issues
- Merger and acquisition announcements

- New product announcements
- Strategic alliances.

The textual data was from Capital IQ companies' news reports (Capital IQ, 2010, 2011), which includes 583 sources. Some source examples are individual company websites, Reuters, Dow Jones News Service, and Capital IQ Transaction Database. The large number of documents for each business event type provided a basis for rich insights into a company's characteristics.

Validation of our taxonomy was accomplished by assessing the extent to which the text mining results agreed with Capital IQ's manual analysis of the same data set. We continued to refine our taxonomy until agreement was quite high. A key factor in achieving this match was the design of rules that enabled correct interpretation of terms. Mergers, acquisitions, and legal issues are pretty straightforward. Business alliances, for example, are more subtle. Company X may mention Company Y in a press release because Y is a new alliance partner or just because Y is a large customer—they may do this without using the word alliance or customer, or synonyms.

Figure 4.6 shows Nokia's story. There were not many Business Expansion or Downsizing news announcements around 2001–2002, as Nokia maintained its leading position for several years. The net income decrease in 2001 represented a downsizing effect due to the market bubble more than a company internal effect for ranking change. Between 2003 and 2008, Nokia kept expanding according to the text mining results. However, Nokia's ranking decreased from the market leader range. This might appear contradictory until one looks at what other companies were doing. For example, Apple's expansion was much more vigorous. Starting from the end of 2008, the text mining results show that there was a decline in Nokia's business expansion while an increase in downsizing and discontinued operations. This aligns with the change of ranks, as well as the effects of the economic recession.

This example, and many others discussed by Yu, Serban, and Rouse (2013), show that evidence-based surveillance of the story playing out in a company can be automated and provide numerous insights. I hasten to emphasize the fact that the evidence includes

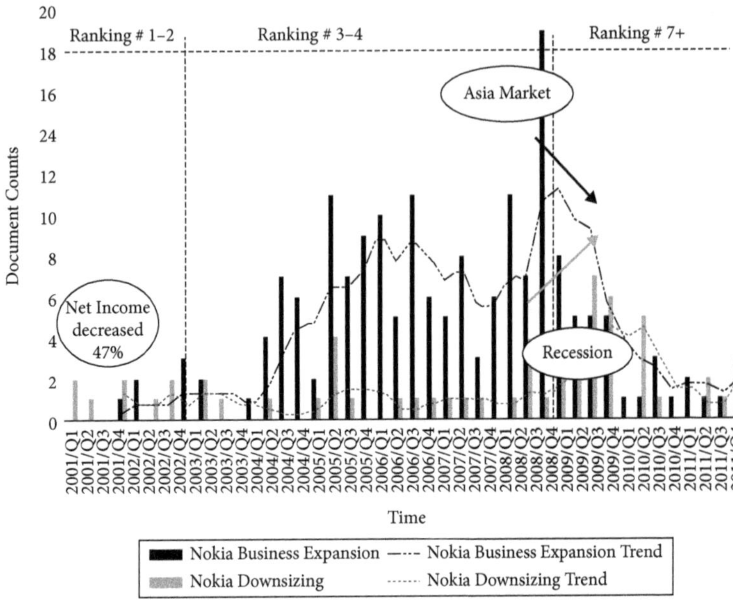

Figure 4.6 Evidence-based story for Nokia for 2001–2011

both company press releases and thousands of other third-party assessments of what is happening in a company. This representation is much richer than typical self-portrayals of a company's financial performance.

Change Strategies

Using one of more of the approaches discussed thus far in this section, a company may be ready to pursue fundamental change. There are several strategies a company might adopt. The choice depends on enterprises' abilities to predict their futures, as well as their abilities to respond to these futures. What strategies might enterprise decision makers adopt to address alternative futures? As shown in Figure 4.7, we have found that there are four basic strategies that decision makers can use: optimize, adapt, hedge, and accept.

If the phenomena of interest are highly predictable, then there is little chance that the enterprise will be pushed into unanticipated

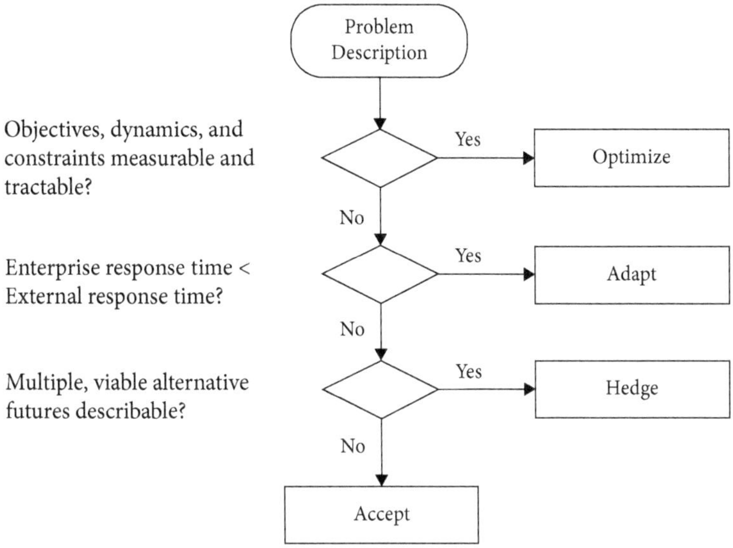

Figure 4.7 Strategy framework for enterprise decision makers
Source: Pennock and Rouse (2016).

territory. Consequently, it is in the best interest of the enterprise to optimize its products and services to be as efficient as possible. In other words, if the unexpected cannot happen, then there is no reason to expend resources beyond process refinement and improvement.

If the phenomena of interest are not highly predictable, but products and services can be appropriately adapted when necessary, it may be in the best interest for the enterprise to plan to adapt. For example, agile capacities can be designed to enable their use in multiple ways, to adapt to changing demands, e.g., the way Honda did but other automakers could not in response to the Great Recession. In this case, some efficiency has been traded for the ability to adapt.

For this approach to work, the enterprise must be able to identify and respond to potential issues faster than the ecosystem changes. For example, consider unexpected increased customer demands that tax capacities beyond their designed limits. Design and building of new or expanded facilities can take considerable time. On the other hand, reconfiguration of agile capacities should be much faster.

If the phenomena of interest are not very predictable and the enterprise has a limited ability to respond, it may be in the best interest of the enterprise to hedge its position. In this case, it can explore scenarios where the enterprise may not be able to handle sudden changes without prior investment. For example, an enterprise concerned about potential obsolescence of existing products and services may choose to invest in multiple, potential new offerings. Such investments might be pilot projects that enable learning how to deliver products services differently or perhaps deliver different products and services.

Over time, it will become clear which of these options makes most sense and the enterprise can exercise the best option by scaling up these offerings based on what they have learned during the pilot projects. In contrast, if the enterprise were to take a wait and see approach, it might not be able to respond quickly enough, and it might lose out to its competitors.

If the phenomena of interest are totally unpredictable and there is no viable way to respond, then the enterprise has no choice but to accept the risk. Accept is not so much a strategy as a default condition. If one is attempting to address a strategic challenge where there is little ability to optimize the efficacy of offerings, limited ability to adapt offerings, and no viable hedges against the uncertainties associated with these offerings, the enterprise must accept the conditions that emerge.

There is another possibility that deserves mention—stay with the status quo. Yu, Rouse, and Serban (2011) developed a computational theory of enterprise transformation, elaborating on the qualitative theory presented earlier in this chapter (Rouse, 2005, 2006). They employed this computational theory to assess when investing in change is attractive and unattractive. Investing in transformation is likely to be attractive when one is currently underperforming and the circumstances are such that investments will likely improve enterprise performance. In contrast, if one is already performing well, investments in change will be difficult to justify. Similarly, if performance cannot be predictably improved—due to noisy markets and/or highly discriminating customers—then investments may not be warranted despite current underperformance.

How do the choices in Figure 4.7 align with the choices made by the six companies highlighted in this chapter? Their primary choices seemed to be to optimize the efficiency of current offerings, even though they recognized the technology forces they were facing. Kodak, Xerox, and Motorola had invested in options for digital photography, personal computing, and digital cell phones, but either exercised these options far too late or failed to exercise them at all. Milking current cash flows was just too compelling.

Creative Destruction

This chapter addressed Kodak, Polaroid, Digital, Xerox, Motorola, and Nokia as examples of companies that did not change, did not remediate their emerging value deficiencies. All of these companies had periods of great success, when revenues, profits, and share prices were soaring. Then they were overtaken by creative destruction (Schumpeter, 1942).

From a broad perspective, creative destruction is a powerful, positive force. New value propositions, often enabled by new technologies, led by new, innovative competitors take markets away from established players. Jobs are created. The economy grows. People can, therefore, afford cars, TVs, smartphones, etc.

The story is not as positive for the incumbents. They are under constant pressure. They have to face the dilemma of running the company they have while they try to become the company they want. But the company they have is usually consuming all the money and talent. They need to address the balance between investing in getting better at what they are already doing versus investing in doing new things.

It is very difficult to achieve this balance. Most of the stakeholders are strongly committed to the status quo. They need resources and attention to keep the status quo functioning. Many of the stakeholders in the future have yet to arrive. Consequently, they are not very demanding. Creating a sense of urgency is usually essential to addressing this stalemate.

Various pundits express this in the sense of needing a "burning platform." A key is to identify leading indicators of both positive and negative changes. Then, one should look for evidence of these indicators, both externally in the economy and marketplace and internally in the enterprise and intraprise. The result can be stories of change that, hopefully, everyone can understand and find compelling (Yu, Serban, and Rouse, 2013).

Examples of Success

Fundamental change can be successfully pursued and achieved. IBM moved from relying on mainframe computer sales to selling software and services. Microsoft moved beyond milking Windows and Microsoft Office to embrace the Internet. Apple transformed itself from selling computers to providing elegant digital devices.

IBM had its highest share price in 1990 but was on the path to losing billions in 1993. Louis Gerstner, IBM CEO, "is widely credited with transforming IBM into a customer-focused global enterprise dedicated to leadership in services and technology. Mr. Gerstner joined IBM in April 1993. Through year-end 2001, the company's share price increased more than 800 percent, and its market value grew by $180 billion. The company also gained market share in key strategic areas, including servers, software, storage, and microelectronics. IBM had received more US patents than any other company for nine consecutive years" (IBM, 2002).

Microsoft at first dismissed the Internet and Netscape's web browser, introduced in 1994. By May of 1995, however, Microsoft CEO Bill Gates had thrown his company wholeheartedly into joining the "Internet tidal wave." They released Internet Explorer as an add-on for Windows 95. More recently, Microsoft introduced Azure cloud computing services in 2010 and now is second in market share behind Amazon Web Services.

Apple was on the brink of fizzling out, struggling to find a consistently profitable source of revenue. Instead of continuing to aimlessly pursue marginal product ideas, Apple, with Steve Jobs again leading, began to focus once more on creating beautiful consumer electronics, starting with the iMac in 1998. The iPod was an even bigger success, selling over 100 million units within six years of its 2001 launch. The iPhone, another smash hit, was released in 2007 and resulted in enormous year-over-year increases in sales. The iPad followed in 2010. Apple changed its name in 2007 from Apple Computer to just Apple.

Success is possible. However, as is evident from these three examples, leadership is crucial. If top leaders remain stewards of the status quo, fundamental change will not happen. Leadership is the most important competency along with vision, communications, and collaboration (Rouse, 2011).

Conclusions

Technology transitions are difficult for successful incumbents to address. The norm is for such companies to fall prey to creative destruction. While this fate lurks on the horizon, management tends to stick to the knitting until time and resources do not allow effective responses.

There are strong impedances to change. Assessments of market situations are often premised on outdated assumptions. Strategic delusions about customers, competitors, and the company itself often undermine strategic thinking. There is also the compelling nature of the status quo, especially when revenues and profits are still strong.

However, disciplined surveillance and control can compensate for these natural tendencies. Business intelligence should include market and technology trends, as well as evidence-based research on the story playing out in the company. There are analytical methods that can enable rigorous assessment of this story, or set of stories, and their likely implications.

References

Anthony, S.D. (2016). Kodak's downfall wasn't about technology. *Harvard Business Review*, July 15.

Anthony, S.D., Viguerie, S.P., Schwartz, E.I., and Van Landeghem, J. (2018). *2018 Corporate Longevity Forecast: Creative Destruction Is Accelerating*. Lexington, MA: Innosight.

Bonanos, C. (2012). *Instant: The Story of Polaroid.* Princeton, NJ: Princeton Architectural Press.

Capital IQ (2010). *The Premier Solution for Quantitative Analysis.* Retrieved from S&P Capital IQ: https://www.capitaliq.com/home/what-we-offer/information-you-need/financials-valuation/premium-financials.aspx.

Capital IQ (2011). *Analyze and Anticipate the Impact of News on Market Prices.* Retrieved from S&P Capital IQ: https://www.capitaliq.com/home/what-we-offer/information-you-need/qualitative-data/key-developments.aspx.

CNET (2014). Farewell Nokia: The rise and fall of a mobile pioneer. *CNET*, April 25.

CNN (1999). Nokia overtakes Motorola. *CNN Money*, February 8.

Collins, M. (2018). *A Telephone for the World: Iridium, Motorola, and the Making of a Global Age.* Baltimore, MD: Johns Hopkins University Press.

Dautovic, G. (2019). Smartphone market share: Past, present and future. *Fortunly*, August 19.

Doz, Y., and Wilson, K. (2018). *Ringtone: Exploring the Rise and Fall of Nokia in Mobile Phones.* Oxford: Oxford University Press.

Economist, The (2012). The last Kodak moment? *The Economist*, January 14.

Ellis, C.D. (2006). *Joe Wilson and the Creation of Xerox.* New York: Wiley.

Fishman, T.C. (2014). What happened to Motorola? *Chicago Magazine*, August 25.

Hessledahl, A. (2004). Motorola vs. Nokia. *Forbes*, January 19.

Hiltzik, M. (2011). Kodak's long fade to black. *Los Angeles Times*, December 4.

IBM (2002). Samuel J. Palmisano elected IBM CEO; Louis V. Gerstner, Jr. to remain chairman through 2002. IBM Press Release, January 29.

IBM (2019). The birth of the IBM PC. IBM Archives. Accessed 16/10/2019.

Isaacson, W. (2011). *Steve Jobs.* New York: Simon & Schuster.

Linge, N. (2016). Motorola bought us the mobile phone, but ended merged out of existence. *The Conversation*, January 13.

McAfee, A., and Brynjolfsson, E. (2017). *Machine Platform Crowd: Harness our Digital Future.* New York: Norton.

MIT (2011). Lessons from Ken Olsen and Digital Equipment Corporation. *Sloan Management Review*, February 17.

Pennock, M.J., and Rouse, W.B. (2016). The epistemology of enterprises. *Systems Engineering*, 19 (1), 24–43.

Press, G. (2018). Apple, Xerox, IBM, and fumbling the future. *Forbes*, January 14.

Reeves, M., and Harnoss, J. (2015). Don't let your company get trapped by success. *Harvard Business Review*, November 19.

Rockman, S. (2012). What killed Motorola? Not Google! It was Moto's dire software. *The Register*, November 29.

Rouse, W.B. (1996). *Start Where You Are: Matching your Strategy to your Marketplace*. San Francisco, CA: Jossey-Bass.

Rouse, W.B. (1998). *Don't Jump to Solutions: Thirteen Delusions that Undermine Strategic Thinking*. San Francisco, CA: Jossey-Bass.

Rouse, W.B. (2001). *Essential Challenges of Strategic Management*. New York: Wiley.

Rouse, W.B. (2005). A theory of enterprise transformation. *Systems Engineering*, 8 (4), 279–95.

Rouse, W.B. (ed.) (2006). *Enterprise Transformation: Understanding and Enabling Fundamental Change*. New York: Wiley.

Rouse, W.B. (2007). *People and Organizations: Explorations of Human-Centered Design*. New York: Wiley.

Rouse, W.B. (2011). Necessary competencies for transforming an enterprise. *Journal of Enterprise Transformation*, 1 (1), 71–92.

Rouse, W.B. (2019). *Computing Possible Futures: Model-based Explorations of "What if?"* Oxford: Oxford University Press.

Schein, E.H., DeLisi, P.S., Kampas, P.J., and Sonduck, M.M. (2004). *DEC Is Dead, Long Live DEC: The Lasting Legacy of Digital Equipment Corporation*. New York: Berrett-Koehler.

Schumpeter, J. (1942). *Capitalism, Socialism, and Democracy*. New York: Harper.

Seuss, C.D. (2011). Teaching search engines to interpret meaning. *Proceedings of the IEEE*, 99 (4), 531–5.

Sheetz, M. (2017). Technology killing off corporate America: Average life span of companies under 20 years. *CNBC*, August 24.

Siebel, T.M. (2019). *Digital Transformation: Survive and Thrive in an Era of Mass Extinction*. New York: Rosetta.

Smith, D.K., and Alexander, R.C. (1988). *Fumbling the Future: How Xerox Invented, Then Ignored, the First Personal Computer*. New York: Morrow.

Snyder, P. (2013). *Is This Something George Eastman Would Have Done? The Decline and Fall of Eastman Kodak Company*. New York: CreateSpace.

Yu, X., Rouse, W.B., and Serban, N. (2011). A computational theory of enterprise transformation. *Systems Engineering*, 14 (4), 441–54.

Yu, X., Serban, N., and Rouse, W.B. (2013). The demographics of change: Enterprise characteristics and behaviors that influence enterprise transformation. *Journal of Enterprise Transformation*, 3 (4), 285–306.

5

Failures of Complex Ecosystems

Introduction

In this chapter, we transition from technologies and organizations to ecosystems that involve many organizations and millions of people, often across global borders. Failures of these complex ecosystems can take significant time to detect, diagnose, compensate, and remediate.

Table 5.1 summarizes the six ecosystem failures discussed in this chapter. These ecosystems—in health, the economy, and the environment—have faced or will likely face enormous losses of life, human suffering, and economic disruptions.

These case studies involve distributed failures, in contrast to point failures. Point failures, as illustrated in Chapter 3, are latent in engineered systems due to their design, development, and deployment as well as how they are operated, maintained, and managed. Point failures are much more quickly recognized, typically leading to immediate responses and eventual remediation.

Distributed failures are usually not readily apparent until their consequences have been manifested over time. Recognition and diagnosis are often quite delayed. Design, development, and deployment are in reaction to such failures. Operations, maintenance, and management relate to delivery of interventions intended to remediate the failures.

Failures of complex organizations, as considered in Chapter 4, tend to be hybrids of point and distributed failures. Specific things may go wrong, e.g., releases of poorly received product offerings. However, this usually occurs in the context of overall corporate

Failure Management: Malfunctions of Technologies, Organizations, and Society. William B. Rouse, Oxford University Press (2021). © William B. Rouse. DOI: 10.1093/oso/9780198870999.003.0005

Table 5.1 Consequences of failures of complex ecosystems

Case study	Domain	Proximal consequences
AIDS	Health	75 million infected globally, 32 million deaths, treatment of HIV now effective, cost of treatment of $8 billion annually.
Opioids	Health	27 million addicted globally, 50,000 deaths in 2017, costs of substance abuse in United States of $0.75 trillion annually.
Depression	Economy	Half of US banks failed; 15 million (25 percent) of US population unemployed, US economy shrunk by 50 percent.
Recession	Economy	$8 trillion stock market wealth lost and $6 trillion in home value lost, 4 million mortgages foreclosed.
Population	Environment	795 million people undernourished. 9 million annual global deaths from hunger and hunger-related diseases
Climate	Environment	Weather changes, sea level rise, salinization of groundwater and estuaries, decrease in freshwater availability, ocean acidification affects sea life, food supply and health degraded

cultures and rules of the game. Consequently, it may require considerable time before the enterprise realizes and accepts that a failure has emerged.

Thus, point failures tend to manifest themselves relatively quickly, while distributed failures emerge over time and are slowly recognized as failures. This difference significantly affects methods for addressing failures, including approaches to surveillance and control. It also tends to affect the breadth of stakeholders involved in addressing failures.

For distributed failures, consequences are typically unexpected, so control has usually been ignored. For example, clinicians were treating pain, making money, and living life, but bad things happened. Eventual risks were not anticipated and were years beyond any planning horizon. Design decisions, e.g., the structure of financial derivatives, occurred long before problems emerged and were recognized; crisis management decisions occurred after the failure. Operational management decisions occurred as an unrecognized failure was emerging; remediation decisions occurred after the failure.

Point failures are amenable to engineering approaches to system design. However, these approaches are not particularly useful for distributed failures of systems for which there are no blueprints, i.e., systems that were not really designed. Distributed failures have to be addressed differently.

Surveillance of the state of the system focuses on detecting anomalies, i.e., unexpected system states. There are surveillance methods for population health, the economy, and the environment. The data and methods employed for surveillance in these different domains are discussed after the six case studies in this chapter are reviewed.

AIDS and Opioids Epidemics

HIV is a virus spread by physical contact; untreated it can result in AIDS. Opioid addiction is a disease spread socially, both by marketing processes and peer groups. Both diseases were slowly detected as deaths multiplied. We have determined how best to address HIV. Addressing opioid addiction is a work in progress.

AIDS Epidemic

HIV (human immunodeficiency virus) is a virus that attacks cells that help the body fight infection, making someone more vulnerable to other infections and diseases. The virus is spread by contact with certain bodily fluids of a person with HIV. If not treated, HIV can lead to the disease AIDS (acquired immunodeficiency syndrome).

It is believed that HIV originated in Kinshasa, in the Democratic Republic of Congo around 1920 when HIV crossed species from chimpanzees to humans. The chimpanzee version of the immunodeficiency virus (called simian immunodeficiency virus or SIV) was most likely transmitted to humans and mutated into HIV when humans hunted these chimpanzees for meat and came into contact with their infected blood.

The AIDS epidemic, caused by HIV, emerged in the United States perhaps by 1960, but was first noticed after doctors discovered clusters of Kaposi's sarcoma and pneumocystis pneumonia in gay men in Los Angeles, New York City, and San Francisco in 1981. In 1983, doctors at the Pasteur Institute in France reported the discovery of a new retrovirus called LAV (Lymphadenopathy-Associated Virus) that was likely the cause of AIDS.

In April 1984, the National Cancer Institute announced they had found the cause of AIDS, the retrovirus HTLV-III. In a joint conference with the Pasteur Institute, they announced that LAV and HTLV-III were identical and the likely cause of AIDS. In May 1986, the International Committee on the Taxonomy of Viruses said that the virus that causes AIDS would officially be called HIV.

In 1989, the number of reported AIDS cases in the United States reached 100,000. By the end of 1993, there were an estimated 2.5 million AIDS cases globally. The estimated number of people living with HIV was 23 million by the end of 1996. Roughly 38 million people were living with HIV globally by 2018.

In June 1995, the FDA approved the first highly active antiretroviral treatment (HAART). Once incorporated into clinical practice, this brought about an immediate decline of between 60 percent and 80 percent in rates of AIDS-related deaths and hospitalization—in those countries that could afford it. In September 1997, the FDA approved Combivir, a combination of two antiretroviral drugs, taken as a single daily tablet, making it easier for people living with HIV to take their medication.

In August 2011, the FDA approved Complera, the second all-in-one fixed-dose combination tablet, expanding the treatment options available for people living with HIV. In July 2012, the FDA approved PrEP for HIV-negative people to prevent the sexual transmission of HIV. In 2012, for the first time, the majority of people eligible for treatment were receiving it (54 percent).

The Economist (2019) reported on the steady progress to thwart HIV, currently at a cost of $8 billion per year. The operative goals are that by the end of 2020 are:

- 90 percent of those infected will know they are

- 90 percent of this group will be receiving antiretroviral therapy
- 90 percent of those receiving therapy will have had the virus effectively suppressed.

They report that progress towards these goals is on course, but these targets are unlikely to be hit in 2020. Bernstein (2019) discusses factors impeding progress including the number of people without health insurance and the costs of the drugs.

Multi-level Interpretations. These findings and conclusions can be framed in the multi-level framework discussed in Chapter 2, where the levels for this case study are people, processes, organizations, and society:

- Society: Society slowly became aware of the pervasiveness and consequences of the problem and recognized the broader population risks and needs to address these risks.
- Organizations: National health organizations and medical research institutions led the efforts to understand the causes of HIV and AIDS; pharmaceutical organizations led the development of drugs.
- Processes: Surveillance processes slowly detected the epidemic; medical research processes diagnosed the causes; pharmaceutical research processes yielded the needed drugs.
- People. People slowly became aware of how their behaviors affected becoming afflicted with HIV and then AIDS; more recently they recognized the drugs they needed to combat HIV.

Why am I characterizing this as a "failure?" The fact that millions of people have died seems a sufficient justification. However, despite the inherent slowness of progress, society has succeeded in addressing this failure.

A key point is that unanticipated failures happen. Proper surveillance can eventually detect such public health challenges. Research can unearth the causes of these challenges. Further research can develop interventions to remediate these causes. This is one of several approaches to failure management discussed in Chapter 7.

Opioid Epidemic

Sam Quinones' *Dreamland* (2015) provides a portrayal of the panorama of substance abuse epidemic in America. Pharma's business model for pain pills included misleading advertising, an aggressive sales force, and incentives for doctors to prescribe opioids. Central to this was the delusion that opioids are not addictive, based on a one-paragraph letter to the editor of the prestigious *New England Journal of Medicine* (Porter and Jick, 1980).

Once addicted, people found heroin to be much cheaper than prescription drugs, and more powerful. Unfortunately, heroin laced with fentanyl has become increasingly deadly. Product supply chains, whether for prescription or illicit drugs, are highly integrated. However, the service supply chain for treating substance abuse is highly fragmented (Rouse, Johns, and Pepe, 2019).

DeWeerdt (2019) traces the US opioid crisis to its roots. The epidemic arose through a confluence of well-intentioned efforts to improve pain management by doctors and aggressive—even fraudulent—marketing by pharmaceutical manufacturers. Characteristics of the US healthcare system, regulatory regime, culture, and socio-economic trends all contributed to what is now a full-blown crisis.

The foundation for the crisis was laid in the 1980s, when pain increasingly became recognized as a problem that required adequate treatment. US states began to pass intractable pain treatment acts, which removed the threat of prosecution for physicians who treated their patients' pain aggressively with controlled substances. These substances were substituted for pain treatment centers that payers found too expensive.

Before the present epidemic, opioids were prescribed mainly for short-term uses such as pain relief after surgery or for people with advanced cancer or other terminal conditions. But in the United States, the idea that opioids might be safer and less addictive than was previously thought began to gain credibility, in part prompted by the previously noted Porter and Jick letter.

Prescriptions for opioids increased gradually throughout the 1980s and early 1990s. In the mid-1990s, pharmaceutical companies introduced new opioid-based products. Of particular note is Purdue Pharma's OxyContin, a sustained-release formulation of oxycodone. Prescriptions surged and the use of opioids to treat chronic pain became widespread.

The claim that OxyContin was less addictive than other opioid painkillers was not true. Despite the Porter and Jick letter, Purdue Pharma knew that OxyContin was addictive. It admitted this in a 2007 lawsuit that resulted in a US$635 million fine for the company. Doctors and patients were unaware of that at the time and did not question what they were told by pharmaceutical representatives.

The structure of the healthcare system in the United States also contributed to the over-prescription of opioids. Because many doctors are in private practice, they can benefit financially by increasing the volume of patients that they see, as well as by ensuring patient satisfaction, which can incentivize the over-prescription of pain medication. Prescription opioids were also cheap in the short term. Patients' health-insurance plans often covered pain medication but not pain-management approaches such as physical therapy.

The hardest-hit communities are in the US states in the Ohio River Valley and northern New England, particularly communities with a problem of under-employment and a problem of concentration of poverty. The notion of "deaths of despair" arose to describe the suicides and opioid-overdose deaths of people affected by de-industrialization and economic decline. The increased deaths in these regions have resulted in decreasing life expectancy in the United States for the past three years (Woolf and Schoomaker, 2019).

The opioid epidemic has played out in three phases (DeWeerdt, 2019; Rich et al., 2019). The first phase was dominated by prescription opioids, the second phase by heroin, and the third phase by cheaper—but more potent—synthetic opioids such as fentanyl. All of these forms of opioid remain relevant to the current crisis. "Basically, we have three epidemics on top of each other," Keith Humphreys says. "There are plenty of people using all three drugs. And there are plenty of people who start on one and die on another" (DeWeerdt, 2019).

The National Institute on Drug Abuse (2018) reports on drug overdose deaths involving any opioid--prescription opioids (including methadone), synthetic opioids, and heroin. Deaths rose from 18,515 in 2007 to 47,600 in 2017; 68 percent of deaths occurred among males. NIH (2016) estimates that substance abuse, including tobacco, alcohol, and drugs, in the United States costs US$0.75 trillion annually.

We recently addressed substance abuse as a population health problem (Rouse, Johns, and Pepe, 2019). Population health involves integration of health, education, and social services to keep a defined population healthy, to address health challenges holistically, and to assist with the realities of being mortal. The fragmentation of the US population health delivery system was of particular interest. The impacts of this fragmentation on the treatment of substance abuse were addressed in detail. We proposed innovations to overcome this fragmentation.

More specifically, we addressed treatment capacity issues, including scheduling practices, as well as costs of treatment and lack of treatment. We reviewed models of integrated care delivery. We considered potential innovations from systems science, behavioral economics, and social networks, as well as the implications of these innovations in terms of IT systems and governance.

We found that enormous savings are possible with more integrated treatment. Based on a range of empirical findings, we argued that investments of these resources in integrated delivery of care have the potential to dramatically improve health outcomes, thereby significantly reducing the costs of population health.

In conjunction with this research, I conducted a series of interviews with front-line health professionals at MedStar Health in Baltimore. Interviewees included nurses, social workers, and recovery coaches. My interview notes include litanies of needs for better integration of care across health, education, and social services.

One nurse complained of the enormous percentage of her time she spends on the phone trying to coordinate the services needed by patients. A social worker commented that substance abuse was typically just one of a patient's problems. Other problems included mental health challenges, joblessness, and homelessness. A recovery coach noted one patient who had been in the Emergency Department several hundred times over a two-year period.

There have been concerted efforts to limit opioid prescription in terms of both numbers of pills and refills. This will likely limit the growth of the number of new addicts. However, as noted earlier, it forces existing addicts to seek new and less safe sources of opioids and heroin. A much more integrated approach to population health is needed to assist these people.

Multi-level Interpretation. These findings and conclusions can be framed in the multi-level framework discussed in Chapter 2, where the levels for this case study are people, processes, organizations, and society:

- Society: The fragmented nature of the US healthcare system, regulatory practices, a culture of independence, and socio-economic trends aligned to enable creation of roughly 10 million addicts in the United States.
- Organizations: Physicians increased their revenues by prescribing opioids. Pharma companies invested in creating opioid offerings as well as massive marketing campaigns that avoided mention of any risks of addiction.
- Processes: Approaches to treating pain included physical therapy, exercise, and drugs. Insurers found physical treatments too expensive and limited reimbursements to drugs. Multiple supply chains emerged.
- People: People thought that opioids provided a safe approach to managing pain; once addicted, their brains demanded continued fixes, leading to growing numbers of overdoses and deaths.

The opioid epidemic represents a massive distributed failure, the causes of which seem to be understood. Failure management needs to address the social determinants of health that accompany and exacerbate substance abuse. The fragmented US healthcare ecosystem is poorly prepared to do this.

Great Depression and Recession

The next two case studies address the economy. Both cases involved rampant speculation, undisciplined banks, and enormous economic losses. The government played a very different role in these two cases. They could not bail out the banks in the 1930s but did in the 2000s, with the gold standard no longer in the way. People were more directly supported by the New Deal in the 1930s than by government expenditures in the 2000s.

Great Depression

There was an unprecedented growth of stock prices throughout the 1920s. Unemployment was low. The automobile industry was thriving. Speculation was rampant with people mortgaging their homes to invest in stocks.

Outrageously overpriced shares, it is argued, precipitated a four-day market crash starting on October 24, 1929. The crash destroyed confidence in the market. In addition, just weeks before the crash, the Federal Reserve had raised interest rates. In the days after the stock market crash, hordes of people rushed to banks to withdraw their funds. In a number of such "bank runs" customers were unable to withdraw their money because the banks had also invested the money in the stock market.

This led to massive bank failures and worsened an already dire financial situation. The Federal Reserve could not the increase money supply sufficiently as it was tied to gold reserves. The United States did not abandon the gold standard until 1933.

Half of US banks failed. 15 million (25 percent) of the US population was unemployed. The US economy shrunk by 50 percent. Consumers reigned in expenditures. Industrial output decreased and prices dropped.

Inexpensive US products led to a trade surplus. Foreign banks had to compensate for this surplus by sending gold to United

States. To avoid this, foreign banks increased interest rates, further depressing their economies. Consequently, the United States imposed steep tariffs on agricultural and industrial goods. Other countries retaliated.

President Franklin Roosevelt's New Deal increased social welfare programs, including the Resettlement Administration (RA), the Rural Electrification Administration (REA), rural welfare projects sponsored by the Works Progress Administration (WPA), National Youth Administration (NYA), Forest Service and the Civilian Conservation Corps (CCC). These programs helped but the defense economy of World War II brought the United States out of Depression, which lasted 10 years (1929–1939).

Depression Mentality

My grandparents, George and Marian Peirce, lived in Boston in Back Bay. George was a major investor and executive in a furniture company. The crash and subsequent depression resulted in the company going bankrupt. Everything was lost.

They had a summer house on the shore in Portsmouth, RI. They moved there, living on the second floor. The first floor became the Wharf Tavern. The whole family worked there. This strategy worked for a while until the 1938 New England Hurricane completely destroyed the Wharf Tavern.

They rebuilt about a mile away, renaming this much smaller restaurant Peirce's Tavern. It burned down a year later. Soon after, George succumbed to cancer. Marian opened an antique shop she ran for several years to make ends meet.

My mother and her four brothers and sisters experienced the Depression, 1938 Hurricane, and then World War II, all in a bit over a decade. They all developed some version of a "depression mentality," namely, if something can go wrong, it will. I experienced this legacy throughout the 1950s and 1960s.

Multi-level Interpretation. These findings and conclusions can be framed in the multi-level framework discussed in Chapter 2, where the levels for this case study are people, processes, organizations, and government:

- Government: The gold standard prevented the Federal Reserve from bailing out the banks. A 50 percent increase of federal spending in 1932 had little impact. New Deal spending focused on directly helping citizens.
- Organizations: Speculation by all players was rampant, betting on profits to service loans. All investments, whether good or bad, suffered from dramatic decreases of stock prices.
- Processes: Banks used people's money to take the same risks in the stock market, subjecting the financial system to the risk of "common mode" failures. The money supply was linked to and limited by the gold standard.
- People: People thought the bull market would continue indefinitely and expected they would use profits from share price increases to pay loans used to buy shares. After the crash, people sharply curtailed spending.

Great Recession

Bubbles eventually burst, whether joyful children playing with soapy water create them, or greedy people playing with other people's money fashion them. One of the earliest economic bubbles concerned tulip bulbs in Holland (Dash, 2001). Tulipomania involved speculative buying and selling of rare tulip bulbs in the 1630s by Dutch citizens. Coveted bulbs changed hands for amazingly increasing sums, until single bulbs were valued at more than the cost of a house. When the bubble burst, the value of bulbs quickly plummeted and fortunes were lost.

We recently experienced a real estate bubble (Lewis, 2011; Blinder, 2013). In real estate mortgage markets, impenetrable derivative securities were bought and sold. The valuations and ratings of these securities were premised on any single mortgage default being a random event. In other words, the default of any particular mortgage was assumed to have no impact on the possible default of any other mortgage.

The growing demand for these securities pressured mortgage companies to lower the standards for these loans. Easily available mortgages drove the sales of homes, steadily increasing home prices. Loans with initial periods of low, or even zero, interest, attracted home buyers to adjustable rate mortgages. Many of these people could not possibly make the mortgage payments when the rates were adjusted after the initial period.

This was of less concern than one might think because people expected to flip these houses by selling them quickly at significantly increased prices. This worked as long as prices continued increasing, but as more and more lower quality mortgages were sold, the numbers of defaults increased and dampened the increasing prices, which led to further increases of defaults. The bubble quickly burst.

The defaults were not random events as assumed by those valuing these securities. They constituted what is termed a "common mode failure" where a common cause results in widespread failure. Thus, these securities were much more risky than sellers had advertised. The consequences of such misinformation were enormous.

Origins of Crisis

An extraordinary rise in housing asset prices and an associated boom in demand characterized the years leading up to the crisis, both while interest rates were very low. The US "shadow" banking system of non-depository financial institutions such as investment banks had grown to rival the depository system yet was not subject to the same regulatory oversight.

US mortgage-backed securities, which involved packaging of risks that were hard to assess, offered higher yields than US government bonds and were marketed globally. Pricing of securities was based on the assumption that any particular mortgage default was independent of any other. "Common mode" failures were not considered.

Many of these securities were backed by subprime mortgages, which collapsed in value when the US housing bubble burst during 2006 and homeowners began to default on their mortgage payments in large numbers starting in 2007. On November 17, 2006, the Commerce Department warned that October's new home permits were 28 percent lower than the year before.

The government did not realize the gravity of these early warning signs. They thought the strong money supply and low-interest rates would limit any problems to the real estate industry. However, banks had become reliant on derivatives, or contracts whose value is derived from other assets, assuming that these assets will perform well. Banks and hedge funds sold mortgage-backed assets securities to each other as investments, not realizing that the underlying mortgages were often quite risky.

Mortgages of interest-only loans were offered to subprime borrowers. These high-risk people were most likely to default on a loan. The banks offered them initial low interest rates, but this loan type escalates to a much higher rate after a certain period. Home prices fell at the same time interest rates reset. Their defaults caused the subprime mortgage crisis.

The emergence of sub-prime loan losses in 2007 began the crisis and exposed other risky loans and over-inflated asset prices. The value of derivatives plummeted. Lehman Brothers fell on September 15, 2008. A major panic soon broke out in the interbank loan market. There was the equivalent of a bank run on the shadow banking system.

The result was many large and well-established investment banks and commercial banks in the United States and Europe suffered huge losses and faced bankruptcy. This led to massive public financial assistance in terms of government bailouts. Governments and central banks responded with fiscal policy and monetary policy initiatives to stimulate national economies and reduce financial system risks.

Commission Conclusions

The US Financial Crisis Inquiry Commission reported its findings in January 2011 (CCFEC, 2019), concluding:

The crisis was avoidable and was caused by:

- Widespread failures in financial regulation, including the Federal Reserve's failure to stem the tide of toxic mortgages;
- Dramatic breakdowns in corporate governance including too many financial firms acting recklessly and taking on too much risk;

- An explosive mix of excessive borrowing and risk by households and Wall Street that put the financial system on a collision course with crisis;
- Key policy makers ill prepared for the crisis, lacking a full understanding of the financial system they oversaw; and systemic breaches in accountability and ethics at all levels.

Quick Response from National Academies

The National Academies of Science, Engineering, and Medicine formed a "quick response" panel that was given two weeks to suggest how the causes of this crisis should be addressed. I was a member of this 10-member panel. We ended up suggesting two approaches. Five members of the panel backed each approach.

One approach involved formulating "bullet proof" oversight and regulatory functions so that it was impossible for either depository or investment banks to stray. A central question, of course, was how to accomplish this and avoid the inevitable gaming of the system.

The second approach, of which I was an advocate, was to assure that the banking system was transparent. Thus, any games being played would be obvious. Bad games would be preempted, but good games might be innovations that could be encouraged and communicated broadly.

I do not know the eventual impact of these quick response recommendations. However, I remain a fan of transparency, whether the system is a nuclear power plant, corporate financial statements, or banking system transactions. Of course, a fundamental question here is: "Who gets to monitor and assess the goodness of alternative ideas?" I review our organizational infrastructure for surveillance later in this chapter.

Multi-level Interpretation. These findings and conclusions can be framed in the multi-level framework discussed in Chapter 2, where the levels for this case study are people, processes, organizations, and government:

- Government: Congress and the Federal Reserve bailed out banks deemed "too big to fail." Little was done to help homeowners; 4 million mortgages were foreclosed, decimating the net worth of many.

- Organizations: Banks created packages with derivatives of mortgages. Credit rating companies rated these packages as low risk, ignoring correlated risks. These packages became toxic as "common mode" defaults spread.
- Processes: Mortgage approval processes became extremely lenient, with applicants having to provide little, if any, evidence that they could make mortgage payments, especially after initial rates were adjusted upward.
- People: People thought house prices would continue to increase indefinitely and expected they would use profits from flipping houses to pay loans used to buy the houses. As prices dropped, the money owed exceeded house value.

Population and Climate

The next two case studies are interrelated. Population growth tends to result in increased use of fossil fuels, which increases carbon in the atmosphere that leads to higher temperatures. These temperature increases result in melting glaciers that raise sea levels, threatening coastal populations in terms of loss of land and degraded water and food supplies. We have a fairly good understanding of how to address population growth. Climate change is a bit trickier, due to the time lags involved.

Population Growth

Population growth is affected by fertility rate and mortality rate. Population is also affected by immigration rate. In the United States, the fertility rate is less than the replacement value of 2.1 births per woman. In addition, life expectancy has been decreasing for the past three years (Woolf and Schoomaker, 2019). Consequently, the population of the United States will eventually start decreasing unless we increase the immigration rate. The population of Japan, for example, is already in decline due to limited immigration.

World population has been rising continuously since the end of the Black Death in the fourteenth century. Population began growing rapidly in the Western world during the industrial revolution, in part due to better nutrition. The most significant increase in the world's population has been since the 1950s, mainly due to improved public health and increases in agricultural productivity.

Developed nations have seen a decline in their population growth rates in recent decades, though annual growth rates remain high in many of the world's countries. Sub-Saharan Africa, the Middle East, South Asia, and South East Asia, have seen a sharp rise in population since the end of the Cold War. The concern is that high population numbers will put substantial strain on natural resources, food supplies, fuel supplies, employment, housing, etc. in some of the less fortunate of these countries.

Figure 5.1 show the United Nations' projection of population growth through the year 2100 (UN, 2019). The range is from a bit over 7 billion to almost 16 billion people in 2100. The median shows a diminishing returns curve to roughly 11 billion. Why would population growth slow? The answer is that the fertility rate tends

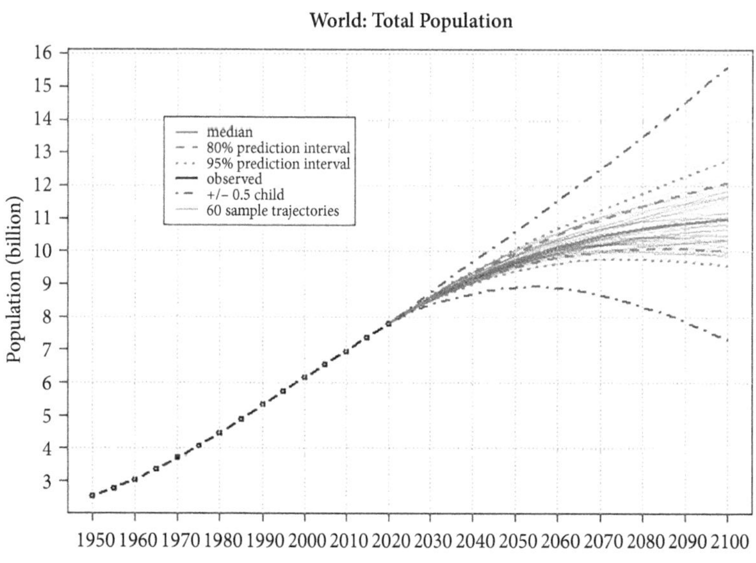

Figure 5.1 World population projections
Source: UN (2019).

to decrease as people's economic situation improves. In fact, many developed countries have fertility rates below the replacement value of 2.1.

Using data from Ethiopia, Ghana, and Kenya, Pradhan (2015) shows that the higher the level of a woman's educational attainment, the fewer children she is likely to bear. Fewer children per woman and delayed marriage and childbearing could mean more resources per child and better health and survival rates for mothers and children.

Emergence in Cities

People can often improve their economic situation by moving to cities. Society is increasingly dominated by cities, as people globally move to cities seeking such prosperity. To provide a sense of the concentration of resources in cities, metropolitan New York City, defined broadly, generates roughly 10 percent of the GDP in the United States. Edward Glaeser, in his book *Triumph of the City* provides an insightful treatise on the nature and roles of cities (Glaeser, 2011).

Cities have been seen as dirty, poor, unhealthy, and environmentally unfriendly. This was certainly true before modern urban infrastructure emerged replacing, for example, New York City's 100,000 horses and 1,200 metric tons of horse manure daily. Glaeser argues that cities are now actually the healthiest, greenest, and—economically speaking—the richest places to live. He argues that cities are humanity's greatest creation and our best hope for the future.

Barber (2013) agrees and would let city mayors rule the world. He contrasts dysfunctional nations with rising cities. Mayors, he argues, have no choice but make sure that schools are open, traffic lights work, and the garbage is picked up. Otherwise, they will be turned out in the next election. Members of national legislative bodies, on the other hand, can manage to accomplish nothing and still be reelected.

Daniel Brook (2013) provides a fascinating look into developing "instant cities" like Dubai and Shenzhen. He anticipates development of such cities by referencing previous instant cities—St. Petersburg, Shanghai, and Bombay, now Mumbai. Tsar Peter the

Great personally oversaw the construction of St. Petersburg in the early eighteenth century. In the middle of the following century, the British facilitated Shanghai becoming the fastest-growing city in the world, an English-speaking, Western-looking metropolis. During the same period, the British Raj invested in transforming Bombay into a cosmopolitan hub.

All three cities were gleaming exemplars of modernity, all with ambiguous legacies. Impoverished populations surrounded these cities. These populations could daily see what they did not have. Eventually they revolted in one manner or another, providing evidence that development can have both positive and negative consequences. The visionaries who planned these cities and supervised their construction had likely not imagined these emergent phenomena.

Despite such hiccups, the steady migration to cities will improve people's economic circumstances; decrease fertility rates over time; moderate population growth; and decrease energy use per capita. As noted above, education is the key to the success of this transition.

National Academy Workshop

In 2014, the National Academy of Sciences conducted a workshop on the question of "Can Earth's and Society's Systems Meet the Needs of 10 Billion People?" All the members of the planning committee were elected members of the US Academy of Sciences. I was appointed chair of this endeavor, although my membership is in the US Academy of Engineering. The workshop report (Mellody, 2014) addresses several themes.

Several demographic variables that influence sustainability were discussed, including education, fertility, and aging, urbanization, and migration. Also of interest were the economic and policy variables that influence sustainability, including economic incentives, costs, and consumption habits associated with food, land use, and technological change. There was considerable discussion of suitable metrics for sustainability, including overall human well-being, environmental indicators, impacts of climate on humans, demographic changes, and returns on investments.

A topic of great debate was the "carrying capacity" of Earth. While the conversation started with the notion that population growth was a threat to Earth, the planning committee quickly challenged this idea. The Earth is going to be fine, with population growth, ice ages, asteroids, etc. The threat is to civilization—to people—not to the Earth.

We discussed constraints. Land is certainly not an issue. It was noted that the whole global population could fit into townhouses in Texas. Water could be a constraint unless desalinization is affordable, which it could be if renewable energy sources continue to mature. The most difficult constraint is protein to feed the world's population. We cannot afford enough cows to feed everyone beef. The largest source of protein in the world is insects, which will likely be reconstituted in some way to make such protein palatable.

Multi-level Interpretation. These findings and conclusions can be framed in the multi-level framework discussed in Chapter 2, where the levels for this case study are people, processes, organizations, and government:

- Government: Society needs to require government to work across siloed agencies and constituencies to promote integrated and effective means to foster population health and economic well-being.
- Organizations: The private and public sectors, including non-governmental organizations, need resources and incentives to invest in the well-being of populations in terms of health, education, and productivity.
- Processes: Improved urbanization processes are needed to assimilate, educate, and employ immigrants. Research processes need to mature renewable energy sources, as well as address protein availability and palatability.
- People: People have larger families when child mortality is high and child labor is important to the family. As people gain education, their economic circumstances improve and fertility decreases.

Climate Change

Humanity has always exploited natural resources for food, shelter, energy, etc. This exploitation emerged on an industrial scale in the nineteenth century as the extraction and processing of raw materials blossomed during the Industrial Revolution. During the twentieth century, energy consumption rapidly increased.

Today, the vast majority of the world's energy consumption is sustained by the extraction of fossil fuels, including oil, coal, and gas. Intensive agriculture also exploits the natural environment via degradation of forests and water pollution. As the world population rises, the depletion of natural resources will become increasingly unsustainable.

New England's Wood Economy

New England was heavily forested when the colonists arrived in the seventeenth century. It is heavily forested today, particularly in northern states. However, the forests one sees today are "new growth." The earlier forests were denuded to support the region's wood economy.

The colonists used wood for everything. They cut down trees to build homes, roads, bridges, and ships. Shipbuilding in New England was a major industry. My great, great grandfather founded a shipyard and later was superintendent of construction for a steamship line, originally with wooden ships but later iron and then steel.

Ships were also built for fishing and hunting whales. This affected what goods people in New England could trade. There was much trade between New England and other regions or countries such as England. New England would export resources like fish and lumber. In return, unfortunately, New England would receive slaves that were sold to plantations in the south.

New England and the rest of the country moved from a wood economy to a fossil fuel economy. Coal, oil, and gas fueled industry. Private automobiles emerged in the early twentieth century, enabling by mid-century vast suburbs and increasing traffic and congestion. This has resulted in vast amounts of carbon dioxide (CO_2) emitted into the atmosphere.

Consequences of CO_2

Almost 90 percent of all human-produced CO_2 emissions come from the burning of fossil fuels like coal, natural gas, and oil. Deforestation also increases CO_2 in atmosphere by destroying trees that consume CO_2.

The CO_2 in the atmosphere increases greenhouse warming that results when atmosphere traps solar radiation. Consequently, the Earth's temperature increases. This leads to ice melting and sea level rise.

Beyond threatening coastal buildings, rising sea levels lead to salinization of groundwater and estuaries. This decreases the availability of freshwater. Ocean acidification also affects sea life. Consequently, the food supply and human health are degraded.

Reducing CO_2 Emissions

A multi-faceted approach to CO_2 reduction involves reducing, reusing, and recycling. Using less heat and air conditioning, using less hot water, replacing incandescent light bulbs, and buying energy-efficient products are elements of this approach. Using the off switch on lights and appliances is also of value.

Transportation is a large producer of CO_2. Compared to an average single-occupant car, the fuel efficiency of a fully occupied bus is six times greater and a fully occupied train car is 15 times greater. In general, we need to drive less and ride smarter. Increased migration to cities should help this, as the feasibility of mass transit increases with population density.

Urban living is, in general, more energy efficient than suburban or rural living. For example, apartment living involves more shared walls and fewer exposed walls, reducing energy consumptions for heating and cooling. Green spaces in cities are also important both for people's well-being and the CO_2 that trees consume.

Progress and Problems

The recently published Production Gap Report (SEI et al., 2019) provides a stark assessment of progress toward constraining temperature increases:

- Governments are planning to produce about 50 percent more fossil fuels by 2030 than would be consistent with a 2°C pathway and 120 percent more than would be consistent with a 1.5°C pathway.
- The global production gap is even larger than the already-significant global emission gap, due to minimal policy attention on curbing fossil fuel production.
- The continued expansion of fossil fuel production—and the widening of the global production gap—is underpinned by a combination of ambitious national plans, government subsidies to producers, and other forms of public finance.

Lenton and colleagues (2019) argue that we are already at climate tipping points in terms of artic warming, ice collapses, and ocean heat waves. Waterman (2019) reports on emerging consequences for US national parks in terms of climate change and invasive species, as well as overcrowding and money woes. The consequences of global warming are no longer hypothetical.

Lightbody and colleagues (2019) consider flood mitigation efforts across the United States and argue for the cost effectiveness of mitigation. Lempert and colleagues (2018) focus on climate restoration. As compelling as such proposals may be, they face fundamental economic hurdles.

Flavelle and Mazzei (2019) recently reported on efforts to estimate the costs of raising roads in the Florida Keys to escape rising ocean levels. Route 1 in the Keys is 113 miles long. Raising all of it by 1.3 feet by 2025 will cost $2.8 billion; elevating it by 2.2 feet by 2045 will cost $4.8 billion; and by 2060 the cost would be $6.8 billion. With 13,300 people living in the Keys, this amounts to a range of $215,000 to $523,000 per person. They conclude that: "As sea levels rise, some places can't be saved."

The implications are clear. We cannot deal with global warming by simply restoring everything that is damaged, and then restoring it again after the next flood, for example. We either have to stem the use of fossil fuels or prepare for disruptive and eventually different living conditions.

Earth as a System

Looking at the overall system that needs to be influenced can facilitate addressing the challenges of climate change and likely consequences. As shown in Figure 5.2, the Earth can be considered as a collection of different phenomena operating on different time scales (Rouse, 2014a). Loosely speaking, there are four interconnected systems: environment, population, industry, and government. In this notional model, population consumes resources from the environment and creates by-products. Industry also consumes resources and creates by-products, but it also produces employment. The government collects taxes and produces rules. The use of the environment is influenced by those rules.

Each system component has a different associated time constant. In the case of the environment, the time constant is decades to centuries. The population's time constant can be perhaps a few months. Government's time constant may be a bit longer, thinking in terms of years. Industry is longer still, on the order of decades. These systems can be represented at different levels of abstraction and/or aggregation.

A hierarchical representation does not capture the fact that this is a highly distributed system, with all elements interconnected. It is difficult to solve one part of the problem, as it affects other pieces. By-products are related to population size, so one way to reduce by-products is to moderate population growth. Technology may help to ameliorate some of the by-products and their effects, but it is also possible that technology could exacerbate the effects. Clean technologies lower by-product rates but tend to increase overall use, for instance.

Sentient stakeholders include population, industry, and government. Gaining these stakeholders' support for such decisions will depend upon the credibility of the predictions of behavior, at all levels in the system. Central to this support are "time value" and "space value" discount rates. The consequences that are closest in time and space to stakeholders matter the most and have lower discount rates; attributes more distributed in time and space are more highly discounted. These discount rates will differ across stakeholders.

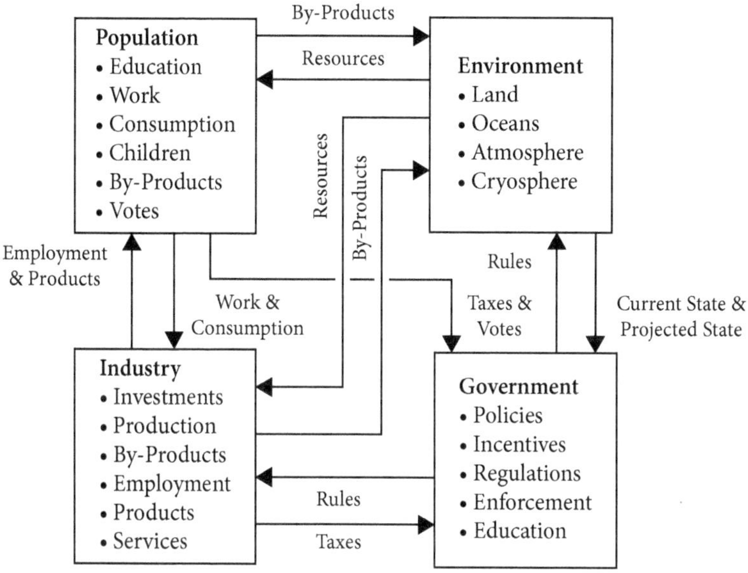

Figure 5.2 Earth as a system

People will also try to "game" any strategy to improve the system, seeking to gain a share of the resources being invested in executing the strategy. The way to deal with that is to make the system sufficiently transparent to understand the game being played. Sometimes gaming the system will actually be an innovation; other times, prohibitions of the specific gaming tactics will be needed.

The following three strategies are likely to enable addressing the challenges of climate change and its consequences:

- *Share Information*: Broadly share credible information so all stakeholders understand the situation.
- *Create Incentives*: Develop long-term incentives to enable long-term environmental benefits while assuring short-terms gains for stakeholders.
- *Create an Experiential Approach*: Develop an interactive visualization of these models to enable people to see the results.

An experiential approach can be embodied in a "policy flight simulator" that includes large interactive visualizations that enable stakeholders to take the controls, explore options, and see the sensitivity of results to various decisions (Rouse, 2014b).

Multi-level Interpretation. These findings and conclusions can be framed in the multi-level framework discussed in Chapter 2, where the levels for this case study are people, processes, organizations, and government:

- Government: Elected officials have great difficulty trading off short-term versus long-term costs and benefits, due to a large extent to the concerns, values, and perceptions of their constituents—citizens and companies.
- Organizations: The vested interests in energy extraction, refinement, and use are enormous and are naturally inclined to sustain status quo business models, and the benefits these models provide to these organizations.
- Processes: Processes for extracting, refining, and utilizing fossil fuels are well developed, employ millions of people, and represent trillions of dollars of stock market capitalization.
- People: People have long exploited natural resources and come to depend on the benefits of these resources in terms of both consumption and employment. Changing consumption habits is very difficult.

Comparison Across Case Studies

Table 5.2 summarizes the causal chains of these case studies of failures of six complex ecosystems. They all begin with humans' sexual activities, economic optimism, and consumption inclinations. The unexpected happens, but emerges slowly and is only recognized once the consequences are irreversible, but can—or may be—mitigated and remediated. The end results, often years later, are managed outcomes for five of the six case studies. It is not clear how we will eventually address climate change. We seem to know what to do, but do not have the will to do it.

Table 5.3 summarizes the multi-level analyses of the six case studies. People play central roles in all of these ecosystems.

Table 5.2 Causal chains of ecosystem failures

Aids	Opioids	Depression	Recession	Population	Climate
HIV arises in primates	Palliative pain medicine developed	10-year rise of stock market	Low interest rates	Lack of family planning	Burning of fossil fuels increases CO_2
Humans encounter primates	Pain more broadly recognized	Crash, bank rushes, bank failures	Booming housing market	Large families produced	Deforestation increases CO_2 in atmosphere
Initially observed in gay males	Pharma aggressively markets	Increased interest rates	Mortgage-backed securities	Malnutrition, starvation, and deaths	Greenhouse warming increases
Aids epidemic grows	Prescriptions increase, then controlled	Decreased monetary liquidity	Increased mortgage defaults	Education of young women	Earth's temperature increases
HIV virus identified	Addicts revert to cheaper street drugs	Decreased spending and deflation	MBS increasingly toxic	Smaller families produced	Ice melting and sea levels rise
Anti-retroviral therapy	Overdoses and deaths increase	Decreased employment and income	Financial companies bankrupt	Educated women enter workforce	Salinization of groundwater and estuaries
Deaths due to Aids decreases	Causes of substance abuse tackled	Increase of homeless people	Government bails out companies	Economic growth increases	Decrease in freshwater availability
Population with HIV increases	Population health services provided	New Deal initiates programs	Net worth of families demolished	Family planning adopted	Ocean acidification affects sea life
Managed as chronic disease	Managed as chronic disease	WWII fuels economic growth	Economy eventually recovers	Global population stabilizes	Food supply and health degraded

Table 5.3 Multi-level analysis of failures of six complex ecosystems

Level of analysis	Health		Economy		Environment	
	AIDS	Opioids	Depression	Recession	Population	Climate
Society	Society slowly became aware of the pervasiveness and consequences of the problem and recognized the broader population risks	The fragmented nature of the US healthcare system, regulatory practices, a culture of independence, and socio-economic trends aligned to enable creation of roughly 10 million addicts in the United States	Gold standard prevented bailout; New Deal focused on directly helping citizens	Banks deemed "too big to fail" were bailed out by Congress and the Federal Reserve	Society needs to require government to work across siloed agencies and constituencies to promote integrated and effective services	Elected officials have great difficulty trading off short-term versus long-term costs and benefits
Organizations	National health organizations and medical research institutions led the efforts to understand the causes of HIV and AIDS; pharmaceutical organizations led the development of drugs	Physicians increased their revenues by prescribing opioids. Pharma companies invested in creating opioid offerings as well as massive marketing campaigns	Speculation by all players was rampant, betting on profits to service loans	Banks created packages with derivatives of mortgages. Credit rating companies rated these packages as low risk	Private and public sector, including non-governmental organizations, need resources and incentives to invest in the well-being of populations	Vested interests in energy extraction, refinement, and use are enormous and are naturally inclined to sustain status quo business model

Processes	Surveillance processes slowly detected the epidemic; medical research processes diagnosed the causes; pharmaceutical research processes yielded the needed drugs	Approaches to treating pain included physical therapy, exercise, and drugs. Insurers found physical treatments too expensive and limited reimbursements to drugs	Banks used people's money to take the same risks in the stock market	Mortgage approval processes became extremely lenient, with applicants having to provide little, if any, evidence that they could make mortgage payments	Improved urbanization processes are needed to assimilate, educate, and employ immigrants	Processes for extracting, refining, and utilizing fossil fuels are well developed, employ millions, and represent trillions of dollars
People	People slowly became aware of how their behaviors affected becoming afflicted with HIV and then AIDS	People thought that opioids provided a safe approach to managing pain; once addicted, their brains demanded continued fixes, leading to growing numbers of overdoses and deaths	People thought the bull market would continue indefinitely; After the crash, people sharply curtailed spending	People thought house prices would continue to increase indefinitely and expected they would use profits from flipping houses to pay loans used to buy the houses	People have larger families when child mortality is high and child labor is important. As people gain education, fertility decreases	People have long exploited natural resources; changing consumption habits is very difficult

Processes both precipitate and remediate consequences. Organizations own and exploit processes, but also invest in remediation. Government or society provides the overall context for recognizing situations and acting, or sometimes denying, delaying, or avoiding action.

The four levels provide insights into the levers for detecting, diagnosing, compensating, and remediating failures. It is unlikely that these six failures could have been completely avoided. They were unexpected and only detected after consequences were broadly manifested. Nevertheless, the multi-level system did eventually manage the failures, although climate is a work in progress.

Anticipating Failures

In this section, I address the range of organizations charged with anticipating and managing the types of failures discussed in this chapter. The national and international organizational infrastructure charged with these tasks is extensive and rather impressive. There is, however, some room for improvement.

Health Monitoring—CDC and WHO

The US Centers for Disease Prevention and Control monitors and reports on the frequency of mortality, causes of death, and disability (Thacker et al., 2006). The three major categories of reports and a few examples of each include:

- Mortality: Heart disease, cancer, cerebrovascular disease, respiratory disease, injuries, diabetes, influenza, Alzheimer's disease
- Causes of Death: Tobacco, poor diet, physical inactivity, alcohol, microbial agents, toxic agents, accidents, firearms
- Disability: Arthritis, back problems, heart trouble, respiratory problems, hearing problems, limb stiffness, mental health problems, diabetes

CDC also reports on health in terms of "healthy days" (CDC, 2000). Often, the CDC also conducts targeted epidemiological studies to address new questions such as emerged with AIDS and opioids. The *CDC Field Epidemiology Manual* provides guidance for such studies (Hedberg and Maher, 2019).

The World Health Organization (WHO) monitors and reports on a range of metrics far wider than just health (WHO, 2017, 2019):

- Strategic Development Goals: health and health-related targets
  - Mortality and global health estimates
  - Health Equity Monitor
- Maternal Mortality: Maternal and reproductive health
- Newborn and Child Mortality: Child health and mortality
- Communicable Diseases
  - HIV/AIDS
  - Tuberculosis
  - Malaria
  - Neglected tropical diseases
  - Cholera
  - Influenza
  - Meningitis
  - Other vaccine-preventable communicable diseases
  - Sexually transmitted infections
- Non-communicable Diseases and Mental Health
  - Non-communicable diseases
  - Mental health
- Substance Abuse
  - Global information system on alcohol and health
  - Resources for the prevention and treatment of substance use disorders
- Road Traffic Injuries: Road safety
- Sexual and Reproductive Health: Universal access to reproductive health
- Universal Health Coverage: Universal health coverage data portal
- Mortality from Environmental Pollution

  - Public health and environment
  - Joint effects of air pollution
- Tobacco Control: Tobacco control
- Essential Medicines and Vaccines
  - Essential medicines
  - Priority health technologies
  - Immunization
- Health Financing and Health Workforce
- National and Global Health Risks: International health regulations
- Child Malnutrition: Child malnutrition country survey results
- Drinking Water
- Sanitation and Hygiene: Water and sanitation
- Clean Household Energy
- Clean Cities
  - Public health and environment
  - Urban health
  - Ambient air pollution
- Violence: Violence prevention and violence against women.

The US National Academies of Science, Engineering, and Medicine conduct a wide range of studies that result in reports to Congress, the Executive Office, and other sponsors. A good recent example is *Guiding Cancer Control*, which employed the multi-level modeling approach advocated in this book (Johns et al., 2019). I was a member of this study committee.

A highly relevant study is *US Health in International Perspective: Shorter Lives and Poorer Health* (Woolf and Laudan, 2013). They report that the US fares poorly, compared to 16 high-income peers, in terms of:

- Adverse birth outcomes
- Injuries and homicides
- Adolescent pregnancy
- HIV and AIDS
- Drug-related mortality
- Obesity and diabetes

- Heart disease
- Chronic lung disease
- Disabilities.

As impressive as the entire surveillance infrastructure is, it is not as broad and integrative as it should be. In recognition of this, the Blue Ridge Group of Academic Health Centers proposed a United States Health Board (BRAHG, 2008). Modeled on the Federal Reserve (see below), they argue for a high-level, independent organization with powers to foster high-value integrated health services, and compensate for the effects of the currently highly fragmented US health system.

Economy Monitoring—Federal Reserve

The Federal Reserve frequently (many times per day) accesses data about the economy—see Table 5.4. This is done to make sure nothing is happening in the economy that the Fed does not know about. The Fed can also tap into a network of business contacts that provide insight into a wide range of businesses, revealing who is buying what and in what amounts. By staying on top of where the economy is right now and where it is going, the Fed can project future changes and act accordingly (Federal Reserve, 2019).

All developed countries have their equivalent of the Federal Reserve. Also important is the World Bank and the International Monetary Fund (IMF). The World Bank provides loans and grants to the governments of poorer countries for the purpose of pursuing capital projects. The IMF fosters global monetary cooperation, secure financial stability, and international trade, with emphasis on high employment, sustainable economic growth, and poverty reduction.

Climate Monitoring—IPCC

The Intergovernmental Panel on Climate Change provides access to observed data covering the physical climate (e.g., global distributions temperature and rainfall), atmospheric composition, socio-economic information (e.g., national population and income data), and impacts of climate change (IPCC, 2019). Their reports include:

- Data Compilations
- Climate System Scenario Tables
- Climate Observations: Global mean temperature, climatology data set
- Carbon Dioxide: Observed atmospheric concentrations
- Socio-economic Baseline Dataset
- Observed Climate Change Impacts
- Computational Models
- Climate System Scenario Tables
- Emissions Scenarios from Integrated Assessment Models
- Carbon Dioxide: Projected emissions and concentrations
- Global Climate Model Outputs: Period averages and global means

Failure Management

The organizational infrastructure for surveillance of health, economy, population, and climate seems rather robust. The central issue here is how to address failures once they become apparent. If a pump fails in a power plant, once you detect, you repair it. If a balance sheet is going south in an enterprise, approaches to remediation are well known, once management admits it has a problem.

As shown in Figure 5.3 (repeated from Chapter 1), the distinction between point failures and distributed failures is important in terms of how failures are addressed. Point failures are often anticipated or at least imagined if not expected. Distributed failures emerge. When an anomaly is detected, emphasis soon shifts to diagnosis (what is causing the anomaly) and remediation (how to counteract the causes).

It can require additional, well-designed, experimentation to assess the merits of alternative diagnoses and possible remediations. For

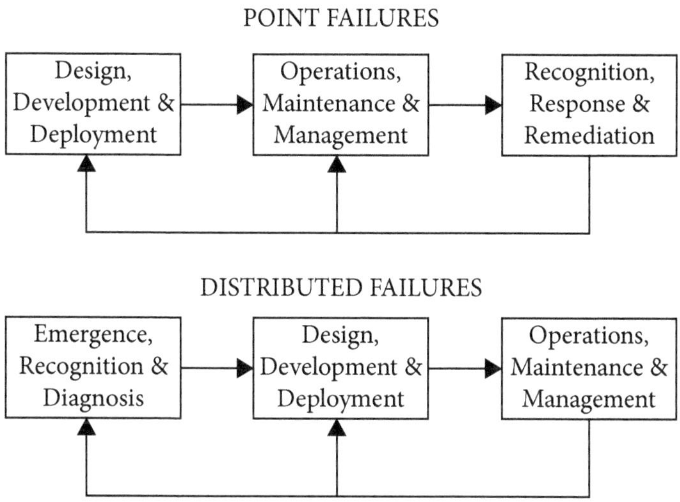

Figure 5.3 Addressing point vs. distributed failures

example, doctors did not examine the first few AIDS patients and conclude they had AIDS. It took quite some time to determine that the cause of the disease was the HIV virus. The increasing drug overdoses due to opioids did not immediately present itself as due to aggressive marketing by pharmaceutical companies.

Implementation of the best remediations can face enormous economic, political, and social resistance, particularly when change threatens a major stakeholder's income. A good example here is the trillion-dollar-plus energy industry. If you are a major investor in oil wells or coal mines, you do not look forward to solar and wind energy replacing your fossil fuels. You do not look forward to charging stations replacing gas stations. You are likely to argue against the evidence that such changes are needed.

Threatened stakeholders may mount substantial disinformation campaigns and very strong, and well-financed, lobbying campaigns, including arguments that the evidence constitutes fake news. People whose livelihoods are at risk—at the bench level or in corporate suites—are likely to push back. It can take considerable creativity and determination to make progress in such situations.

Table 5.4 Measures monitored by the US Federal Reserve

Measure	Definition
Consumer Price Index (CPI)	The change in price for a fixed set of merchandise and services intended to represent what a typical consumer might purchase over a given period.
Real Gross Domestic Product (GDP)	The total of all of the goods produced in the United States, regardless of who owns them or the nationality of the producers.
Housing Starts	Because housing is very sensitive to interest rates, this measure indicates how financial changes are affecting consumers.
Nonfarm Payroll Employment	Measures the total number of payroll jobs that are not in the farming business.
S&P Stock Index	The Standard & Poor Index indicates changes in price in a very wide variety of stocks.
Industrial Production/ Capacity Utilization	Measures industrial output both by product and by industry.
Retail Sales	The total of all merchandise sold by retail merchants in the United States.
Business Sales and Inventories	A measurement of the total sales and inventories for the manufacturing, wholesale, and retail sectors.
Light-Weight Vehicle Sales	Changes in car sales can account for a large portion of the change in the GDP from quarter to quarter.
Yield on 10-year Treasury Bond	The current market rate for US Treasury bonds that will be maturing in 10 years.
M2	Because there is often a link between the supply of money and the growth of the GDP, this measurement is yet another indicator considered when making decisions about monetary policy.

Source: Federal Reserve (2019).

Conclusions

This chapter has addressed failures of complex ecosystems. These were failures in that bad things happened to many people. This affected millions of people's health and livelihoods. Some of the effects are still playing out and will continue to evolve for many years.

We have the organizational infrastructure to detect anomalies, often not quickly but eventually. There are methods and tools to enable diagnosis of the causes of the detected anomalies. There are also approaches to researching and refining ways to compensate for and remediate the consequences of distributed failures such as discussed here.

Considering the six case studies in this chapter, it seems reasonable to argue that we will continue to encounter such surprises. We cannot engineer a world free of failures. However, we can design processes, methods, and tools for failure management that enable timely and accurate detection, diagnosis, compensation, and remediation of the bad things that inevitably happen.

Success in this process will require two important human ingredients—trust and will. We all need to trust the people and processes associated with failure management. Then, we need the will to act on the recommendations that result. I am not suggesting that we immediately deploy the findings, but that we determine trajectories of changes that make sense over time for all the stakeholders in the failures. Finally, doing nothing should not be an option.

References

Barber, B.R. (2013). *If Mayors Ruled the World: Dysfunctional Nations, Rising Cities*. New Haven, CT: Yale University Press.

Bernstein, L. (2019). Trump administration pushes efforts to wipe out HIV amid stalled progress. *The Washington Post*, December 3.

Blinder, A.S. (2013). *After the Music Stopped: The Financial Crisis, the Response, and the Work Ahead*. New York: Penguin.

BRAHG (2008). *A United States Health Board*. Atlanta, GA: Blue Ridge Group of Academic Health Centers.

Brook, D. (2013). *A History of Future Cities*. New York: Norton.

CCFEC (2019). *The Financial Crisis Inquiry Report*. Washington, DC: National Commission on the Causes of the Financial and Economic Crises in the US.

CDC (2000). *Measuring Healthy Days: Population Assessment of Health-related Quality of Life*. Atlanta, GA: Centers for Disease Prevention and Control.

Dash, M. (2001). *Tulipomania: The Story of the World's Most Coveted Flower and the Extraordinary Passions It Aroused.* New York: Broadway Books.

DeWeerdt, S. (2019). Tracing the US opioid crisis to its roots. *Nature*, 573, S10–S12.

Economist, The (2019). AIDS: Slowly HIV is being beaten. *The Economist*, November 30.

FED (2019). *About the Federal Reserve Bank.* https://www.federalreserve.gov/aboutthefed.htm, accessed 12/11/19.

Flavelle, C., and Mazzei, P. (2019). Florida Keys deliver a hard message: As seas rise, some places can't be saved, *New York Times*, December 5.

Glaeser, E.L. (2011). *Triumph of the City: How our Greatest Invention Makes Us Richer, Smarter, Greener, Healthier, and Happier.* New York: Penguin.

Hedberg, K., and Maher, J. (2019). *The CDC Field Epidemiology Manual.* https://www.cdc.gov/eis/field-epi-manual/chapters/collecting-data.html, accessed 12/08/19.

IPCC (2019). *IPCC Data Distribution Center*, Intergovernmental Panel on Climate Change. https://www.ipcc-data.org/observ/index.html, accessed 12/11/19.

Johns, M.M.E., Madhavan, G., Amankwah, F., and Nass, S. (eds) (2019). *Guiding Cancer Control: A Path to Transformation.* Washington, DC: National Academies Press.

Lempert, R.J., Marangoni, G., Keller, K., and Duke, J. (2018). *Is Restoration an Appropriate Climate Policy Goal?* Santa Monica, CA: RAND.

Lenton, T.M., et al. (2019). Climate tipping points—too risky to bet against. *Nature*, 575, 592–5.

Lewis, M. (2011). *The Big Short: Inside the Doomsday Machine.* New York: Norton.

Lightbody, L., Fuchs, M., and Edwards, S. (2019). *Mitigation Matters: Policy Solutions to Reduce Local Flood Risk.* Philadelphia, PA: The Pew Charitable Trusts.

Mellody, M. (2014). *Can Earth's and Society's Systems Meet the Needs of 10 Billion People? Summary of a Workshop.* Washington, DC: National Academies Press.

NIDA (2018). *Overdose Death Rates.* Washington, DC: National Institute on Drug Abuse, https://www.drugabuse.gov.

NIH (2016). *Trends and Statistics*. Washington, DC: National Institute on Drug Abuse.

Porter, J., and Jick, H. (1980). Addiction rare in patients treated with narcotics. New *England Journal of Medicine*, 302, 123.

Pradhan, E. (2015). *Female Education and Childbearing: A Closer Look at the Data*. Washington, DC: The World Bank, November 24.

Quinones, S. (2015). *Dreamland: The True Tale of America's Opiate Epide*mic. New York: Bloomsbury Press.

Rich, S., Kornfield, M., Mayes, B.R., and Williams, A. (2019). How the opioid epidemic evolved. *The Washington Post*, December 23.

Rouse, W.B. (2014a). Earth as a system. In M. Mellody, ed., *Can Earth's and Society's Systems Meet the Needs of 10 Billion People?* (pp. 20–3). Washington, DC: National Academies Press.

Rouse, W.B. (2014b). Human interaction with policy flight simulators. *Journal of Applied Ergonomics*, 45 (1), 72–7.

Rouse, W.B., Johns, M.M.E., and Pepe, K. (2019). Service supply chains for population: Overcoming fragmentation of service delivery ecosystems. *Journal of Learning Health Systems*, 3 (2), https://doi.org/10.1002/lrh2.10186.

SEI, IISD, ODI, Climate Analytics, CICERO, and UNEP (2019). *The Production Gap: The Discrepancy between Countries' Planned Fossil Fuel Production and Global Production Levels Consistent with Limiting Warming to 1.5°C or 2°C*. http://productiongap.org/.

Thacker, S.B., Stroup, D.F., Carande-Kulis, V., Marks, J.S., Roy, K., and Gerberding. L.L. (2006). Measuring public health. *Public Health Reports*, 121, 14–22.

UN (2019). *World Population Prospects 2019*. New York: United Nations, Department of Economic and Social Affairs.

Waterman, J. (2019). Our national parks are in trouble: Overcrowding, invasive species, climate change, and money woes. *New York Times Magazine*, November 22.

WHO (2017). *Tracking Universal Health Coverage*. Geneva: World Health Organization.

WHO (2019). *Global Health Observatory Data Repository*. Geneva: World Health Organization. http://apps.who.int/gho/data/node.home, accessed12/11/19.

Woolf, S.H, and Laudan, A. (eds) (2013). *US Health in International Perspective: Shorter Lives and Poorer Health*. Washington, DC: National Academies Press.

Woolf, S.H., and Schoomaker, H. (2019). Life expectancy and mortality rates in the United States, 1959–2017. *Journal of the American Medical Association*, 322 (20), 1996–2016.

6
Multi-Level Analyses

The multi-level framework introduced in Chapter 2 was applied to elaborating the phenomena associated with each of the 18 failures in Chapters 3–5. These phenomena include those contributing to the failures and those resulting from the failures. Tables 6.1–6.4 provide summaries of how this framework was applied to each of the case studies.

Findings

Table 6.1 summarizes the findings at the people, products, and technologies level of the framework, i.e., the lowest level. This illustrates how levels can have different meanings in differing contexts. Thus, the multi-level framework is not a fixed construct and can be adapted to the particulars of the problem at hand.

Interpretation of the results in Table 6.1 suggests several findings. First, as illustrated in Chapter 3, human operators' and maintainers' displays, controls, and procedures, as well as training, can support or undermine people's performance. Human-centered design should be a central methodology for addressing this (Rouse, 2007).

Second, human consumers adopt new technologies faster than providers can adapt and change their offerings to incorporate these technologies. As illustrated in Chapter 4, this can lead to "creative destruction," whereby high performing market leaders are marginalized by new offerings that render their current offerings obsolete (Schumpeter, 1942; Christensen, 1997).

Third, human lifestyles, speculative habits, and overall consumption of resources present challenges to health and well-being.

Failure Management: Malfunctions of Technologies, Organizations, and Society. William B. Rouse, Oxford University Press (2021). © William B. Rouse. DOI: 10.1093/oso/9780198870999.003.0006

Table 6.1 Case studies versus people, products, and technologies

Case study	People, products, technologies
Three Mile Island	Serious design flaws—human factors, procedures, training
Chernobyl	Serious design flaws—human factors, procedures, training
Challenger	Serious design flaws, O-rings
Columbia	Serious design flaws, e.g., foam
Valdez	Inoperable detection system; not repaired after a year
Horizon	Concatenation of malfunctions; inadequate procedures and training
Kodak	Invented digital camera, but film-based photography dominated
Polaroid	Invented instant camera; digital photography is inherently instant
Digital	Dominated minicomputer market; PC market seemed obvious next step
Xerox	Desktop metaphor, GUI, computer mouse, and desktop computing
Motorola	Developed analog and later digital cell phones; late to smartphones
Nokia	Initial digital cell phones led market; smartphones were too late and limited
AIDS	People slowly became aware of how their behaviors affected risks
Opioids	Opioids considered safe; once addicted, brains wanted continued fixes
Depression	People thought the bull market would continue indefinitely
Recession	People thought house prices would continue to increase indefinitely
Population	As people gain education, their fertility decreases
Climate	People long exploited natural resources; changing habits very difficult

Epidemics, economic panics, and environmental degradation can result, as described in Chapter 5.

Overall, we need to consider humans as performers of tasks, consumers of market offerings, investors in economic risks, pursuers of various lifestyles, and consumers of food, water, energy, etc. Humans were intimately involved in all the failures discussed in this book, but were not the ultimate causes of these failures. Nevertheless, surveillance of human behaviors is a primary means of detecting failures.

Table 6.2 summarizes findings on processes and operations associated with the 18 case studies. Processes and operations both

Table 6.2 Case studies versus processes and operations

Case study	Processes and operations
Three Mile Island	Lack of consideration of complex failure scenarios
Chernobyl	Lack of consideration of complex failure scenarios
Challenger	Flawed launch procedures
Columbia	Flawed launch and re-entry procedures
Valdez	Crew size halved, production driven
Horizon	Focus on production, ignoring tests and results
Kodak	Business process improvement was inadequate for challenge faced
Polaroid	Business process improvement was inadequate for challenge faced
Digital	Business processes did not support outsourcing
Xerox	Computing was an orphan to document management
Motorola	Inadequate software development process
Nokia	Inadequate software development process
AIDS	Surveillance processes slowly detected the epidemic and its causes
Opioids	Insurers limited reimbursements to drugs rather than therapy
Depression	Banks used people's money to take risks in the stock market
Recession	Mortgage approval processes became extremely lenient
Population	Improved processes to assimilate, educate and employ immigrants
Climate	Processes for extracting, refining, and utilizing fossil fuels

enable and constrain human behaviors at both the people level below and the organization level above.

Interpretation of these findings suggests three conclusions. First, processes were seldom designed to fully support the complete range of possible failure scenarios. Put simply, the types of things that could go wrong, including combinations of things going wrong, did not receive adequate attention during design and testing.

Second, business processes undermined organizations' abilities to adapt to new opportunities. They often obscured the seriousness of competitive threats. Further, new opportunities could not be successfully pursed within the constraints of incumbent business processes. A good example is outsourcing practices that delayed time to markets.

Third, business processes led to poor decisions regarding prescribing drugs, investing in stocks and homes, and consumption choices. These processes often misled consumer decision making. A counter example is the impressive business processes associated with public sector surveillance.

Overall, it is important that processes deliver the right information and capabilities to enable decision making and actions in the range of situations that will be realistically encountered. Well-designed processes can enhance performance at both the people and organization levels of the system of interest. Poorly designed processes can hinder performance as several case studies well illustrate.

Table 6.3 summarizes findings on organizations, management, and markets associated with the 18 case studies. Decision making at this level occurs in the context of the level above, and influences investments in the process level below.

Three conclusions are suggested by the results in Table 6.3. First, pressures for production and meeting schedules, and ignoring lessons learned and safety issues, lead to poor decisions. This includes decisions about how processes are designed and operated, as well as strategic decisions on future directions.

Second, there is a strong tendency for management to focus on sustaining existing lines of business and operational plans, despite awareness of the risks associated with this. Even in cases where management realizes that this strategy will eventually fail, there are many cases where waiting too long was fatal.

Third, vested interests and rampant speculation obscured or delayed recognition of increasing risks. The economic and social costs of recognizing and addressing change were deemed too high. Public sector organizations often led efforts to increase awareness of risks, but translating awareness to action was often quite difficult.

Overall, it is very important that executives and managers have well-informed perceptions of the states of their systems and understand the likely current and future risks. Deficiencies in these areas can result in poor investment decisions, as well as poor operational

Table 6.3 Case studies versus organizations, management, and markets

Case study	Organizations, management, markets
Three Mile Island	Production pressures; lack of incorporation of lessons learned
Chernobyl	Production pressures; lack of incorporation of lessons learned
Challenger	Schedule driven; lack of incorporation of lessons learned
Columbia	Schedule driven; lack of incorporation of lessons learned
Valdez	Driven by economics, not safety, e.g., no iceberg detection
Horizon	Failure to incorporate lessons learned
Kodak	Kept digital camera on shelf to sustain sales of photographic film
Polaroid	Failed to compete with new photographic technologies and products
Digital	Dismissed PC market; lacked needed business processes to catch up
Xerox	Failed to capitalize on desktop technology investment
Motorola	Delayed transition from analog to digital cell phone technology
Nokia	Focused on low-priced cell phones; surprised by smartphones
AIDS	Health organizations led efforts to understand the causes and drugs
Opioids	Physicians prescribed opioids; Pharma massively marketed
Depression	Rampant speculation, betting on profits to service loans
Recession	Banks created derivatives; credit companies rated them low risk
Population	Resources and incentives needed for well-being of populations
Climate	Enormous vested interests in energy extraction, refinement, and use

decisions. As several case studies illustrate, it can result in the demise of the system, organization, or ecosystem.

Table 6.4 summarizes findings at the level of society, government, and industry associated with the 18 case studies. This level sets the tone for all the lower levels. It usually determines the incentives and inhibitions within which the lower levels must operate.

The findings in Table 6.4 suggest three conclusions. First, lack of oversight, regulations, and inspections, while focused on delivering missions rather than safety, can enable and exacerbate failures. Allowing unsafe design practices can undermine safe operations. Lack of consequences can allow the organization level to skew priorities away from safety.

Table 6.4 Case studies versus society, government, and industry

Case study	Society, government, industry
Three Mile Island	Lack of oversight
Chernobyl	Lack of oversight, repression of communications
Challenger	Focus on delivering missions rather than safety
Columbia	Focus on delivering missions rather than safety
Valdez	Lack of inspections, communications about practices
Horizon	Lack of oversight
Kodak	Photography transitioned from cameras to digital devices
Polaroid	Photography transitioned from cameras to digital devices
Digital	Steady transitions between computing generations
Xerox	Steady transitions between computing generations
Motorola	Transition between cell phone generations happened quickly
Nokia	Transition between cell phone generations happened quickly
AIDS	Society aware of the pervasiveness and consequences of the problem
Opioids	Fragmented nature of healthcare system created 10 million addicts
Depression	No bailout; New Deal focused on directly helping citizens
Recession	Banks deemed "too big to fail" were bailed out by government
Population	Government needs to provide integrated and effective services
Climate	Elected officials unable to tradeoff short-term versus long-term

Second, markets can transition relatively quickly and substantially. However, the leading players often avoid recognizing and accepting looming changes. There is a likely tendency to pursue short-term rewards and discount the likelihood of long-terms losses, especially if leadership is likely to change before losses are experienced.

Third, the public sector is much better at recognizing problems than solving them. This is mainly due to the stewards of the status quo pushing back against change. This tends to be accepted as normal within our economic, political, and social system, but the negative consequences for millions of people seem a high price to pay for the great benefits gained by a few.

Overall, this level sets the "rules of the game." It plays a strong role in the economics, health, and safety of the other levels. It can act in ways that the other levels cannot. The nature of this level differs substantially across countries, hopefully providing opportunities to learn from others' experiences.

Observations

It is particularly important to look beyond the operators, maintainers, and managers involved in the failures of complex systems to consider how designers and their managers influenced the nature of the system of interest. Further, their enterprises were subject to economic and political pressures that strongly affected decision making.

Flawed strategic thinking, a focus on near-term revenues and profits, and hubris bred by past success were important contributors to the failures of complex enterprises. These six highly successful enterprises succumbed to similar forces that undermined their abilities to leverage competitive advantages in which they had invested.

Failures of complex ecosystems were more influenced by policy than by design. For example, limiting prescription drugs leads to increased reliance on more deadly street drugs. Promoting home ownership results in criteria for mortgages being loosened. In both examples, entrepreneurs took advantage of the resulting economic opportunities.

It is important to keep in mind that none of the 18 failures were intentional. Consequently, we need to consider the designers of the sensors, the producers of the drugs, and the originators of the mortgage products. These people put bad things into the environment. There were potential downstream consequences that they likely did not understand.

Thus, many of failures either resulted from poor design, inadequate evaluation, or mismanagement, or the consequences were exacerbated by these factors. These are among the things that need improvement—design, evaluation, and management. Recommended practices in these three areas are discussed in Chapter 7.

Amended Multi-Level Framework

The findings in Tables 6.1–6.4 help to reformulate the multi-level framework as shown in Figure 6.1. The phrases from the baseline framework in Chapter 2 have been amended to reflect the findings from the 18 case studies.

On the lowest level, people make operational decisions, or decisions to adopt products and technologies, or lifestyle decisions. These decisions are based on the capabilities and information available, and result in behaviors, for example, how tasks are performed, what investments are made, or interpersonal actions exhibited.

At the next level, processes and operations provide capabilities and information and are affected by people's decisions and behaviors. The capabilities and information are influenced by investments and operational policies of organizations, management, and markets from the level above. The result is process and operational performance outcomes and consequences.

The highest level determines the economic models available and incentive structures, which influence the investment strategies and policies decided by the level below. These decisions, over time, strongly affect population impacts and economic effects such as revenues, profits, investment losses, and costs of failure remediation.

Computational Modeling

We would like to be able to predict the variables summarized in Figure 6.1 as functions of different scenarios and policies. These predictions will serve as a baseline against which we can compare the performance assessed by surveillance to detect anomalies that will be subject to failure management as discussed in Chapter 7.

We would like to make these predictions computationally. Not surprisingly, there is no single monolithic model that can capture each level of Figure 6.1, independent of context. Table 6.5 summarizes example phenomena to be represented. Computational models of these phenomena can serve as component models in overall models of each domain. The goal in this chapter is not to discuss

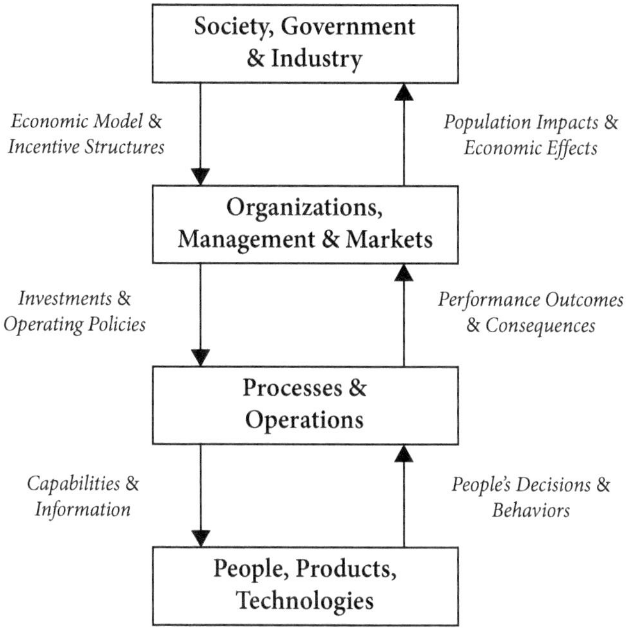

Figure 6.1 Amended multi-level framework

particular models, but simply to illustrate that the ingredients are available for doing so. Those interested in more technical details might consult my recent books (Rouse, 2015, 2019).

There is a variety of ways to formulate these representations as illustrated in Table 6.6. Examples of a few classes of models include:

- Macroeconomics: Rule-based policies and regulation; systems dynamic representation of broad economic processes
- Microeconomics: Decision theory models of company choices of investment; game theory models of competition
- Discrete-event Models: Flow of people and materials, capacity and inventories of capabilities, waiting lines
- Agent-based Models: Decision theory models of independent actors, influenced by networks of relationships and information
- Dynamics and Control Models: Manual or automatic control of evolving states of dynamic systems; decision theory models of failure detection and diagnosis.

Table 6.5 Example phenomena to represent in computational models

Levels of analysis	Types of failures		
	Failures of complex technologies	**Failures of complex organizations**	**Failures of complex ecosystems**
Society, government, industry	Design and safety statutes, regulations, oversight, inspections, penalties	Dynamics of technology changes and market product transitions	Oversight of health, economy, population, and climate; government policy and intervention
Organizations, management, markets	Design, training, and operational policy decision making; incentives and rewards	Market strategy and technology investment decision making; change management	Public sector oversight; private sector exploitation of opportunities
Processes and operations	Design and evaluation practices; training, operations, safety, recovery, and learning processes	Value management, product development, including software; partnering strategy and outsourcing practices	Social interactions, Infection spread, economic panic, population growth, climate change
People, products, technologies	Human operational and detection/ diagnosis behaviors and performance	Dynamics of competitor technology adoption; consumer product transitions	Human choices of social behaviors, investments, consumption

Table 6.6 Example issues, concerns, and models

Level	Issues and concerns	Models
Society, government, industry	GDP, Supply/Demand, Policy Economic Cycles Intra-Firm Relations, Competition Population and Climate Health	Macroeconomic System Dynamics Network Models Statistical Models
Organizations, management, markets	Profit Maximization Competition Investment Technology Adoption	Microeconomic Game Theory Discounted Cash Flow, Real Options
Processes and operations	Design and Evaluation Patient, Material Flow Process Efficiency Workflow, Safety Disease Infection and Propagation	System Design Matrices Discrete-event Models Learning Models Network Models Statistical Models
People, products, technologies	Operator Behavior Patient Behavior Disease Progression Risk Aversion Consumer Choice	Agent-based Models Manual Control Models Utility Models Bayes Models Markov Models

There is a very rich corpus of models that can be drawn upon to address particular domain questions.

One of the challenges in developing computational models is representation of behavioral and social phenomena, which are pervasive in the 18 case studies. My latest books address such phenomena in some detail. Recent books by Sheridan (2017), Tolk et al. (2018), and Davis et al. (2019) discuss these phenomena in great depth.

Interactive Visualizations

In Chapter 2, I outlined a brief methodology for designing and developing interactive visualizations. In this section, I discuss two examples that illustrate typical results of applying this methodology. My purpose here is to simply illustrate these two outcomes, not provide a tutorial on how to create such interactive visualizations.

Emory Prevention and Wellness

This case study addressed the employee prevention and wellness program of Emory University (Park et al., 2012). The application of the multi-level model focused on the roughly 700 people in this cohort and their risks of diabetes mellitus (DM) and coronary heart disease (CHD). The Human Resources Department of Emory University (HR) was the payer responsible for healthcare costs for university employees, while the Predictive Health Institute (PHI) was the provider focused on prevention and maintenance of employee health.

The Ecosystem level allowed decision makers to test different combinations of policies from the perspective of HR. For instance, this level determines the allocation of payments to PHI based on a hybrid capitated and pay-for-outcome formula. It also involves choices of parameters such as projected healthcare inflation rate, general economy inflation rate, and discount rate that affect the economic valuation of the prevention and wellness program. One of the greatest concerns of HR was achieving a satisfactory return on investment (ROI) on any investments in prevention and wellness.

The concerns at the Organization level include the economic sustainability of PHI—their revenue must be equal to or greater than their costs. To achieve sustainability, PHI must appropriately design its operational processes and rules. Two issues are central. What risk levels should be used to stratify the participant population? What assessment and coaching processes should be employed for each stratum of the population? Other Organization level considerations include the growth rate of the participant population, the age ranges targeted for growth, and the program duration before participants are moved to "maintenance."

Runs of the multi-level simulation were set up using the dashboard in Figure 6.2. Beyond the decision variables discussed above, decision makers could decide what data source to employ to parameterize the models—either data from the American Diabetes Association (ADA) and American Heart Association (AHA), or data specific to Emory employees. Decision makers

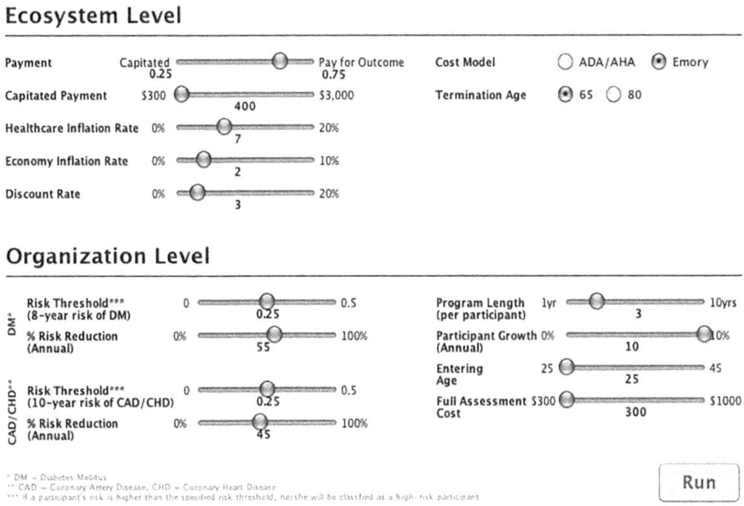

Figure 6.2 Multi-level simulation dashboard

could choose to only count savings until age 65 or also project post-retirement savings.

The bottom half of the dashboard provided inputs from Organization level decision makers, namely PHI. Beyond the variables mentioned above, these decision makers must choose how to stratify the participant population into low- and high-risk groups for each disease. Once they choose a level using the risk threshold slider, a set point appears on the percent risk reduction slider that represents what PHI is actually achieving based on analysis of their ongoing assessment data. Decision makers can choose to operate at the set point by moving the slider to this point, or they can explore the consequences of larger or smaller risk reductions.

Figure 6.3 shows the predictions for the Ecosystem and Organization levels of the model. The ROI from PHI's services is shown in net present values using the discount rate shown in Figure 6.2. PHI's delivery processes were significantly redesigned computationally to increase the annual ROI from –96% to 7%. Interestingly, the leaders of PHI commented that they never would have thought to do this computationally.

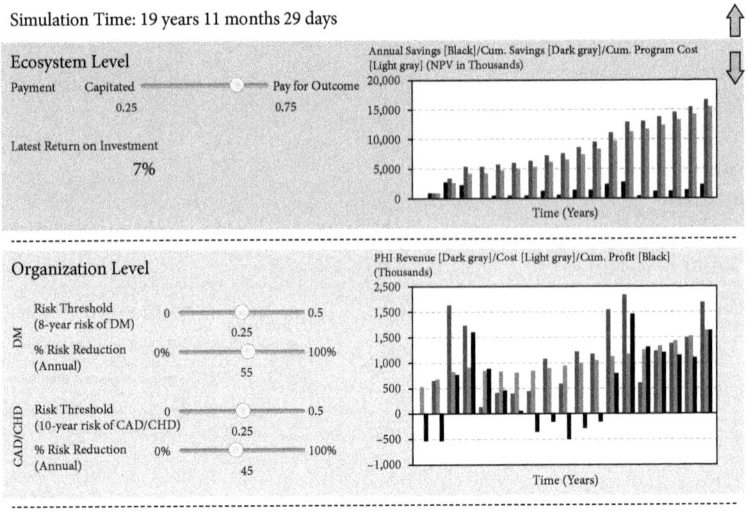

Figure 6.3 Ecosystem and organization levels of model

New York City Health Ecosystem

The Affordable Care Act (ACA) is causing a transformation of the healthcare industry. This industry involves complicated relationships among patients, physicians, hospitals, health plans, pharmaceutical companies, healthcare equipment companies, and government. Hospitals are uncertain about how they should best respond to threats and opportunities. This is particularly relevant for hospitals located in competitive metropolitan areas such as New York City, where a large number of hospitals compete—many among the nation's best.

In this case study, we developed a data-rich agent-based simulation model (Yu et al., 2016) to study dynamic interactions among healthcare systems in the context of merger and acquisition (M&A) decision making, driven by the US Affordable Care Act. By "rich" we mean extensive rule sets and information sources, compared to traditional agent-based models. The computational model included agents' revenues and profitability (i.e., financial statements), operational performance, and resource utilization, as well as a more detailed set of objectives and decision-making rules to address a variety of what-if scenarios.

The results from the simulation model facilitated M&A decision making, particularly in identifying desirable acquisition targets, aggressive and capable acquirers, and frequent acquirer–target pairs. The frequencies of prevalent pairs of acquirer and target appearing under different strategies in our simulation were of particular interest. The frequency level is a relative value in that it depends on number of strategies included and hospitals involved. A high frequency suggests a better fit and also repeated attraction.

The key value of the overall model and set of visualizations is, of course, the insights gained by the human users of this environment—see Figure 6.4. For example, they can determine the conditions under which certain outcomes are likely. They can then monitor developments to see if such conditions are emerging. Thus, they know what *might* happen, even though they cannot be assured what will happen. The greatest insights are gained not only from simulation, but also from interactive visualizations that enable massive data exploration, which moves from a "one-size-fits-all" static report to more adaptable and useful decision process.

Figure 6.4 Simulation of New York City health ecosystem

Summary

These two examples illustrate several important points:

- Key stakeholders need to be able to explore the complexity of the system of concern. They need to be able to conduct "what if?" experiments.
- Their explorations can help to validate the models. Especially early on, these explorations can help to identify misconceptions and errors.
- Once stakeholders are looking at predictions based on their own assumptions, their confidence tends to steadily increase.
- Over time, they tend to become advocates for the simulated world and attract other stakeholders to participate in these explorations.
- Many, and perhaps most, of the important insights that arise from such explorations are due to the humans creatively experimenting.
- We have *not* encountered anyone who says, "I do not understand these predictions. They do not make intuitive sense. But I will accept this advice because the model produced it."

Conclusions

Surveillance for failure management begins with comparing what you thought would happen with what did happen, i.e., comparing your predictions to your observations. This chapter has integrated the findings of the 18 case studies to identify central phenomena that need to be predicted to enable this comparison. I also provided examples of component models that could serve as elements of an overall computational model. Finally, a couple of examples of model-based interactive visualizations served to illustrate how models are employed.

Key enablers of failure management are predictions of future outcomes and comparisons of these predictions to measured outcomes.

Chapters 3–5 summarized how this is accomplished to detect failures of complex technologies and organizations, as well as broader societal failures. This chapter generalized across domains.

This is not to suggest that the same computational model can be applied to this full range of failures. The particular component models employed will vary substantially across domains. However, as Chapter 7 outlines, the same conceptual model can be employed to formulate a computational approach to failure management in any domain, perhaps even domains broader than represented by the case studies explored here.

My objective in this chapter was to convince readers that computational approaches to surveillance are feasible. The objective of Chapter 7 is to show how to employ these mechanisms for failure management. One particular hindrance deserves early mention. Will organizations be willing to invest in the requisite computational models?

The "cost of entry" has been a hurdle in the past. However, the perspectives of executives and managers have rapidly evolved over recent years. As discussed in Chapter 4, infusions of cloud computing, big data, artificial intelligence, and the Internet of Things have caused decision makers to entertain and pursue business models that are much more efficient and better serve consumers (Siebel, 2019). The maturity of these technologies has increased their confidence.

Of course, once we cut across organizational boundaries, especially across private companies and public agencies, adoption of new approaches becomes much more complicated. I return to such considerations in Chapter 8.

References

Christensen, C.M. (1997). *The Innovator's Dilemma: When New Technologies Cause Great Firms to Fail*. Boston, MA: Harvard Business Review Press.

Davis, P.K., O'Mahony, A., and Pfautz, J. (eds) (2019). *Social-behavioral Modeling for Complex Systems*. New York: Wiley.

Park, H., Clear, T., Rouse, W.B., Basole, R.C., Braunstein, M.L., Brigham, K.L., and Cunningham, L. (2012). Multi-level simulations of health delivery systems: A prospective tool for policy, strategy, planning and management. *Journal of Service Science*, 4 (3), 253–68.

Rouse, W.B. (2007). *People and Organizations: Explorations of Human-centered Design*. New York: Wiley.

Rouse, W.B. (2015). *Modeling and Visualization of Complex Systems and Enterprises: Explorations of Physical, Human, Economic, and Social Phenomena*. New York: Wiley.

Rouse, W.B. (2019). *Computing Possible Futures: Model-based Explorations of "What If?"* Oxford: Oxford University Press.

Schumpeter, J. (1942). *Capitalism, Socialism, and Democracy*. New York: Harper.

Sheridan, T.B. (2017). *Modeling Human System Interaction: Philosophical and Methodological Considerations, with Examples*. New York: Wiley.

Siebel, T.M. (2019). *Digital Transformation: Survive and Thrive in an Era of Mass Extinction*. New York: Rosetta.

Tolk, A., Diallo, S., and Saurabh Mittal, S. (eds) (2018). *Emergent Behavior in Complex Systems Engineering: A Modeling and Simulation Approach*. New York: Wiley.

Yu, Z., Rouse, W.B., Serban, S., and Veral, E. (2016). A data-rich agent-based decision support model for hospital consolidation. *Journal of Enterprise Transformation*, 6 (3/4), 136–61.

7
Failure Management

It is important to distinguish accident prevention from failure management. Accident prevention is a great goal, but there will inevitably be failures that are not prevented. This is particularly true for new, less than fully mature technologies. Driverless cars provide a contemporary example. When failures are likely, particularly unforeseen failures, an approach to failure management is needed.

This chapter begins with a brief review of the rich history of research in failure management, where the emphasis was much more on detection and diagnosis than management. This leads to consideration of failure management tasks, and how they differ for point and distributed failures. I then consider failure surveillance and control, which leads to an outline of an integrated decision support system for failure management. I finally consider the potential role of artificial intelligence in failure management.

Background

Starting in the mid 1970, I became fascinated with human abilities to address failures. This interest led us to report on 26 studies of failure detection and diagnosis between 1978 and 1986. We studied aircraft powerplant mechanics, communications network operators, supertanker engineering officers, nuclear powerplant operators, and space shuttle crews.

A close colleague in this endeavor was Jens Rasmussen of the Riso National Laboratory in Denmark. We met in Greece in 1977, knew of each other's research, and soon joined forces to organize a NATO Conference on Human Detection and Diagnosis of System

Failure Management: Malfunctions of Technologies, Organizations, and Society. William B. Rouse, Oxford University Press (2021). © William B. Rouse. DOI: 10.1093/oso/9780198870999.003.0007

Failures in Denmark in 1980. An edited book with the same title was published the next year (Rasmussen and Rouse, 1981).

The domains addressed in this conference naturally included defense systems, but also nuclear power and process plants; electronics, computer and software maintenance; aircraft operations and maintenance; and ship navigation. Detecting and diagnosing systems failures was clearly a pervasive problem.

This insight led me to subsequently compile a set of empirically validated models of human failure detection and diagnosis (Rouse, 1983). I identified six models of human failure detection: four based on anomaly thresholds, one based on filter residuals, and one based on pattern recognition. There were eleven models of human failure diagnosis: four based on the notion of "half split" tests, one based on half splits using information theory, two based on symbolic rules (i.e., if–then rules), two based on fuzzy set theory, one based on Bayesian probabilities, and one based on repair time probabilities.

I have updated this compilation in two more recent books (Rouse, 2007: Ch. 5; Rouse, 2019: Ch. 6). There is clearly a rich knowledge base to draw upon. However, almost all of this research focused on detection, diagnosis, and repair, i.e., once one figured out what had failed, one fixed it. It did not consider management of failure situations after detection and diagnosis, particularly when the idea of simply fixing things was not feasible. Such management was central to most of the 18 case studies discussed in this book. This is the focus in this chapter.

Failure Management Tasks

There are four tasks associated with failure management:

- Detection: Determination that the state of the system is off normal
- Diagnosis: Determination of the cause(s) of the off-normal states

Table 7.1 Failure management tasks for point and distributed failures

Failure management	Point failures	Distributed failures
Detection	Determination that system states are off normal	Comparison with projections that assume no anomalies
Diagnosis	Identification of the source(s) of the off-normal states	Determination of the source(s) of the anomalies
Compensation	Returning system to acceptable states despite failure(s)	Maintaining acceptable system states despite anomalies
Remediation	Correcting or counteracting the failure(s)	Correcting or counteracting the sources of anomalies

- Compensation: Controlling the system to achieve acceptable states
- Remediation: Repairing or countering the cause(s) of the failure.

Early detection, rapid (correct) diagnosis, timely compensation, and eventual remediation are key. These things could have been done better for 15 of the 18 failures. There was no way for Chernobyl or the space shuttles to recover, although subsequent designs of plants and shuttles were significantly improved.

As shown in Table 7.1, these tasks are addressed rather differently for point and distributed failures. For point failures, consequences were usually anticipated during system design. During operations, it was typically assumed that the state of the system was under control. In other words, decision makers knew such outcomes could happen but they thought they were under control. Design decisions occurred long before the system was deployed; crisis management decisions occurred after the failure. Operational management decisions occurred somewhat before failures; remediation decisions occurred after failures.

For distributed failures, consequences are typically unexpected, so control had usually been ignored. For example, clinicians were treating pain, making money, and living life, but bad things happened. Eventual risks were not anticipated and were years beyond any planning horizon. Design decisions, e.g., the structure of financial derivatives, occurred long before problems emerged and were recognized; crisis management decisions occurred after the failure. Operational management decisions occurred as an unrecognized failure was emerging; remediation decisions occurred after the failure.

Summarizing, engineered systems usually anticipate the possibilities of failures, e.g., of pumps, but they are not really expected; the consequences are initiated at one point, e.g., the pump. Social systems, e.g., healthcare, anticipate infectious diseases but usually do not know what specifically to expect, e.g., AIDS, and the consequences are distributed over time across populations.

Failures manifest themselves at one or more levels of systems, enterprises, and ecosystems. Detection, diagnosis, compensation, and remediation are affected by decision making across these levels. Anticipated point failures are addressed rather differently than unexpected distributed failures that slowly emerge.

As noted earlier, many of the 18 failures resulted from or were exacerbated by poor design, inadequate evaluation, or mismanagement of operations. Improvements in these areas are also broad elements of failure management as indicated in Table 7.2. The interpretations of the elements of this table depend on context.

Usability, aiding, training, and evaluation are similar for technological systems, complex enterprises, health systems, and the economy. People need to be able to do their jobs well, and outcomes need to be assured and monitored. These objectives may seem obvious, but the case studies starkly illustrate the consequences of underinvesting in these goals.

Interpretation of the operations columns in Table 7.2 differs across the case studies. The entries in these cells are well aligned with operation of complex technological systems discussed in Chapter 3. However, the construct of safety needs a different interpretation for complex organizations and ecosystems.

I will define safety as assurance of the acceptability of future states of systems, as well as the consequences of these states. Clearly, the futures states of the six enterprises in Chapter 4 were unacceptable. In that sense, these enterprises were unsafe. However, my

Table 7.2 Broad elements of failure management

	Design			Evaluation		Operations	
	System	**Aiding**	**Training**	**Test**	**Ongoing**	**Culture**	**Incentives**
People	Usability and usefulness assured	Directly augment performance	Augment potential to perform	Usability testing	In-use testing	Safety culture embraced	Balance of safety and performance
Processes	Human-centered design	Procedures, job aiding	Simulators, team training	Extreme scenarios explored	Capture activities	Safe practices enabled	Timely feedback provided
Organizations	Investment in design expertise	Investment in aiding technology	Investment in training technology	Oversight of testing integrity	Oversight of ongoing integrity	Safe practices exalted	Balanced performance reviews
Society	Required design practices	Required personnel aiding plan	Required training plan	Publication of testing results	Publication of ongoing evaluations	Safety culture required	Transparent incentives and rewards

knowledge of these enterprises suggests that management was totally focused on performance, not safety as I have defined it.

What is a safe health system, economy, or environment? I think the same definition of safety applies. Millions of people dying, losing their homes, and being inundated by rising sea levels reflect unsafe ecosystems. The surveillance mechanisms discussed in Chapter 5 are able to detect the emergence of unsafe system states. However, with the possible exception of the health system, we seem willing to let bad things happen and try to fix them later, often much later.

Failure Surveillance and Control

We would like to design systems, organizations, and ecosystems that anticipate the possibility of failures and incorporate mechanism for managing these failures. The goal is resilience. The approaches and methods summarized in Chapters 3–5 are the starting point. Point failures are amenable to engineering approaches to system design. However, these approaches are not particularly useful for distributed failures of systems for which there are no blueprints, i.e., systems that were not really designed.

Distributed failures have to be addressed differently. Surveillance of the state of the system focuses on detecting anomalies, i.e., unexpected system states. As discussed in Chapter 5, there are surveillance methods for population health, the economy, and the environment. We reviewed the data and methods employed for surveillance in these different domains.

There can be passive, active, or predictive surveillance, as well as predictive control. Table 7.3 summarizes the technologies needed to implement these levels of surveillance and control. The Internet of Things (IoT) denotes our rapidly advancing abilities to sense things remotely.

With passive surveillance via IoT, off-normal situations are detected and reported, inherently after the fact. Active surveillance involves proactively probing systems looking for emergent anomalies. This enables reporting trends that possibly portend failures. In

Table 7.3 Interventions vs. types of failures

Interventions	Types of failure	
	Point failures	**Distributed failures**
Passive surveillance	Internet of Things (IoT)	Early warning measures (EWM)
Active surveillance	Optimized IoT (OIoT)	Optimized EWM (OEWM)
Predictive surveillance	OIoT and one model	OEWM and one model
Predictive control	OIoT and two models	OEWM and two models

other words, passive and active surveillance measure what *has* happened. Predictive surveillance focuses on what *might* happen.

Predictive surveillance and predictive control involve model-based approaches to surveillance and control as depicted in Figure 7.1. The central idea is to use the differences between expected and actual system outputs, i.e., the residuals, to drive the control of the system to minimize the residuals, i.e., to minimize "surprise."

Predictive surveillance uses a model of the system to predict outputs. Predictive control adds an optimization model to minimize residuals. There is a possibility that the optimizer in Figure 7.1 may be trying to overcome deficiencies of the systems model in this figure. Thus, ideally, the system model would be adapted to make better predictions, which would also reduce residuals.

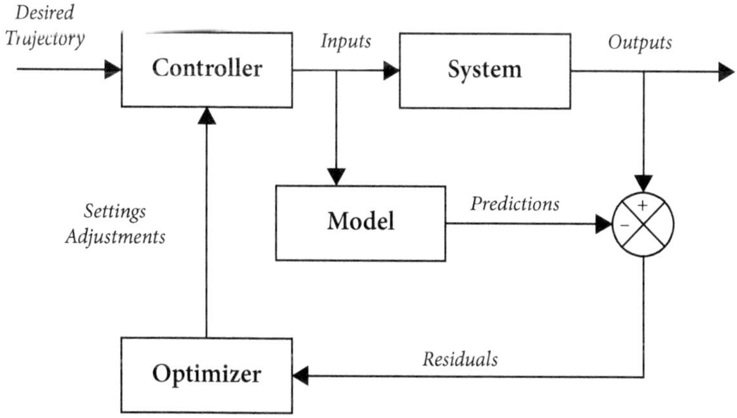

Figure 7.1 Model-based predictive control

Table 7.4 Surveillance and control strategies

Case study	Elements of surveillance and control strategy
Three Mile Island	Support to detect and diagnose energy imbalances
Chernobyl	Support to detect and diagnose energy imbalances
Challenger	Design and testing for wide range of malfunctions
Columbia	Design and testing for wide range of malfunctions
Valdez	Collision detection and avoidance system, which was turned off
Horizon	Support to detect and diagnose energy imbalances
Polaroid	Support to detect and diagnose change of photography market
Kodak	Support to detect and diagnose change of photography market
Digital	Support to detect and diagnose change of computing market
Xerox	Support to detect and diagnose change of computing market
Motorola	Support to detect and diagnose change of cell phone market
Nokia	Support to detect and diagnose change of cell phone market
Aids	Health, education, and social services; incentives for safe sex
Opioids	Health, education, and social services; alternative pain management
Depression	Banking insurance
Recession	Regulations on mortgage qualifications
Population	Education, incentives for family planning
Climate	Education, incentives for energy conservation

The evolving system model would likely be of great interest to management because it would inform them of the nature of the system they actually have versus what they thought they had. They might learn, for example, that the performance characteristics of their system have degraded, or perhaps the nature of the market, health system, economy, or environment has changed.

Table 7.4 summarizes a few key elements of a possible surveillance and control strategy for each of the 18 case studies. Cases 1–6 involve technological interventions to make detection and diagnosis of failures much easier. For example, the three interventions that involve graphically portraying energy imbalances would make it immediately clear that something was wrong and, depending on where the energy was imbalanced, provide clear evidence of what was wrong.

Cases 7–12 all involved misreading of markets. These companies undoubtedly noticed a softening of the markets for their products but were quite slow to consider scenarios that would eventually decimate their businesses. Scenario planning support that caused them to consider a wider range of alternative futures could, at the very least, have caused them to recognize market threats much earlier. Of course, this might require top management to entertain futures that they did not want to admit were possible.

Cases 13–18 are much more varied than the other two sets of cases. For the health-related cases, the consequences of the failures were very much exacerbated by the fragmentation of the US health system. Integrated delivery of health, education, and social services was almost impossible. Integrated delivery, enabled by integrated information systems and incentives for care coordination are key elements of efficient and effective surveillance and control strategies.

The failures of the economic system were subject to different problems. Pervasive greed and misunderstandings of risks were central determinants of bad investment decisions that taxpayers had to bail out. For the most part, financial institutions were bailed out while individual investors had to suffer the consequences. Appropriate regulations could have countered these tendencies, but vested interests strongly opposed regulation, squirrelling away their winnings while everyone else suffered.

The precipitation of population and climate failures reflects people not understanding the consequences of their actions. Large families and consumption of fossil fuels were not intended to undermine economies and environments. They were local decisions about economic needs and priorities that had consequences that few people imagined. They were just living their lives and trying to get by. Of course, citizens, managers, and politicians do this all the time.

Complications

There are various complications that make failure management more difficult. Failures that emerge over time, the hallmark of distributed failures, can also happen with point failures where, for example, a subsystem degrades for a period before it fails, e.g., a slow leak that eventually ruptures. Another complication is multiple failures where more than one thing goes wrong, often independently, although this may not be readily apparent.

Human error frequently seems to be the identified cause. Jens Rasmussen (1986) and Rasmussen and colleagues (1994) have characterized human error as often involving an unfortunate experiment in an unkind environment. W. Edwards Deming (1982) argues that human performance failures are often attributable to the design of the system. Thus, errors are frequently organizational as illustrated in the recent HBO special *Chernobyl*. Organizational errors are pervasive throughout the 18 case studies discussed in this book.

We have explored the notion of error tolerant interfaces and developed the technology to enable these interfaces (Rouse, 2007; Rouse and Spohrer, 2018). The basic idea is that errors are less a problem than consequences. If errors can be recognized and remediated before there are consequences, errors are much less a problem. The key, of course, is the ability to recognize observed information and actions as anomalous. This requires a more intelligent interface.

We first studied this possibility for aircraft operating procedures. The question was whether one could infer which procedure was being executed and whether it was being executed correctly. As aircrew cockpit operation procedures are very well structured and most steps involve pushing buttons, turning switches, etc., we were able to experimentally show that procedure execution was substantially enhanced by an intelligent error-tolerant interface (Rouse, 2007).

Rarely do such academic findings make it quickly to actual practice. I was a member of the advisory committee for design of the cockpit of the Boeing 777 aircraft. During each meeting, we flew the B777 simulator and commented on its functions and features. When I commented to a Boeing engineer that their electronic checklist shared some features with ours, he responded that they had read our papers and our findings influenced their design.

Finally, we need to consider the possibility of malicious failures, situations where competitors, adversaries, or villains consciously cause systems to fail. We have, of late, seen numerous instances of such failures. This possibility does not seem to really change surveillance, detection, and diagnosis. One still has to determine what went wrong and why.

However, compensation and remediation are likely to be quite different. One has to counter the adversary, both to eliminate the current threat and minimize the likelihood of similar future threats. This is still about safety, as broadly defined above, but also includes the design of countermeasure to thwart adversaries. Cybersecurity is, of course, a major example of such threats. Unfortunately, this topic is beyond the scope of this book.

Integrated Decision Support

Integrated decision support for failure management must achieve several objectives, First, it has to represent both running the enterprise you have while trying to create the enterprise you want, In other words, keeping the current engine running while you design and deploy the future engine.

There are three levels of operations of interest. Level four provides societal context:

- Plans for future operations
- Current operations
- Detection and diagnosis within current operations.

Failure management has to balance all three levels of operations, while monitoring level four (society) for changes of the rules of the game. This balance is very difficult to achieve—the present almost always dominates the future.

Figure 7.2 portrays these three levels of support. This integrated decision support concept was motivated, in part, by a much more constrained view of integration in a production-systems setting (Rouse, 1988). Of course, the findings for the 18 case studies were the primary drivers of the functionality depicted in Figure 7.2.

The dashed lines differentiate the three levels. The roles of the three levels are:

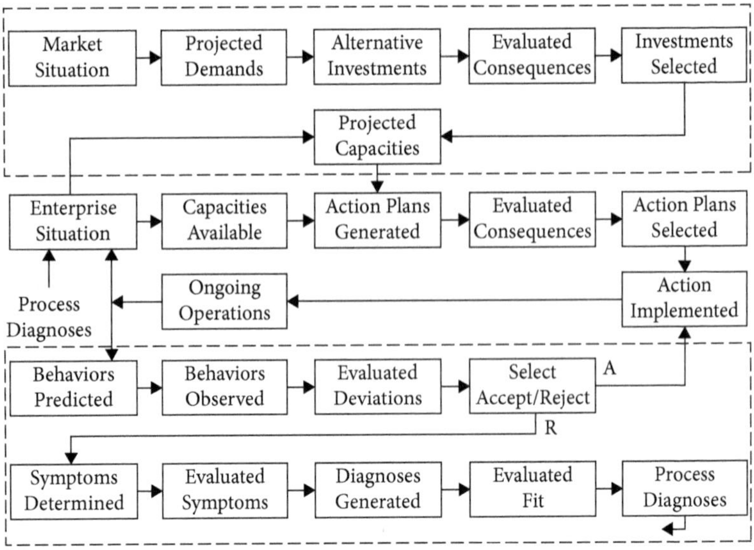

Figure 7.2 Integrated decision support for failure management

- The top level monitors the "market" and "enterprise" and invests accordingly, with market and enterprise broadly defined
- The second level executes the top-level plans, employing existing and new capacities, the latter due to the above investments
- The lowest level addresses anomalies, decides whether something has failed, diagnoses sources of failures, which contributes to situation assessment.

What does "failure" mean in this depiction? Operational failures of technology reflect Cases 1–6. Failure of product and/or service offerings relate to Cases 7–12. Failure to deter phenomena and often delayed failure management are central to Cases 13–18. Conceptually, Figure 7.2 can address all of these but, of course, the details of the instantiation of this support concept vary significantly with the context.

These are the proximate causes of failures. Distal or ultimate causes include:

- Failures to correctly assess markets and enterprise situations and trends

- Failures to invest appropriately in products and processes, including training, procedures, etc., where products and processes include interventions, e.g., drugs, regulations, incentives
- Failures to recognize situations and act despite compelling evidence of the need to respond.

These distal or ultimate causes often resulted in transforming easily managed failures into complex, high consequence problems epitomized by the cases discussed here.

Figure 7.3 shows a version of this functionality for population health (Madhavan et al., 2018) that was derived from a multi-level model of population health. This "dashboard" was included in the National Academies' recommendations for cancer control (Johns et al., 2019). This diagram could warrant an enormous amount of explanation. However, I include it here primarily to illustrate the extent to which context plays a major role in how decision support is manifested.

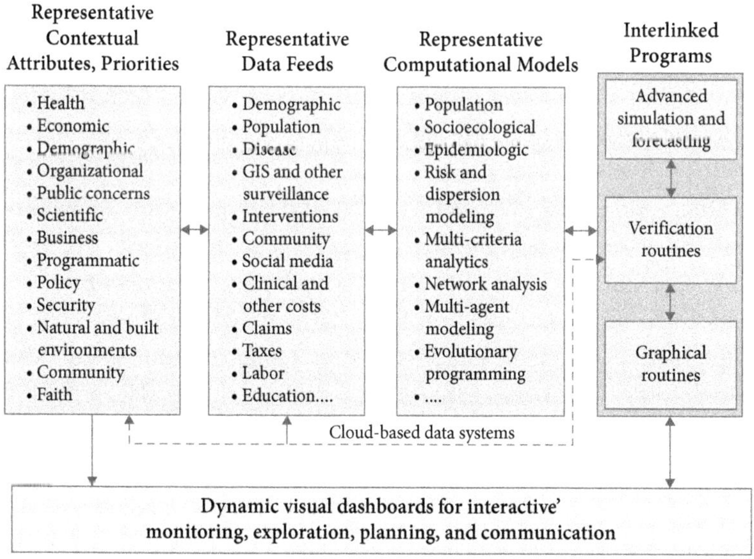

Figure 7.3 Example dashboard for population control
Source: Madhavan et al. (2018).

AI For Failure Management

How might artificial intelligence (AI) help with this? In Chapter 4, I discussed the perspectives of McAfee and Brynjolfsson (2017) and Siebel (2019) on likely disruptions by AI and related technologies. Can we reasonably expect to automate the processes in Figure 7.2? My sense is that augmented, rather than automated, intelligence is a much more reasonable aspiration (Rouse and Spohrer, 2018; Rouse, 2019).

AI could help in recognizing unusual circumstances and overcoming natural human tendencies to force observed patterns into standard scripts. Physicians, for example, have said they would value AI assistance in determining that a patient with a particular morbidity is not presenting the usual pattern of symptoms. On the other hand, if the AI is intended to recommend what to do for this patient, then it needs to be able to provide a physician-understandable explanation. This is beyond the current state of the art.

The underlying issue is trust. *The Economist* (2019), interviewing Gary Marcus (Marcus and Davis, 2019), discusses how AI is prone to failures, lacks transparency, and cannot explain its recommendations. For these reasons, it often cannot be trusted. This distrust of AI accompanies wariness of related technologies, e.g., the surveillance and harassment enabled by Facebook and Twitter (Eveleth, 2019).

Obermeyer and Weinstein (2020) address adoption in healthcare. Their survey results indicate that AI is being aggressively oversold to clinicians. They are most confident in augmentation via pattern recognition, based on large data sets where phenomena of interest have repeatable patterns. Where standardization is desirable and feasible, they believe that AI can find anomalies. Nevertheless, they conclude that it is difficult to teach machines ethics, intuition, and empathy.

Fontaine, McCarthy, and Saleh (2019) address organizing for AI. They argue that slow adoption reflects failures to rewire organizations and the fact that AI is not plug and play with immediate returns—this expectation precipitated earlier disaffections with AI (Rouse and Spohrer, 2018). They articulate three needed shifts. Organizations need to move from siloed work to interdisciplinary collaboration, from experience-based leader-driven decision making to data-driven decision making at the front line, and from being rigid and risk-averse to becoming agile, experimental, and adaptable. I return to these issues in Chapter 8.

Given the above technology trends, will human detection, diagnosis, compensation, and remediation become obsolete? Let's ask Jack Tuttle. Robert De Niro plays Jack Tuttle in Terry Gilliam's dystopian 1985 film *Brazil* (1985). Here is a snippet of dialog:

SAM LOWRY (JONATHAN PRYCE): Are you from central services?
HARRY TUTTLE (ROBERT DE NIRO): Hah! They're a little overworked these days. Luckily I intercepted your call.
SAM LOWRY: Can you fix it?
HARRY TUTTLE: No, but I can bypass it with one of these.

The complexity had become overwhelming and a primary strategy for addressing it was to find workarounds. Humans are good at this. I expect we will long depend on such abilities.

Conclusions

This chapter addressed the 18 case studies in terms of how the failures manifested in these cases could be addressed. There are obvious merits in avoiding such failures in the first place. However, this book is about managing failures and their consequences once they occur.

A central premise of this chapter is that failure management can be pursued in an integrated manner, regardless of the context. The thinking need not change, although the specific interventions will obviously be context dependent. In other words, the conceptual design of integrated decision support can be generalized, while the detailed design of the support depends on the context.

Thus, model-based predictive surveillance and control can be employed for all the contexts represented by the 18 cases. The integrated decision support concept presented broadly applies as well. The concept is general; the specifics are context dependent. Moreover, specific design decisions need to deliver the functions and features implied by Figure 7.2.

This chapter has articulated a technical solution to the broad problem of failure management. It would be straightforward to argue the economic benefits of this approach (Rouse, 2010; Sage and Rouse, 2011), but beyond the scope of this book. Thus, this chapter has provided the technical and economic rationale for failure management.

Diesing (1971) articulates four types of rationality—economic, legal, political, and social. His classification embeds technical rationality within the economic category. To fully address and enable failure management, we need to consider behavioral, social, political, and legal perspectives. These are addressed in Chapter 8.

References

Brazil (1985). Film, directed by Terry Gilliam, produced by Embassy International Pictures N.V.

Deming, W.E. (1982). *Out of Crisis*. Cambridge, MA: MIT Press.

Diesing, P. (1971). *Reason in Society*. Urbana, IL: University of Illinois Press.

Economist, The (2019). Don't trust AI until we build systems that earn trust. *The Economist*, December 18.

Eveleth, R. (2019). The architects of our digital hellscape are very sorry. *Wired*, December 28.

Fontaine, T., McCarthy, B., and Saleh, T. (2019). Building the AI-powered organization. *Harvard Business Review*, July-August.

Johns, M.M.E., Madhavan, G., Nass, S.J., and Amankwah, F.K. (eds) (2019). *Guiding Cancer Control: A Path to Transformation*. Washington, DC: National Academies Press.

Madhavan, G., Phelps, C.E., Rouse, W.B., and Rappuoli, R. (2018). A vision for a systems architecture to integrate and transform population health. *Proceedings of the National Academy of Sciences*, 115 (50), 12,595–602.

Marcus, G., and Davis, E. (2019). *Rebooting AI*. New York: Pantheon.

McAfee, A., and Brynjolfsson, E. (2017). *Machine Platform Crowd: Harness our Digital Future*. New York: Norton.

Obermeyer, Z. and Weinstein, J. (2020). Adoption of artificial intelligence and machine learning is increasing, but irrational exuberance remains. *New England Journal of Medicine Catalyst*, 1 (1), January.

Rasmussen, J. (1986). *Information Processing and Human–machine Interaction*. New York: North-Holland.

Rasmussen, J., Pejtersen, A.M., and Goodstein, L.P. (1994). *Cognitive Systems Engineering*. New York: Wiley.

Rasmussen, J., and Rouse, W.B. (eds) (1981). *Human Detection and Diagnosis of System Failures*. New York: Plenum Press.

Rouse, W.B. (1983). Models of human problem solving: Detection, diagnosis, and compensation for system failures. *Automatica*, 19 (6), 613–25.

Rouse, W.B. (1988). Intelligent decision support for advanced manufacturing systems. *Manufacturing Review*, 1 (4), 236–43.

Rouse, W.B. (2007). *People and Organizations: Explorations of Human-centered Design*. New York: Wiley.

Rouse, W.B. (ed.) (2010). *The Economics of Human Systems Integration: Valuation of Investments in People's Training and Education, Safety and Health, and Work Productivity*. New York: John Wiley.

Rouse, W.B. (2019). *Computing Possible Futures: Model-based Explorations of "What If?"* Oxford: Oxford University Press.

Rouse, W.B., and Spohrer, J.C. (2018). Automating versus augmenting intelligence. *Journal of Enterprise Transformation*, https://doi.org/10.1080/19488289.2018.1424059.

Sage, A.P., and Rouse, W.B. (2011). *Economic System Analysis and Assessment*. New York: Wiley.

Siebel, T.M. (2019). *Digital Transformation: Survive and Thrive in an Era of Mass Extinction*. New York: Rosetta.

8
Enabling Change

Introduction

Failures are inevitable. As the technological complexity of our world continually increases, the complexity of failures will increase as well. We can do our best to prevent these failures, but there will always be surprises. These surprises will need to be managed to minimize negative consequences.

The management of failures should both mitigate consequences and provide insights and lessons learned. This knowledge should increase enterprises' abilities to continually improve their management of failures. However, these improvements will require concerted efforts by enterprises.

This book has articulated an integrated approach to realizing these benefits. A key issue is the affordances and impedances to adopting this approach. In other words, what are the likely avenues to success and what barriers can impede progress? We need to understand avenues and barriers and how best to address them.

We have, at this point in this book, a rather thorough understanding of the nature of failures and we have derived an overall conceptual model for failure management. The next step concerns how to get organizations to adopt what we have learned to improve their approaches to failure management and the outcomes they experience.

How can we enable the changes articulated in Chapters 6 and 7? To begin, we need to consider the processes whereby technologies are invented, and sometimes succeed to become market innovations. Technology learning curves affect when mature capabilities are available. With rare exceptions, technology adoption tends to be

Failure Management: Malfunctions of Technologies, Organizations, and Society. William B. Rouse, Oxford University Press (2021). © William B. Rouse. DOI: 10.1093/oso/9780198870999.003.0008

slow, i.e., years rather than months. Many of the case studies in this book involved technological innovation, often embraced but sometimes avoided.

There are progressions of change from needs, occasionally prompted by failures, to technological innovation, formation of companies, creation of jobs, and resulting outcomes. These outcomes typically provide great benefits to people, the economy, and society. However, these changes often germinate the seeds of future failures. Some are point failures when advanced technology breaks down. Others are distributed failures that slowly emerge and eventually prompt the types of problem solving addressed in this book.

The context of failure is often mature organizations, with entrenched vested interests in the status quo, and dogged pursuit of near-term goals. Despite claims otherwise, productivity is primary and safety is secondary. This context determines who is recruited, how they are trained, and the nature of incentives and rewards. Not surprisingly, failures and their consequences are often not in managers' and executives' plans. Safety science, as discussed in Chapter 3, argues that safety metrics should influence incentives and rewards.

Decision Making

We first need to address the behavioral and social nature of decision making. People react to incentives and rewards rather than values and principles. They do not like to admit they are wrong, e.g., misread the market, and do not like conflicts with key stakeholders. People tend to delay major decisions until everyone is on board.

People have various defense mechanisms and limitations. They may deny the situation because it threatens the status quo and threatens various "rice bowls." They may deny acknowledging the situation because it would be socially unacceptable for their reputation or the mood of the organization.

They may distance themselves from the situation due to temporal and spatial discounting. The consequences may be delayed and they can discount them, perhaps because they are unlikely to be there when the consequences are manifested (Story et al., 2014). They may spatially discount the consequences because they will be manifested far away.

Managers may have attention deficits due to preoccupation with status quo, or what Hallowell (2005) terms an attention deficit trait such that "an event occurs when a manager is desperately trying to deal with more input than he possibly can. In survival mode, the manager makes impulsive judgments, angrily rushing to bring closure to whatever matter is at hand. He feels compelled to get the problem under control immediately, to extinguish the perceived danger lest it destroy him."

They may be unable to digest and think through implications of symptoms. Simon (1972) argues that human decision making is limited by information available, cognitive limitations, and the time available—in other words, bounded rationality. Consequently, decision makers "satisfice" rather than optimize. Thus, decision makers allocate resources in a manner that is satisfactory in that it makes sense and is acceptable.

People employ various heuristics and biases that cause them to over- or underestimate probabilities and imagine alternative futures (Kahneman, 2011). They respond to often-subtle nudges, for better or worse (Thaler and Sunstein, 2008). Their intuitions can be powerful in circumstances they have repeatedly experienced (Klein, 2004) or completely misleading in novel situations, which is often the case for failures.

Mintzberg (1975) argues that plan, organize, coordinate, and control are not the right characterization of managers' jobs. "Study after study has shown that managers work at an unrelenting pace, that their activities are characterized by brevity, variety, and discontinuity, and that they are strongly oriented to action and dislike reflective activities." Their work "involves performing a number of regular duties, including ritual and ceremony, negotiations, and processing of soft information that links the organization with its environment."

Within such an interrupt-driven environment, Mintzberg indicates "managers strongly favor verbal media, telephone calls and meetings, over documents." It is easy to imagine technology that might assist managers to balance the many interruptions. However, "the managers' programs—to schedule time, process information, make decisions, and so on—remain locked deep inside their brains."

Consequently, even if they have access to integrated decision support for failure management, managers and executives are likely to delay or avoid taking timely action to address failures. Climate change, for example, threatens powerful stakeholders (i.e., investors, donors, voters) and consequently the evidence is denied and action delayed or possibly avoided.

Figure 8.1 summarizes these observations on decision making by executives who decide where to invest resources and managers who oversee operations. The economic and social environments have enormous impacts, beyond the symptoms and contingencies of the failures anticipated or at hand. There are significant consequences for where and how the organization invests and manages.

Is it important that organizations accurately assess the strategic situation they are facing, including any current failure situation. Our studies of the former suggest that strategic situation assessment is often badly flawed (Rouse, 1996). It is quite common for executives and managers to assume, often only implicitly, that they are in the same situation that led to their past successes.

This mistake was quite evident in the case studies of complex enterprises in Chapter 4. In Chapter 3, we saw several instances of

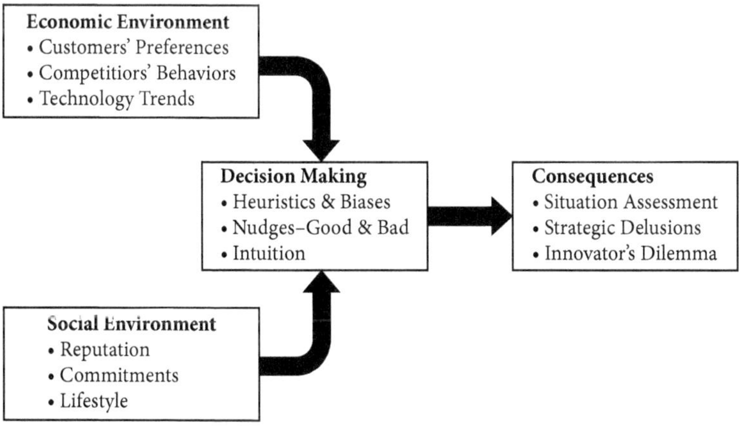

Figure 8.1 Factors affecting decision making and consequences

organizations that believed that they had an adequate culture of safety, but were wrong. In Chapter 5, beliefs in business as usual resulted in significantly delayed responses. In the context of Figure 8.1, these organizations were unwilling or unable to admit that assumptions were wrong.

Our studies of delusions that undermine strategic thinking (Rouse, 1998) suggest other possible difficulties in addressing failures. One delusion is "we just have to make our numbers." Production and performance are paramount. All the processes are in place to achieve this safely. This reflects the delusion that "we have the ducks all aligned." The key is that organizations make implicit assumptions that are no longer justified, but are seldom questioned (Harford, 2011).

Christensen (1997) has addressed a major consequence of inaccurate situation assessments and strategic delusions in terms of the innovator's dilemma. He has studied this phenomenon in business, healthcare, and education. Succinctly, inventions that could become significant market innovations are ignored because they cannot yet compete with the status quo in terms of near-term revenues and profits.

This phenomenon was quite evident in the case studies in Chapter 4. It is subtle in Chapters 3 and 5. However, one climate-related example is renewable energy sources (e.g., solar and wind) that certainly have faced the innovator's dilemma. On the other hand, for the economics case studies, financial companies seemed willing to quickly adopt anything that would rapidly yield substantial revenues and profits, regardless of the risks.

Decision-Making Vignettes

I have often encountered executives and managers affected by the limitations and orientation outlined above. There are many stories, where success was not hindered. Earlier, I discussed IBM moving beyond mainframes to services, Microsoft initially dismissing then pursuing Internet offerings, and Apple transforming from a computer company to a digital device company.

One of my favorite examples involved a large food services company that was mired in a low-margin business of operating internal cafeterias for clients. As I was facilitating their strategy offsite, we wrestled with this situation. The CEO then suggested, "Let's raise prices." There were almost universal skeptical reactions.

He followed, "If we increase the price by $2 per meal, our labor costs will not increase. We could put most, but not all, of this increase into better quality ingredients and advertise this to those eating in the cafeterias." They rolled out this upgrade with great fanfare and enormous success.

Working with the executive team of a large health-related nonprofit, we discussed how best to employ their resources. Many donors wanted the monies to be invested in medical research, but their pool of resources was very small compared to ongoing federal investments. We decided to focus on those aspects of health where the government did not invest, e.g., patient education and advocacy. In those areas, this organization could be a much larger player and seriously address issues that tended to fall through the cracks.

There are also many examples of flawed decision making. In Chapter 4, I related my experiences at Digital where the first goal of every product planning engagement was keeping the alpha chip in the Guinness Book of Records. The culture had evolved to first focusing on technical success and then addressing market success.

In a strategic planning engagement focused on new defense capabilities, I commented to the team that we needed to include concepts that did not involve airplanes, missiles, or satellites. A senior member of the team commented, "Bill, that's what we sell." Consequently, discussion avoided concepts enabled by new technologies that would better do the job, faster, and cheaper.

Two of my aviation and automotive clients independently made comments that, at the time, surprised me. I was engaged to bring new ideas to the discussion, in part from the wide range of experiences that I had been accumulating. In both companies, executives responded, "If those were good ideas, we would have already had them." Such hubris was pervasive. Both of them later stumbled significantly, but have survived.

One of my automotive clients provided vehicles in every product category. The high-end SUVs and specialty vehicles were immensely profitable. The passenger cars lost enormous sums. I suggested they exit the passenger car business. They responded, "But then we would not be a full scope automobile manufacturer." Within a couple of years, they were sold to a much larger player, who did exactly what I had imagined.

I met with one of my aviation clients on the first day of the new fiscal year. I began by asking if they were glad that this year's production goals were set. One executive responded, "Do you mean are we happy that we agreed to goals that are completely unachievable?"

I asked, "Are you saying that on the first day of the new fiscal year, you have already failed?" He affirmed this and I asked, "How could you agree to these goals?" Another executive responded: "We had no choice but agree with Corporate. They need to project the revenues that Wall Street expects and we need to keep our jobs—at least until the end of this year."

I have experienced many instances of choosing the wrong goals, adopting bad assumptions, assuming business as usual, and not recognizing latent delusions. Organizations tend to think they can muddle through such mistakes—until they cannot. At that point, time and resources have been wasted and recovery is very difficult.

Reflections on Maintenance

Maintenance is an important aspect of the concerns evidenced by the case studies. We are well aware of corrective maintenance of our bodies, vehicles, appliances, etc. We are less inclined to preventive maintenance to avoid or forestall failures. This is often referred to as delayed maintenance, implying that it will eventually be conducted. However, we often wait for failures before we fix things, as evidenced by several case studies.

Howard (2015) addresses delayed infrastructure maintenance. US infrastructure is in need of enormous investments to update 50–100-year-old bridges, tunnels, subways, etc. Both money and permits are constraints. Silos have their own rules and territorial instincts. Of course, politicians are afraid to ask taxpayers to foot such huge bills with benefits accruing to their children and grandchildren who are not yet voters.

Maintenance of health and well-being is obviously important, but only recently is receiving concerted attention, e.g., (Madhavan et al., 2018; Rouse, Johns, and Pepe, 2019). Prevention and screening for early detection can greatly decrease needs for expensive healthcare expenditures. The economic case is straightforward to make except, in the United States, providers and payers are two separate industries. There are few incentives for providers to invest to save money for payers. Thus, health maintenance is much less a priority than it should be.

Figure 8.1 might be interpreted as executives and managers being afraid of failing. This is, of course, to an extent true. However, considering cultural perspectives on failure (Bryant, 2019), risk taking is a hallmark in the United States, emergent in India, and negatively viewed in Germany, Japan, Mexico, and Islamic countries. Interestingly, Germany and Japan may be better at maintaining systems because failures are viewed so negatively.

Broader Perspectives

As noted in Chapter 7, Diesing (1971) articulates four types of rationality—economic, legal, political, and social. His classification embeds technical rationality within the economic category. To fully address and enable change, we need to consider behavioral, social, political, and legal perspectives.

Behavioral and social forces that inhibit change were summarized earlier in this chapter. When considering alternative futures, the status quo is very compelling. It requires no investment, is already in place, and everyone knows how to proceed. For most people, there needs to be a compelling argument why the status quo will no longer be tenable.

Beyond the technical and economic arguments, there are political considerations. I recently interviewed a former White House official in the Bush and Obama administrations. After we finished discussing the topic at hand, I asked him why the two parties couldn't agree on just a few good ideas, whose merits are obvious.

He countered by hypothesizing that one party had a really good idea that the other party agreed was a great idea. The party without the idea would work to defeat it because the other party would get credit for the great idea. This might help them in the next election. Getting reelected has become the primary jobs of politicians. Benefits to the public are very much secondary. This was quite a lesson.

Legal perspectives can also hinder change. I recently helped to conduct a series of three workshops on accessibility of driverless cars for disabled and older adults. The first workshop addressed needs, the second technologies, and the third policy and economic issues. Participants included advocacy groups, automakers, and a range of government agencies.

The third workshop included considerations of statutes and regulations that would likely affect deployment of driverless cars. Speakers included senior executives from the US Departments of Health and Human Services, Justice, Labor, and Transportation, the Federal Communications Commission, and other agencies that were new to me.

Listening to their outlines of relevant statutes and regulations led the person next to me to comment, "There does not seem to be anything you can do that is not illegal." The legal "rules of the game" in these agencies have evolved rather independently over many decades, almost always for reasons unrelated to driverless cars. Nevertheless, change and innovation will have to make their ways through these wickets.

Recent years have seen increased polarization in the United States between blue and red states, rural and urban constituencies, and various other distinctions (Rausch, 2019; Mann and Ornstein, 2020). Polarization has also emerged in Europe. People have come to increasingly identify with their tribes, regardless of the policies articulated.

Such tribalism has led to different groups having their own sets of facts and their favored media. Social media is a major contributor to these phenomena. Tribalism exacerbates all the difficulties discussed in this chapter, making discussion and debate near impossible. However, diseases, economies, and environments march on, for better or worse.

Joseph Schumpeter, an Austrian economist, outlined another force affecting change—"creative destruction" (Schumpeter, 1942). As technologies and markets change, older established products and services are displaced by new offerings. A vivid example is the opening of the 363-mile long Erie Canal in upstate New York in 1825. Bernstein (2006) reports that the stagecoach businesses along that route disappeared almost overnight. We saw this in all six case studies in Chapter 4.

Creative destruction, over time, is great for the economy. Many new enterprises emerge, some prosper, and a few become major players. In the near term, however, creative destruction can be very disruptive. People who have invested their life savings in New York City taxi medallions, for example, have seen their investments evaporate. Families who have worked at local factories for several generations see their jobs exported to low wage countries. They find such changes threatening.

Such forces have political ramifications for issues ranging from trade to immigration. Most of these issues do not affect failure management concerns. However, the overall political stalemates that result can lead to barriers to the changes needed for adopting best failure management practices. For example, Shulkin (2019) in a recent memoir vividly describes how such forces have stymied healthcare practices in the Department of Veterans Affairs. In the next section, I suggest an approach to overcoming such barriers.

Enabling Change

Harford (2011) convincingly argues for an evolutionary approach to learning from inevitable failures. Put simply, as noted throughout this book, failures will happen. Sometimes, they will have been anticipated, but not expected, as illustrated in Chapter 3. Other times, they will not have been imagined and we will be surprised, as demonstrated by some of the cases in Chapter 5.

Harford's emphasis on learning from failures is undoubtedly the right thing to do. Better yet would be learning about failures before they happen. The idea is to explore possible failures computationally. The goal is not to predict what will happen but explore what *might* happen. I briefly outlined an approach to this in Chapter 5. I elaborate and illustrate this approach in this section.

Share Information

The first step is to broadly share credible information so all stakeholders understand the situation. The discussion and debate should be evidence-based, whether the topic is public policy (Haskins and Margolis, 2015) or engineering (Hybertson et al., 2018). Consequently, data compilation and aggregation are where we usually begin. The integrated data sets we create are usually project specific, but drawn from a wide variety of available data sets on business, health, education, transportation, etc.

It is very important that stakeholders believe in the validity of the data. If they question data validity and provide competing data sets, we welcome this—sooner the better helps. If stakeholders assert "facts" for which there are no data, we park these assertions for later discussion. We have found that computational explorations of portrayals of data can lead stakeholders to abandon beliefs of things they "knew" were true.

I hasten to note that almost all of our projects involve professional stakeholders who value science, engineering, and legal approaches to understanding problems and exploring solutions. Thus, we rarely face people who believe the moon landing or the 9/11 attacks were faked. However, we do often encounter skeptics that ask difficult questions about data integrity, assumptions, and so on. Such challenges typically serve to greatly improve the analyses.

Consistent with Harford's perspective, our initial computational models are often seriously flawed. Once key stakeholders experience the first version, they realize all the various things they did not think to tell us. Interestingly, once we incorporate these things into the next version, stakeholders' sense of ownership increases as they see their ideas on the displays.

Create Incentives

Stakeholders need to see that the solution being created will provide something of value to them. We are often focused on understanding possible failure situations over years rather than days. This is certainly the case for population growth and climate change.

We have found that also addressing some near-term issues often motivates many stakeholders. The data sets we compile can be used to address many issues. In a project where we studied the long-term market adoption of battery electric vehicles (Liu, Rouse, and Hanawalt, 2018), we also considered the near-term impacts of recharging these vehicles using electricity from coal-fired power plants.

Quite often stakeholders want to use our data sets to explore what their competitors are doing, e.g., their prices for products and services. As our data sets are almost always based on publicly available data, these stakeholders are not seeing anything that they could not access if they invested the time to do it. We are simply making it easier for them. In the process, of course, they are also buying into the merits of the overall project.

Provide an Experiential Approach

Interactive visualizations are central to our approach. Such visualizations enable people to experience the results of potential interventions, as illustrated in Figure 8.2. Immersing people in the complexity of their systems, and letting them take the controls, greatly increases their support. When they see projections based on the assumptions they have chosen, their sense of ownership usually increases considerably.

Figure 8.2 shows workshop participants listening to the discussion leader. Quite often, several participants will leave their seats, walk into the 8-foot by 20-foot, 180-degree Immersion Lab, take

Figure 8.2 Simulation of New York City health ecosystem

the controls, and discuss what they find. Typical findings are about how some variables affect others, over periods of time of interest. We have often seen experts discover relationships they had not previously realized, turning to team members with comments like, "Did you realize that personnel mix has such a significant impact on speed of response?"

Example Applications

Here are several examples of where the above approach has worked and the decisions that resulted. Most of our early applications were for companies launching new products or considering entering new markets.

A major test equipment company was launching a new generation of its best-selling equipment. They wanted to determine the best market segment for the initial launch. We compiled information on their competitors' current and anticipated offerings, developing models of all offerings and how well they matched each of the customers' needs in each segment.

After two intense 10-hour days, we had the answer. The team was exhausted. I asked the vice presidents of marketing and engineering how they felt about the results. They both were very positive. I asked them how they would have made this decision without the interactive models. One of them responded, "Normally we would have met several time over many weeks. In the end, we would have done whatever the last person who wasn't tired wanted to do."

Two military electronics companies, on separate occasions, entertained the possibility of moving into commercial electronics. One abandoned the idea quickly, feeling they could not adapt their cost structure. The other company developed business plans using our models for assessing competitive challenges and likely outcomes. After two intense weeks, they decided to not pursue this market.

I met with the vice president leading this effort after this decision was made. I asked whether he felt that all the modeling and analysis had been a waste of time. He responded, "No. This was a major success. We entertained a very appealing opportunity and thoroughly assessed our likely success in pursuing it. We decided we would be unlikely to succeed. We did this all in two weeks. In the past we would have taken months to agonize over this decision."

An aircraft engine company was considering a new small engine product. We spent several days pulling together all the information needed to create the needed models. We explored how they could best compete against rival engines. We conducted extensive sensitivity analysis to determine which assumptions might later bite them. It looked like a great opportunity.

The vice president leading this effort then commented, "I think this analysis is in good shape. Let's try to make a final decision in the next month of so." I asked him what he thought he would know a month from then that he did not know now. He responded by asking, "Do you think we should just decide now?" I nodded yes, as did every member of the team sitting around the table. They decided to proceed.

Working with two automobile companies, on separate occasions, we developed models to help us understand why 20 cars succeeded or failed in marketplace and, in another study, why 12 different cars were removed from market. It was clear that success depended on being able to predict what the market wanted 3–5 years in the future, and having a system development process that assured the targeted car was produced. All but one of the 12 cars was withdrawn due to conditions in the economy, market, and company—unfortunate situations and bad decisions.

We had several engagements where modeling and analysis avoided major investments that seemed like great ideas but would provide no added value in market. Another effort helped a semiconductor company addressing environmental issues due to the toxic waste their manufacturing processes created. Models were used to understand the reasons underlying very strong, differing positions on the real risks and alternative actions. This deeper analysis broke the logjam.

In recent years, we have spent considerable time applying our approach to healthcare delivery. Three applications with major providers involved inefficiencies that did not scale well, i.e., the costs for a few hundred patients were sustainable, but were unsustainable for 50,000 to 100,000 patients. We computationally redesigned delivery processes to assure that benefits to patients could be maintained with affordable investments and operations costs.

After one of these efforts, we asked the clinical team how they would have addressed the scalability issue without the models. The response was, "Normally, we would have formed a committee, met for several months, decided on an approach, rolled it out, and three years later measured whether it worked." With the interactive models, they explored tens of alternatives in a few hours.

The Centers for Medicare and Medicaid Services (CMS) had deployed a policy penalizing hospitals if patients were readmitted within 30 days for the same problem prompting their initial admission. There were interventions that could greatly reduce readmissions, while both improving patient health and saving money. We computationally modeled the impact of this intervention on each of 3,000 Medicare hospitals, tailoring the clinical trial results to each patient population and the economics of each hospital.

Only 10 of 3,000 Medicare hospitals would find it economically reasonable to comply with CMS policy. They were better off accepting the penalties rather than investing in avoiding them. If we varied the baseline intervention, a few hundred hospitals found compliance attractive. Clearly, the penalty policy was flawed. We communicated this finding to key stakeholders. Their main conclusion was that policies needed more rigorous assessments before rolling them out.

Over the past few years, we have applied our approach to higher education, particularly research universities. US universities have been creating a "tuition bubble" with the increasing costs of college education far exceeding increases of incomes. At the same time, research universities are facing stiffer competition for grants and publications, are increasingly dependent on foreign student enrollments (that pay full tuition), and maturing technologies that can increasingly provide high quality online education.

We developed computational models to enable understanding likely failure modes of universities and applied these models in several studies. It is clear that increased competition, declining foreign student enrollments, and educational technologies are going to undermine the finances of all but the best-resourced universities. In fact, these impacts are already emerging with the number of educational institutions failing per year steadily increasing, and accelerating due to the pandemic.

These models were hosted in the Immersion Lab in Figure 8.2. A variety of senior academic administrators explored their universities, standing in the middle of the semicircle of immersive screens. I was a bit surprised with how often they discovered relationships they had not previously considered. It struck me that these leaders had been educated as scientists, engineers, historians, etc., but had little evidence-based understanding of the dynamics of an educational institution. Our policy flight simulator contributed to their better understanding the complexity of their management tasks.

Conclusions

I find it interesting that published advice on addressing failures tends to assume that all the enterprise threats are external, e.g., Stulz (2009) and Demrovsky (2019). Yet, most of the sources and causes of failure discussed in this book were internal. More specifically, failure management problems tend to have internal sources.

The problems arise from imbalanced emphasis on operational priorities, skewed incentive and reward systems, cultures of denial, and a range of behavioral and social forces. There are success stories such as the eventual understanding and successful treatment of AIDS. But the opioid epidemic and climate change are still, at best, works in progress. We tend to delay addressing major problems until failure management is enormously expensive.

Consider climate change. A few years ago, I participated as an invited expert on a two-hour History Channel production named, as I recall, *Threats to Earth*. Failures considered natural calamities, human-caused catastrophes, and even the possibility of alien invasions. Our job, as experts, was to comment on the likelihood and impacts of the envisioned threats. It was a fun assignment.

Later, when leading the National Academy study on population growth that I mentioned in Chapter 5, it struck me that the Earth is not threatened. The Earth is not concerned about rising sea levels, or even ice ages or asteroid impacts. The Earth will be just fine.

Civilization, in contrast, will be profoundly affected. Those who denied the problems to make profits and secure votes will be long gone. Others will have to battle the tides, without the resources skimmed off earlier by the deniers. We need to marshal resources, energize stakeholders, and illustrate the evidence to counter the deniers. Denying major failures does not make them go away. It only delays managing failures and incurs huge costs when finally addressed.

References

Bernstein, P.L. (2006). *Wedding of the Waters: The Erie Canal and the Making of a Great Nation*. New York: Norton.

Bryant, S. (2019). How do different cultures view failure? *Country Navigator*, August 5.

Christensen, C.M. (1997). *The Innovator's Dilemma: When New Technologies Cause Great Firms to Fail*. Boston, MA: Harvard Business Review Press.

Demrovsky, C. (2019). Don't ignore these 10 global business risks in 2019. *Forbes*, January 14.

Diesing, P. (1971). *Reason in Society*. Urbana, IL: University of Illinois Press.

Hallowell, E. (2005). Overloaded circuits: Why smart people underperform. *Harvard Business Review*, 83 (1), 54–62.

Harford, T. (2011). *Adapt: Why Success Always Starts with Failure*. New York: Farrar, Straus and Giroux.

Haskins, R., and Margolis, G. (2015). *Show Me the Evidence: Obama's Fight for Rigor and Results in Social Policy*. Washington, DC: Brookings Institution Press.

Howard, P.K. (2015). The high cost of delaying infrastructure repairs. *Washington Post*, May 14.

Hybertson, D., Hailegiorghis, M., Griesi, K., Soeder, B., and Rouse, W.B. (2018). Evidence-based systems engineering. *Journal of Systems Engineering*, 21 (3), 243–58.

Kahneman, D. (2011). *Thinking, Fast and Slow*. New York: Farrar, Straus and Giroux.

Klein, G. (2004). *The Power of Intuition: How to Use your Gut Feelings to Make Better Decisions at Work*. New York: Currency.

Liu, C., Rouse, W.B., and Hanawalt, E. (2018). Adoption of powertrain technologies in automobiles: A system dynamics model of technology diffusion in the American market. *IEEE Transactions on Vehicular Technology*, 67 (7), 5621–34.

Madhavan, G., Phelps, C.E., Rouse, W.B., and Rappuoli, R. (2018). A vision for a systems architecture to integrate and transform population health. *Proceedings of the National Academy of Sciences*, 115 (50), 12,595–602.

Mann, T.E., and Ornstein, N.J. (2020). Five myths about bipartisanship. *Washington Post*, January 17.

Mintzberg, H. (1975). The manager's job: Folklore and fact. *Harvard Business Review*, July-August.

Rausch, J. (2019). Rethinking polarization. *National Affairs*, 44, Fall. https://www.nationalaffairs.com/publications/detail/rethinking-polarization.

Rouse, W.B. (1996). *Start Where You Are: Matching your Strategy to your Marketplace*. San Francisco, CA: Jossey-Bass.

Rouse, W.B. (1998). *Don't Jump to Solutions: Thirteen Delusions That Undermine Strategic Thinking*. San Francisco, CA: Jossey-Bass.

Rouse, W.B., Johns, M.M.E., and Pepe, K. (2019). Service supply chains for population: Overcoming fragmentation of service delivery ecosystems. *Journal of Learning Health Systems*, 3(2), https://doi.org/10.1002/lrh2.10186.

Schumpeter, J. (1942). *Capitalism, Socialism, and Democracy*. New York: Harper.

Shulkin, D. (2019). *It Shouldn't Be This Hard to Serve your Country*. New York: PublicAffairs.

Simon, H. (1972). Theories of bounded rationality. In C.B. McGuire and R. Radner, eds, *Decision and Organization* (Chap. 8). New York: North Holland.

Story, G.W., Vlaev, I., Seymour, B., Darzi, A., and Dolan, R.J. (2014). Does temporal discounting explain unhealthy behavior? A systematic review and reinforcement learning perspective. *Frontiers in Behavioral Neuroscience*, 8 (76), 1–20.

Stulz, R.M. (2009). Six ways companies mismanage risk. *Harvard Business Review*, 87 (3).

Thaler, R.H. and Sunstein, C.R. (2008). *Nudge: Improving Decisions about Health, Wealth, and Happiness*. New Haven, CT: Yale University Press.

Index

For the benefit of digital users, indexed terms that span two pages (e.g., 52–53) may, on occasion, appear on only one of those pages.

Abandonment, temporary 56
Abbott, R. 15–16, 27–31
Abstraction-aggregation space 26
Abstraction, abstract function 15
Abstraction, functional purpose 15
Abstraction, generalized function 15
Abstraction, levels 6–7, 14–15
Abstraction, physical form 15
Abstraction, physical function 15
Academia, future 20
Accept 94
Accident Investigation Board, Columbia 50
Accident prevention 161
Acquired immunodeficiency syndrome, *See* AIDS
Acquisitions 93
Adapt 94
Adoption, AI 174
Adults, disabled 186
Adults, older 186
Advertising, misleading 108
Aerospace Research and Technology Subcommittee 44
Agent-based models 151, 156
Aggregation, levels 6–7, 14–15
Aging Brain Care Center 18
Aging 121
Agricultural productivity 119
AI, *See* Artificial intelligence
Aiding 33, 164
AIDS epidemic, 2020 goals 106
AIDS epidemic 5, 10–11, 105
AIDS epidemic, growth 106
AIDS 105
Air transportation 20–2
Aircraft engine company 191
Aircraft operating procedures 170
Aircraft operations and maintenance 162
Aircraft powerplant mechanics 161
Airplanes 183
Alarms 33
Alexander, R.C. 78, 99
Alpha chip 183
Alzheimer's disease 18
Amankwah, F.K. 14, 19, 27, 134, 139, 173, 176
Amazon 67, 91
American Diabetes Association 154–5
American Heart Association 154–5
American ingenuity 71
Anadarko 59
Analyses, multi-level 11, 24
Anderson, H. 73
Anomalies 150
Anomaly, detection 172
Anomaly, diagnosis 172
Anthony, S.D. 67, 70, 99
Anticipating failures 60
Apple Computer 73
Apple Lisa 78
Apple Macintosh 78
Apple 79, 83, 98–9, 182
Applications, examples 190
Arguments, overall 8
Artic warming 125
Artificial intelligence 11, 67, 159, 161, 174
Assumption management 16
Assumptions, bad 184
Assumptions 188
AT&T 78
Atmospheric composition 135–6
Attention deficits 180
Augmented intelligence 174
Automobile companies 191–2
Automobile industry 64, 183
Automobiles 124
Aviation industry 183

Bad ideas, eliminated quickly 191
Bailouts, government 116
Bank failures 112
Bank runs 112, 116
Bankes, S.C. 14, 27
Banking system, shadow 115–16
Barber, B.R. 120, 139
Basole, R.C. 12–13, 18, 154, 159
Battery electric vehicles 189
Bayesian probabilities 162
Behavioral economics 110
Behavioral forces 193
Behavioral phenomena 32, 153
Bell, A.G. 79
Bell, M.J. 18
Bell, T. 27
Bennett, J. 64–5
Berman, A.E. 56–7, 65
Bernstein, L. 105–12
Bernstein, P.L. 187, 194
Biases 180
Bifurcations 16, 26
Big data 67, 144
Bigelow, J.H. 14, 27
Biology, theoretical 14
Black death 119
Blackberry Pearl 83
Blinder, A.S. 114, 139
Boeing 777 Aircraft 170
Boeing Company 52
Bombay 120–1
Bonanos, C. 71, 99
Borrowing, excessive 117
Boston, Massachusetts 113
Boudette, N.E. 64–5
Bounded rationality 180
Boustani, M. 18, 27
Boustany, K. 18, 27
BP Company 57, 59
BP Deepwater Horizon 5, 10, 56
BRAHG 135, 139
Braunstein, M.L. 18, 27, 154, 159
Brazil, film 175–6
Brigham, K.L. 18, 27, 154, 159
British Raj 120–1
Brook, D. 120–1, 139
Bryant, S. 185, 194
Brynjolfsson, E. 67, 86, 99, 174, 176
Bubble, economic 114
Bubble, failures 8
Bubble, real estate 114
Bubble, tulip 114
Burning platforms 97–8
Burroughs Company 72
Bush, G.W. 185–6
Business alliances 93
Business decisions, Xerox 77
Business equipment 72
Business processes 84, 145
Busses 124

Cafeterias 183
Calculators 72
Cameras, instant 71
Can Earth's and Society's Systems Meet the Needs of 10 Billion People? 121
Cancer control 14, 19, 173
Cancer, end of life care 19
Cancer, screening 19
Cancer, survivorship 19
Cancer, treatment 19
Capacities, existing 172
Capacities, investment 172
Capacities, new 172
Capital IQ 93, 99
Car-radio receivers 79
Carande-Kulis, V. 132, 139
Carbon dioxide 123
Carbon dioxide, consequences 124
Care coordination, incentives 169
Carlson, C. 77
Case studies 5
Case studies, comparison 60, 84, 128
Case studies, findings 143
Case studies, surveillance and control strategies 168
Cash registers 72
Causes, death 132
Causes, distal 5, 17, 172
Causes, proximate 5, 12, 172
Causes, ultimate 5, 17, 172
CCFEC 116, 139
CDC Field Epidemiology Manual 133
CDC, *See* US Centers for Disease Prevention and Control
CDMA standard 79–80
Cell phones, analog 80–1
Cell phones, digital 80–1
Cement slurries 56–7
Ceremony 180
Change, demographics 92
Change, enabling 11, 187

Change, evolutionary approach 187
Change, impedances 86
Change, management 178
Change, organizational 178
Change, strategies 94
Change, unnecessary 96
Chernobyl 5, 10, 38, 163
Chernobyl, HBO Special 64, 170
Childbearing, delayed 120
Christensen, C.M. 143, 159, 178–9, 182
CICERO 124, 139
Cities, emergence 120
Cities, instant 120–1
Cities, mayors 120
Cities, revolt 121
Citizens 169
Civilian Conservation Corps 113
Civilization 194
Clear, T. 18, 27, 154, 159
Climate analytics 124, 139
Climate change 5, 10–11, 169, 194
Climate monitoring 135–6
Climate restoration 125
Cloud computing 67, 98, 144
CMS, *See* US Centers for Medicare and Medicaid Services
CNET 83, 99
CNN, 1999 82, 91, 99
Cognitive limitations 180
Collaboration 92
Collins, M. 81, 99
Combivir 106
Commission conclusions, BP Deepwater Horizon 59
Commission findings & recommendations 36
Common mode failures 115
Communicable diseases 133
Communications network operators 161
Communications 8
Company formation 179
Compaq 76
Competitive advantage, Digital Equipment Corporation 75
Competitive advantages 149
Competitive analyses 189
Complera 106
Complex ecosystems 103
Complex organizations 68
Complex systems 32
Complex, high consequence failures 173
Complexity, exploration 41
Complexity, overwhelming 175
Complexity, technological 178
Complications 169–70
Computational issues 16
Computational modeling 11, 25, 150
Computational representations 25–6
Computer and software maintenance 162
Computer market, emergence 72
Computers, Macintosh 73
Computers, mainframe 72
Computers, microcomputers 73
Computers, minicomputers 73
Computers, PDP 73
Computers, VAX 73
Congestion pricing 20–2
Consequences 170
Consequences, higher-order 64
Consequences, mitigation 178
Consequences, negative 178
Consequences, unexpected 163–4
Constraints, energy 122
Constraints, land 122
Constraints, protein 122
Constraints, water 122
Consumers, misleading 146
Consumption habits 121
Containment building contamination 36
Contributing factors, Chernobyl 43
Contributing factors, Exxon Valdez 54
Control models 151
Control rods 39
Control rods, design 26–7
Control room user interface 34
Control 161, 180
Control, failure 166
Control, model-based 167
Control, predictive 166
Coordinate 180
Coronary heart disease 154
Corporate fumbles 78
Corporate governance failures 116
Corporate hubris 70
Cortese, D.A. 12, 27
Costs 121
Costs, drugs 107
Costs, economic 146
Costs, social 146
Counterfeit parts 19–20
Craig, D.D. 20, 27
Creative destruction 8, 97, 143, 187

Creative edge 71
Credit 186
Crew rest 54
CSB 56, 65
Culture 92
Culture, corporate 103–4
Culture, denial 193
Culture, values & norms 1
Cunningham, L. 18, 27, 154, 159
Customer-oriented strategy 72
Cybersecurity 171

Darzi, A. 178–80
Dash, M. 114, 139
Data integrity 188
Dautovic, G. 81, 99
Davis, E. 174, 176
Davis, P.K. 14, 27, 153, 159
De Niro, R. 175
Deaths of despair 109
Deaths, drug overdoses 110
DEC, *See* Digital Equipment Corporation
Decision making, behavioral nature 179
Decision making 146, 178
Decision making, data-driven 174–5
Decision making, evidence-based 174–5, 188
Decision making, management 7
Decision making, reluctance 191
Decision making, social nature 179
Decision making, vignettes 11, 182
Decision support concept, integrated 171
Decision support system, integrated 161
Decision support, architecture 1
Decision support 11
Decision support, model-based 174
Decision theory 151
Decision-making processes, NASA 45
Decisions, bad 191–2
Decisions, crisis 163–4
Decisions, delayed 179
Decisions, design 163–4
Decisions, investments 146–7
Decisions, lifestyle 150
Decisions, mergers & acquisitions 157
Decisions, operational 146–7, 150, 163–4
Decisions, product adoption 150
Decisions, technology adoption 150
Defense, capabilities 183
Defense, mechanisms 179
Defense, systems 162
Definition, failure 2
Definition, management 3
Definition, population health 110
Definition, safety 164–6
Definition, system 3
Deforestation 124
Degradation of forests 123
Dekker, S 63, 65
DeLisi, P.S. 75, 99
Dell Company 91
Delusions, latent 184
Delusions, strategic 87, 182
Deming, W.E. 170, 176
Demographic changes 121
Demrovsky, C. 179, 194
Depression mentality 113
Derivatives 114
Design 145
Design, decisions 104
Design, human-centered 143
Design, poor 17–18, 149, 164
Design, practices 1
Design, practices, unsafe 147
Design, principles 1
Design, visualizations 26
Designer's Associate 78
Designers 149
Designers, sensors 149
Detection, passive 166–7
Detection, predictive 166–7
Detection, proactive 166–7
DeWeerdt, S. 108–9, 139
Diabetes mellitus 18, 154
Diallo, S. 14, 153, 159
Diesing, P. 176, 185, 194
Digital Equipment Corporation 5, 10, 73, 183
Digital photography 70
Digital switches 82
Digital transformation 67, 86
Disabilities 132
Disabled adults 186
Discount rates, spatial 126
Discount rates, temporal 126
Discrete-event models 151
Disinformation 137
Disruptive forces 70
Distancing, spatial 179–80
Distancing, temporal 179–80
Distributed computing 75
Distributed failures 2–4, 103, 163, 166
Documents 180–1

Dolan, R.J. 179–80, 194
Don't Jump to Solutions 87–8
Donors 181
Doubleday Executive Book Club 87–8
Dow Jones News Service 93
Doz, Y. 68–72, 82
Dreamland 108
Driverless cars 161, 186
Drugs, costs 107
Drugs, overdose deaths 110
Drugs, supply chain 108
Dubai 120–1
Duke, J. 125, 139
Dynamic models 151

Earth as a system 126
Earth, threatened 194
Eastman Kodak, *see* Kodak
Eastman, G. 69
Economic bubbles 114
Economic disruptions 103
Economic incentives 121
Economic models 150
Economic opportunities 149
Economic panics 143–4
Economic situation 119–20
Economic sustainability 154
Economics 148–9, 176
Economist, The 70, 99, 106, 139, 174, 176
Economy monitoring 135
Economy 105
Economy, wood 123
Edsel, A. 62, 65
Education 121
Education, women 120
Edwards, S. 125, 139
Electric Power Research Institute 33
Electrical power, loss 38
Electronics 162
Electronics, commercial 191
Electronics, military 191
Ellis, C.D. 77, 99
Emergence 15–16
Emergency plans 37
Emergency shutdown, automatic 40
Emergency shutdown, manual 40
Emission reductions 124
Emission reductions, limited progress 124
Emory University 18, 154
Empathy 174
Employee prevention and wellness 18
Enabling change 11
Energy efficiency 124
Engineered systems 164
Engineering the Learning Healthcare Delivery System 12
Engineering 188, 191
Enterprise transformation 84, 88
Enterprise transformation, computational theory 96
Enterprise transformation, context 88–9
Enterprise transformation, costs 91
Enterprise transformation, ends 90–1
Enterprise transformation, framework 90–1
Enterprise transformation, means 90–1
Enterprise transformation, risks 91
Enterprise transformation, scope 90–1
Enterprise transformation, theory 88
Environment 105, 126
Environment, degradation 143–4
Environment, economic 181
Environment, indicators 121
Environment, social 181
Epidemics 143–4
Epistemology 14
EPRI, *See* Electric Power Research Institute
Ericson, C.A. 62, 65
Erie Canal, New York 187
Error-tolerant interfaces 170
Ethics 174
Ethiopia 120
Evaluation 164
Evaluation, inadequate 17–18, 149, 164
Eveleth, R. 174, 176
Events, BP Deepwater Horizon 57
Execution, plans 172
Experiential approaches 127, 189
Explanations 174
Explosion and Fire at Macondo Well: Volume 1 56
Explosion, Chernobyl 41
Exxon Shipping Company 54
Exxon Valdez 5, 10, 54

Facebook 174
Failure Modes and Effects Analysis 62
Failure, adaptation to change 18
Failure, anticipating 60, 84, 132
Failure, bubbles 8
Failure, bypassing 175
Failure, case studies 5

Failure, common mode 115
Failure, compensation 2, 162–3
Failure, complex high consequence 173
Failure, computational exploration 188
Failure, control 2, 11, 166
Failure, corporate governance 116
Failure, cultural perspectives 185
Failure, definition 2
Failure, detection 2, 162
Failure, diagnosis 2, 162
Failure, distributed 2–4, 103, 163, 166
Failure, explanations 8
Failure, hybrid 4–5
Failure, malicious 170–1
Failure, management tasks 162
Failure, management 11, 136, 158, 161
Failure, management, conceptual model 178
Failure, management, history 161
Failure, management, integrated 1, 178
Failure, manifestations 164
Failure, mitigation 2
Failure, multiple 169–70
Failure, organizational 18
Failure, pervasive 8
Failure, point 2–3, 163, 166
Failure, regulations 116
Failure, remediation 2, 162–3
Failure, slow 169–70
Failure, surveillance 2, 11, 166
Failure, technological 18
Failure, types 3
Failure, unforeseen 161
Failures, learning 188
Fake news 137
Family size 169
FDA, *See* Food and Drug Administration
Federal Reserve 112, 135, 139
Fentanyl 109
Fertility rate 118
Fertility rate, decreases 119–20
Fertility 121
Film, instant 71
Financial derivatives 104
Financial difficulties 193
Financial institutions 169
Financial institutions, non-depository 115
Financial statements 156
Findings, shared 189–90
Fire, platform 57
Fish 123
Fishman, T.C. 80–1, 99
Flavelle, C. 125, 139
Flood mitigation 125
Florida Keys 125
Fontaine, T. 174–6
Food and Drug Administration 106
Food services 183
Forces, behavioral 185
Forces, disruptive 70
Forces, social 185
Forest Service 113
Fortune 500, Digital Equipment Corporation 73
Fortune 500, Kodak 69
Fortune 500, Motorola 79
Fortune 500, Nokia 79
Fortune 500, Polaroid 69
Fortune 500, Xerox 73
Fossil fuels 118, 124
Fossil fuels, consumption 169
Fossil fuels, reduction 124
Founding values, Digital Equipment Corporation 75
Framework, analysis 6, 17
Framework, multi-level 6, 12
Fuchs, M. 125, 139
Fuel rods, fracture 41
Fuel rods, melting 36
Fuji Film 70
Fukushima-Daiichi nuclear power station 64
Function, abstract 15
Function, generalized 15
Function, physical 15
Fuzzy set theory 162

Gaffney, C. 16, 27
Galvin Manufacturing Corporation 79
Galvin, J.E. 79
Galvin, P.V. 79
Game theory 151
Gates, W. 98
Generator, diesel 39
Generator, steam 39
Generators 32
Gerberding. L.L. 132, 139
Germany 185
Gerstner, L. 98
Ghana 120
Gillette, K.C. 70
Gilliam, T. 175

Glaeser, E.L. 120, 139
Global distributions of temperature of rainfall 135–6
Global distributions of temperature 135–6
Global warming 124
Goals, corporate 184
Goals, profit 184
Goals, revenue 184
Goals, wrong 184
Gold reserves 112
Gold standard 112
Good ideas 183, 185–6
Goodman, S. 19–20, 27
Goodstein, L.P. 14–15, 27, 170, 176
Google 81
Goolsby, A. 27
Governance 110
Government, bailouts 116
Government 126
Graphical user interface 77
Graphite moderator 41–2
Great Depression 5, 10–11, 112
Great Recession 114
Great Recession, origins 115
Greed 169
Griesi, K. 178–9, 188
Grossman, C. 27
Groundwater, salinization 124
Growth rate 154
GSM standard 79–80, 82
Guiding Cancer Control 134
Guinness Book of Records 74–5, 183
Gulf of Mexico 57

HAART, *See* highly active antiretroviral treatment
Hailegiorghis, M. 178–9, 188
Haimes, Y.Y. 14, 27
Half split tests 162
Half split tests, information theory 162
Hall, A.D. 14, 27
Halliburton 57
Hallowell, E. 180, 194
Haloid Photographic Company 77
Hanawalt, E. 178–9, 194
Handsets 80–1
Hansson, S.O. 63, 65
Harassment 174
Harford, T. 182, 187, 194
Harnoss, J. 71–2, 99
Harrisburg, PA 33
Harvey, D.L. 15, 27
Haskins, R. 188, 194
Hazard Analysis 62
Hazelwood, Joseph 55
Health 148–9
Health, children 120
Health, coverage 133
Health, ecosystem, New York City 156
Health, insurance 107
Health, monitoring 132
Health, risks 133
Health, women 120
Healthcare delivery 17
Healthcare 174, 192
Healthy days 133
Heart Disease 18
Hedberg, K. 133, 139
Hedge 94
Helsinki, Finland 82
Heroin 109
Hessledahl, A. 79–80, 99
Heuristics 180
Hewlett-Packard 76
Heydari, B. 16, 27
Higher education 20, 193
Highly active antiretroviral treatment 106
Hiltzik, M. 70, 99
Hirschman, K.B. 18–19, 27
History Channel 194
HIV 105
Holmberg, J.-E. 63, 65
Home ownership 149
Honda 95
Houses, asset prices 115
Houses, flipping 115
Howard, P.K. 184–5, 194
Hoylan, A. 62, 65
Hubble Space Telescope 49–50
Huber, R.K. 14, 27
Hubris, corporate 70, 149, 183
Human abilities 161
Human consumption of resources 143–4
Human errors 170
Human factors 34–5, 37, 143
Human immunodeficiency virus, *See* HIV
Human lifestyles 143–4
Human speculative habits 143–4
Human suffering 103
Human well being 121
Human-centered design 143
Humphreys, K. 109

Hurricane Sandy 22
Hybertson, D. 178–9, 188

IAEA, *See* International Atomic Energy Agency
IBM 72, 78, 91, 98–9, 182
Ice collapses 125
Ice melting 124
IISD 124, 139
iMac 98–9
Image, automated printing 77
Image, printing process 77
Immersion Laboratory 26–7, 189–90, 193
Immigration 19–20, 118
Impacts of climate change 135–6
Impacts of climate on humans 121
Impulsive judgments 180
Incentive & reward systems 1
Incentive & reward systems, skewed 193
Incentive structures 150
Incentives 17–18, 127, 179, 189
Income data 135–6
Indiana Health 18
Industrial output 112
Industrial Revolution 123
Industry 126
Information systems, integrated 169
Information, sharing 127, 188
Information, validity 188
Innovation, failures 78
Innovation, market 178–9
Innovator's dilemma 182
INSAG-1 38, 43, 65
INSAG-7 38, 40–1, 43, 65
Inspections, lack 147
Instant cities 120–1
Institute of Medicine, *see* National Academy of Medicine
Intel 76
Intellectual property 19–20
Intelligent error-tolerant interface 170
Intelligent interface 170
Intensive agriculture 123
Interactive computing 73
Interactive visualizations 11, 153, 157, 189
Interest rates 112–13
Interface 91
Intergovernmental Panel on Climate Change 135–6
International Atomic Energy Agency 43, 65
International Committee on the Taxonomy of Viruses 106
International Journal of Occupational Safety and Ergonomics 63
International Maritime Organization 56
International Monetary Fund 135
International Nuclear Safety Advisory Group 38
International Ship Management Rules 56
International Space Station 49
Internet of Things 67, 159, 166
Internet 98
Intraprise 89
Intuition 174, 180
Inventions, technology 178–9
Inventories 151
Investment decisions 169
Investment decisions, poor 146–7
Investments 146
Investors 181
iPad 98–9
IPCC 135–6, 139
IPCC, *See* Intergovernmental Panel on Climate Change
iPhone 83, 98–9
iPod 98–9
Iridium 81
Isaacson, W. 77, 99
IT systems 110

Japan 185
Japan, immigration 118
Jick, H. 108, 139
Job creation 179
Jobs, S. 77, 98–9
Johns, M.M.E. 14, 19, 27, 108, 110, 134, 139, 173, 176, 185, 194
Johnson Space Flight Center, Texas 47
Journal of Safety Research 63

Kahan, J.P. 14, 27
Kahneman 180, 194
Kampas, P.J. 75, 99
Kaposi's sarcoma 106
Keller, K. 125, 139
Kennedy Space Center, Florida 44
Kenya 120
Kinshasa, Democratic Republic of Congo 105
Klein, G. 178, 194
Knowledge Navigator 78

Kodak 5, 10, 69
Kodak, market share 70
Kodak, moment 69
Kornfield, M. 109, 139
Kuhlmann, A. 63, 65

Land use 121
Land, E.H. 71
Laudan, A. 134, 139
Launch Control Center 47
Law 188
Le Coze, J-C. 63, 65
Leadership 8, 92, 99, 148
Leadership, experience-based 174–5
Learning from failures 188
Legal issues 93
Lehman Brothers 116
Lempert, R.J. 16, 27, 125, 139
Lenovo 81
Lenton, T.M. 125, 139
Lessons learned 146
Level, organization 7
Level, physical 7
Level, process 7
Level, society 7
Levels of abstraction 14–15
Levels of aggregation 14–15
Leveson, N.G. 55, 62–3, 65
Lewis, M. 114, 139
Life expectancy 118
Life expectancy, decreasing 109
Lightbody, L. 125, 139
Lim, C.P. 62, 65
Limitations 179
Lines of business 146
Linge, N. 80, 99
Liu, C. 14–15, 26–7, 178–9, 194
Lobbyists 137
Lockheed Martin 91
Lombardi, J.V. 20, 27
Loper, M. 19–20, 27
Los Angeles, California 106
Loss of coolant accident 35
Loss of life 103
Lotus 1-2-3 75
Lumber 123
Lumia 83
Lymphadenopathy-associated virus 106

Macintosh 73
Macko, D. 13–14, 27
Macroeconomics 151
Madhavan, G. 14, 19, 27, 134, 139, 173, 176, 178–9
Maher, J. 133, 139
Maintainers 149
Maintenance 11, 55
Maintenance, deferred 184
Maintenance, health 185
Maintenance, infrastructure 184–5
Major investments, avoided 189
Management problems 193–4
Management, decision making 7
Management, definition 3
Management, interrupt driven 180
Managers 149, 169
Mann, T.E. 178–9, 186
Marangoni, G. 125, 139
Marcus, G. 174, 176
Margolis, G. 188, 194
Marine Accident Report: Grounding of the US Tankship Exxon Valdez on Bligh Reef, Prince William Sound, Near Valdez Alaska, March 24, 1989 54
Marine Safety International 53–4
Market, challenges 84
Market, crash 112
Market, leader, Nokia 82
Market, misreading 169, 179
Market, situations 86
Market, situations, unfortunate 191–2
Market, threats 169
Market, transitions 148
Marketing 191
Marks, J.S. 132, 139
Marriage, delayed 120
Marshall Space Flight Center, Alabama 45–6
Materials, recycling 124
Materials, reuse 124
Mayes, B.R. 109, 139
Mazzei, P. 125, 139
McAfee, A. 67, 86, 99, 174, 176
McCarthy, B. 174–6
McDermott, T. 19–20, 27
McDonald, T. 14, 27
McGinnis, J.M. 27
Medical research 183
Medicare 18–19
MedStar Health, Baltimore, Maryland 110
Meetings 180–1
Mellody, M. 121, 139

Mental health 133
Mental stress 37
Mergers & acquisitions 156
Mergers 93
Mesarovic, M.D. 13–14, 27
Methane gas 57
Methodology, modeling 24
Methodology, visualization 24, 26
Mexico 185
Microcomputers 73
Microcomputers, dismissal by Olsen 73–4
Microeconomics 151
Microprocessors, Alpha 74
Microprocessors, AMD 74
Microprocessors, x86 74
Microsoft 82, 98, 182
Microsoft, DOS 75
Microsoft, PowerPoint 52
Middle East 119
Migration 121
Minicomputers 73, 75
Mintzberg, H. 178, 194
Mismanagement 17–18, 149
Missiles 183
Mission Control Center 47
Mission Management Team, NASA 52
MIT 76, 99
Mitsui 59
Mittal, S. 14, 153, 159
Mobile radio telephones 82
Mobile telephone industry 82
Modeling, computational 25
Modeling, epistemology 14
Modeling, methodology 24
Models, agent based 151
Models, composition 26
Models, confidence 41–2
Models, control 151
Models, discrete event 151
Models, dynamic 151
Models, evolution 168
Models, human failure detection 162
Models, human failure diagnosis 162
Models, insights 158
Models, learning 168
Models, optimization 167
Models, validation 41
Möller, N. 63, 65
Money supply 112
Monitoring, enterprise 172
Monitoring, market 172
Mood 179
Mortality 132
Mortality, rate 118
Mortgages, adjustable rate 115–16
Mortgages, criteria 115
Mortgages, defaults 115
Mortgages, interest only 116
Mortgages, subprime 115
Motorola DynaTAC 79
Motorola Mobility 81
Motorola Razr flip phone 79–80
Motorola Solutions 81
Motorola 5, 10, 79
Motorola, demise 81
Muddling through 184
Multi-level analyses 11
Multi-level framework 12
Multi-level interpretation, AIDS epidemic 107
Multi-level interpretation, BP Deepwater Horizon 59
Multi-level interpretation, Chernobyl 43
Multi-level interpretation, Climate change 128
Multi-level interpretation, Digital Equipment Corporation 76
Multi-level interpretation, Exxon Valdez 56
Multi-level interpretation, Great Depression 113–14
Multi-level interpretation, Great Recession 117
Multi-level interpretation, Kodak 70
Multi-level interpretation, Motorola 81
Multi-level interpretation, NASA Challenger 48–9
Multi-level interpretation, NASA Columbia 52
Multi-level interpretation, Nokia 83
Multi-level interpretation, Opioid epidemic 111
Multi-level interpretation, Polaroid 72
Multi-level interpretation, Population growth 122
Multi-level interpretation, Three Mile Island 37
Multi-level interpretation, Xerox 78
Mumbai 120–1

NASA Ames Research Center 44
NASA Challenger 5, 10, 44
NASA Columbia 5, 10, 49

NASA Glenn Research Center 44
NASA Langley Research Center 44
NASA, *see* National Aeronautics and Space Administration
Nass, S.J. 14, 19, 27, 134, 139, 173, 176
Nass, S.J. 173, 176
National Academies of Science, Engineering, and Medicine 19, 117, 134
National Academy of Engineering 12, 121
National Academy of Medicine 12
National Academy of Sciences 121
National Aeronautics and Space Administration 44
National Cancer Institute 106
National Cash Register 72
National forests 125
National Institute on Drug Abuse 110
National population 135–6
National Transportation Safety Board 54, 65
National Youth Administration 113
NATO Conference on Human Detection and Diagnosis of System Failures 161–2
Natural resources 123
Naylor, M.D. 18–19, 27
NCR, *See* National Cash Register
Negotiations 180
Netflix 67
Netherlands Organization for Applied Scientific Research 53–4
Networks 75, 80–1
New Deal 113
New England Journal of Medicine 108
New England, Hurricane of 1938 113
New England, Northern 109
New England, wood economy 123
New York City taxi medallions 187
New York City, New York 106, 156
Newell Rubbermaid 91
NIDA 139
NIH, 2016 110, 139
Nokia 5, 10, 79, 82
Nokia, demise 82
Nokia, limited design options 83
Nokia, market leader 82
Nokia, risk aversion 83
Nokia, story 93
Nokia, Symbian operating system 83
Nokia, US mobile telephone market abandoned 83
Non-profit, health-related 183
Norms 17–18
Northern Light 55
NRC, *See* Nuclear Regulatory Commission
NTSB, *See* National Transportation Safety Board
Nuclear oversight regulations 38
Nuclear power industry 36
Nuclear power plants 162
Nuclear powerplant operators 161
Nuclear reactor, self-destruction 40
Nuclear reactors 32
Nuclear Regulatory Commission 33, 36, 38, 65
Nudges 180
Nurses 110
Nutrition 119

O-ring erosion 45–6
O-ring erosion, history 46
O-ring seals 44–5
O'Mahony, A. 14, 27, 143–9, 153
Obama, B. 185–6
Obermeyer, Z. 174, 176
Ocean transport of oil 53
Oceanography, urban 22
Oceans, acidification 124
ODI 124, 139
Oghbaie, M. 14–15, 26–7
Ohio River Valley 109
Oil and gas platforms 53
Oil tankers 53
Older adults 186
Olsen, K. 73
Olsen, L.A. 27
Operational decisions, poor 146–7
Operational errors 38
Operational performance 156
Operational plans 146
Operational priorities 193
Operations 144–5, 150
Operations, current 171
Operations, current, detection 171
Operations, current, diagnosis 171
Operations, future 171
Operations, future, plans 171
Operations, mismanaged 164
Operator confusion 34
Operator training 35
Operator understanding 43
Operators 149
Opioid epidemic 5, 10–11, 108

Opioid epidemic, roots 108
Opioid epidemic, three phases 109
Opioids, prescription 108–9
Opioids, synthetic 109
Optimization models 167
Optimize 94
Options 96–7
Options, Kodak 96–7
Options, Motorola 96–7
Options, Xerox 96–7
Organization, AI 174–5
Organization, rewiring 174–5
Organizational changes, NASA 49–50
Organizational culture, Digital Equipment Corporation 75
Organizational culture, NASA 45
Organizations, adaptable 174–5
Organizations, agile 174–5
Organizations, complex 68
Organizations, experimental 174–5
Organizations, mature 179
Organizations, risk-averse 174–5
Organizations, siloed 174–5
Organize 180
Originators, mortgage products 149
Ornstein, N.J. 186, 194
Osaba, O. 14, 27
Outcomes 150
Outsourcing processes 145
Oversight, lack 147
Overview, Chapter 1 10
Overview, Chapter 2 10
Overview, Chapter 3 10
Overview, Chapter 4 10
Overview, Chapter 5 10–11
Overview, Chapter 6 11
Overview, Chapter 7 11
Overview, Chapter 8 11
OxyContin 108–9

Pain treatment centers 108
Pain treatment 104, 108
Palast, G. 35, 65
Pandemic, impacts on higher education 193
Park, H. 18, 27, 154, 159
Passenger cars 184
Pasteur Institute, Paris, France 106
Patient advocacy 183
Patient education 183
Pattern recognition 162, 174
Pauly, M.V. 18–19, 27
Payers 185
PDP computers 73
Peirce, G. 113
Peirce, M. 113
Peirce's Tavern 113
Pejtersen, A.M. 14–15, 27, 170, 176
Penalties, readmission 192
Penalty policy, flawed 192–3
Pendleton-Julian, A. 14, 27
Penn Medicine 18–19
Pennock, M.J. 14–16, 18–19, 26–7, 94, 99
People-related problems 37
Pepe, K.M. 18–19, 27, 108, 110, 139, 185, 194
Personal computing market, IBM 75
Perspectives, behavioral 176
Perspectives, disciplinary 8–9
Perspectives, legal 176
Perspectives, operational 8–9
Perspectives, political 176
Perspectives, social 176
Peter the Great 120–1
Pfautz, J. 14, 27, 153, 159
Phelps, C.E. 19, 27, 173, 176, 178–9
Phenomena, behavioral 32, 153
Phenomena 150–1
Phenomena, social 32, 153
Photo sharing 70
Photographic film 69
Photography, instant 71
Physical climate 135–6
Plan 180
Planning 8, 92
Plans, execution 172
Platform companies 67, 86
Pneumocystis pneumonia 106
Point failures 2–3, 163, 166
Polarization 186
Polaroid 5, 10, 71
Polaroid, story 71
Policies 150
Policy flight simulators 26–7, 127–8, 154, 193
Policy, influences 149
Political ramifications 187
Politicians 169
Population growth projections 119–20
Population Growth 5, 10–11, 118, 169
Population health 105, 173
Population health, definition 110
Population health, fragmentation 110

Population 126
Porter, J. 108, 139
Portsmouth, Rhode Island 113
Poverty, concentration 109
Pradhan, E. 120, 139
Predictions 150
Predictive control, model-based 167
Predictive Health Institute 154
Predictive surveillance, model-based 167
PrEP 106
Prescription drugs 149
Prescriptions, opioids 108
Press, G. 78, 99
Pressures, economic 149
Pressures, political 149
Prevention 154, 185
Prices 112
Prices, increases 183
Prince William Sound, Alaska 54
Pripyat, Ukraine 38
Problems, people-related 37
Procedure execution 170
Process information 180–1
Process plants 162
Processes, business 145
Processes 144–5, 150
Processes, outsourcing 145
Processing soft information 180
Producers, drugs 149
Product managers 80
Product Planning Advisor 74–5, 81
Production Gap Report 124
Production pressures 146
Productivity 179
Products, energy-efficient 124
Providers 185
Prudhoe Bay Oil Field 54
Pryce, J. 175
Public health 119
Public sector organizations 146
Purdue Pharma 108–9
Purdue Pharma, fine paid 109
Purpose, functional 15

Qualcomm 80–1
Quinones, S. 108, 139

Radio telephones, mobile 82
Raising roads 125
Rappuoli, R. 19, 27, 173, 176, 178, 194
Rasmussen, J. 14–15, 27, 161–2, 170, 176
Rationality, economic 176, 185
Rationality, legal 176, 185
Rationality, political 176, 185
Rationality, social 176, 185
Rausch, J. 186, 194
Raytheon Collision Avoidance System radar 55
Reactor containment 41–2
Reactor output 41
Reactor test procedure 38
Real estate bubble 114
Recovery coaches 110
Reed, M. 15, 27
Reelection 186
Reeves, M. 71–2, 99
Regulations 169
Regulations, failures 116
Regulations, lack 147
Regulatons, oversight 115
Relief value, pilot-operated 34
Remington Rand 72
Repair time probabilities 162
Replacement value 118–20
Report of the Accident at the Chernobyl Nuclear Power Station 38
Report of the Columbia Accident Investigation Board 49
Report of the President's Commission on the Accident at Three Mile Island 33
Report of the President's Commission on the Space Shuttle Challenger Accident 44
Representations 150–1
Representations, computational 25–6
Reputation 179
Resettlement Administration 113
Residuals, filter 162
Residuals, model 167
Resistance, economic 137
Resistance, political 137
Resistance, social 137
Resource utilization 156
Retrovirus HTLV-III 106
Returns on investments 121, 154
Reuters 93
Rewards 179
Rice bowls 179
Rich, S. 109, 139
RIM 83
Risks, aversion, Nokia 83
Risks 146, 169
Risks, excessive 117

Risks, management 14
Risks, packaging 115
Risks, stratification 154
Riso National Laboratory, Roskilde, Denmark 161–2
Ritual 180
Road traffic injuries 133
Rochester, New York 77
Rockman, S. 80, 99
Rogers Commission 45
Rollenhagen, C. 63, 65
Roosevelt, F.D. 113
Roscosmos State Space Corporation 49
Rosen, R. 14, 27
Rousand, M. 62, 65
Roy, K. 132, 139
Rule-based models 162
Rules of the game 103–4, 148–9, 186
Rules, Nuclear Regulatory Commission 34
Runaway power increase 39
Rural Electrification Administration 113
Rural living 124

S&P 500 67
Safety, analysis 43
Safety 148–9, 164, 179
Safety, culture 43
Safety, definition 164–6
Safety, economy 166
Safety, environment 166
Safety, health systems 166
Safety, metrics 179
Safety, requirements 38
Safety, review 43
Safety, rules 45
Safety, science 63, 179
Safety, standards 43
Safety. issues 146
Sage, A.P. 176
Saleh, T. 174–6
Sales, aggressive 108
Samsung 79, 83
San Francisco, California 106
Sasson, S. 70
Satellites 183
Satisficing 180
Scaling pilot tests 192
Scenario planning 169
Scenarios 150
Schaumburg, Illinois 79
Schedule pressures 146
Schedule time 180–1
Schein, E.H. 75, 99
Schoomaker, H. 109, 118, 139
Schumpeter, J. 97, 99, 143, 159, 178, 194
Schwartz, E.I. 67, 99
Science 188
Scram, *see* emergency shutdown
Screening 185
Sea level rise 124
Sea life, threatened 124
Seals, O-ring 44–5
Securities, mortgage-backed derivatives 114
SEI 124, 139
Serban N. 12, 26–7, 92–4, 96–9, 156, 159
Service model, Fee for service 12–13
Seuss, C.D. 55, 99
Sexual and reproductive health 133
Seymour, B. 178–80
Shanghai 120–1
Share information 188
Sheetz, M. 67, 99
Shenzhen 120–1
Sheridan, T.B. 153, 159
Ship navigation 162
Shulkin, D. 187, 194
Shutdown, automatic emergency 38
Shuttle, breakup 48
Shuttle, foam insulation 49
Shuttle, heat shield 49
Shuttle, history of insulation damage 50
Shuttle, risk assessment 50
Shuttle, sold rocket boosters 45
Siebel, T.M. 67, 86, 99, 159, 174, 176
Simian immunodeficiency virus 105
Simon, H. 178, 194
Situation Assessment Advisor 86–7
Situation assessment 86, 172, 181
Situation assessment, flawed 181
Situations, novel 180
SIV, *See* Simian immunodeficiency virus
Six Sigma 88
Slavery 123
Smartphone market 81
Smith, D.K. 78, 99
Snyder, P. 70, 99
Social forces 193
Social media 186–7
Social networks 110
Social phenomena 32, 153
Social systems 164
Social welfare programs 113

Social workers 110
Society, lack of acceptance 179
Society, monitoring 171
Socio-economic information 135–6
Socio-economic trends 108
Socio-technical systems 12, 14
Soeder, B. 188, 194
Software 80
Software, competencies 80
Software, third party 75
Solar radiation 124
Sonduck, M.M. 75, 99
South Asia 119
South East Asia 119
Space shuttle crews 161
Space shuttle 44, 163
Space shuttle, fuel tank 44
Space shuttle, orbiter 44
Space shuttle, solid rocket boosters 44
Space Systems and Technology Advisory Committee 44
Space Transportation System 44
Spatial discount rates 126
Speculation 146
Speech recognition 75
Spohrer, J.C., 2018 170, 174–6
St. Petersburg 120–1
Stakeholders, ownership 188–9
Stakeholders, powerful 181
Standards, CDMA 79–80
Standards, GSM 79–80, 82
Starbucks 91
State, system 163
Status quo 185
Steam turbines 32
Stewards of the status quo 8, 148
Stock market speculation 112
Story, G.W. 178–80
Story, Nokia 93
Strategic delusions 87, 182
Strategic Development Goals 133
Strategic thinking, flawed 149
Strategies for commitments 127
Strategies, change 94
Strategy 8, 92
Strong, H.A. 69
Stroup, D.F. 132, 139
Stulz, R.M. 193–4
Sub-Saharan Africa 119
Substance abuse 133
Substance abuse, overall costs 110
Suburban living 124
Success, examples 98
Success, trapped by 71–2
Suicides 109
Sunstein, C.R. 180, 194
Supertanker engineering officers 161
Supply chain, drugs 108
Supply chain, fragmentation 108
Supply chain, military systems 19–20
Supply chain, treatment 108
Surveillance, active 166
Surveillance 158, 161, 174
Surveillance, evidence-based 93–4
Surveillance, failure 166
Surveillance, human behaviors 144
Surveillance, mechanisms 166
Surveillance, model-based 167
Surveillance, passive 166
Surveillance, predictive 166
Survival rates, children 120
Survival rates, mothers 120
Sustainability 121
SUVs 184
Switches, digital 82
Symbian 83
Symptoms, implications 180
System state 163
System, decomposition 15
System, definition 3
System, earth 126
Systems science 110
Systems Theoretic Process Analysis 62–3
Systems, behavioral 15
Systems, engineered 164
Systems, social 15, 164
Systems, urban 22

Tabulators 72
Takahara, Y. 13–14, 27
Tariffs 112–13
Tasks, failure management 162
Taxpayers 169
Tay, K.M. 62, 65
Teamwork 92
Technical excellence 74–5
Technology adoption 143, 178–9
Technology Investment Advisor 81
Technology, change 121
Telecommunications infrastructures 82
Telephone calls 180–1
Telephone, invention 79

Temporal discount rates 126
Test equipment 190
Testing 145
Thacker, S.B. 132, 139
Thaler, R.H. 180, 194
Themes 2
Theories, mediation 16
Theory of Multi-level Hierarchical Systems 13–14
Thiokol 45–6
Thomas, J.P. 62–3, 65
Threat to Earth, film 194
Threat, earth 194
Threats, external 193–4
Threats, internal 193–4
Threats, market 169
Three Mile Island 5, 10, 33
Time constants 126
Timeline, BP Deepwater Horizon 57
Timeline, Chernobyl 38
Timeline, Exxon Valdez 54
Timeline, NASA Challenger 44–5
Timeline, NASA Columbia 49
Timeline, Three Mile Island 33–4
TNO, *See* Netherlands Organization for Applied Scientific Research 53–4
Tolk, A. 14, 16, 27, 153, 159
Total Quality Management 88
Trade surplus 112–13
Traffic congestion 20–2
Training deficiencies 37
Training simulators 53–4
Training 33, 164
Training, operator 35
Trains 124
Transformation, digital 67
Transitional Care Model 18–19
Transocean 57
Transparency 117, 174
Transportation 20–2, 124
Treatment, capacity issues 110
Treatment, lack 110
Treatment, scheduling practices 110
Treatment, supply chain 108
Treatments, costs 110
Tribalism 186–7
Triumph of the City 120
Trust 139, 174
Tufte, E.R. 34–5, 65
Tuition cost bubble 193
Tulip bubble 114
Tuttle, J. 175
Twitter 174
Typewriters 72

Ultra large crude carriers 53
Uncertainties, epistemic 16
Uncertainties, ontological 16
Under-employment 109
Underinvestment 164
Undersea extraction of oil 53
Unemployment 112
UNEP 124, 139
United Nations 119–20, 139
United States Health Board 135
United States 185
UPS 91
Urban living 124
Urban oceanography 22
Urban systems 22
Urbanization 121
US Centers for Disease Prevention and Control 132
US Centers for Disease Prevention and Control 133, 139
US Centers for Medicare and Medicaid Services 192
US culture 108
US Department of Commerce 115
US Department of Health and Human Services 186
US Department of Interior 59
US Department of Justice 186
US Department of Labor 186
US Department of Transportation 186
US Department of Veterans Affairs 187
US Federal Communications Commission 186
US Financial Crisis Inquiry Commission 116
US Health in International Perspective: Shorter Lives and Poorer Health 134
US health system, fragmentation 169
US healthcare system 108
US regulatory regime 108
Usability 164

Value deficiencies 89
Values & norms, cultural 1
Values 17–18
Van Landeghem, J. 67, 99
Variables, demographic 121

Variables, economic 121
Variables, policy 121
Vaughan, D. 50, 65
VAX computers 73
Vehicle failures 191–2
Vehicle successes 191–2
Vehicles, specialty 184
Veral, E. 26–7, 156, 159
Verbal media 180–1
Very large crude carriers 53
Vested interests 146, 169
Victoria's Secret 91
Vignettes, decision making 11
Viguerie, S.P. 67, 99
Vision 8, 92
Visualization, methodology 24, 26
Visualizations, interactive 153, 157, 189
Vlaev, I. 178–80
Void coefficient of reactivity 39
Voters 181

Waiting lines 151
Wallerstein, I.M. 14, 16
Walmart 67, 91
Water pollution 123
Waterman, J. 125, 139
Wayfair 67
Weinstein, J. 174, 176
Wellness 154
Wharf Tavern 113
White House 185–6
WHO, *See* World Health Organization
Will to act 139
Williams, A. 109, 139
Williams, J. 56, 65
Wilson, J.C. 77
Wilson, J.R. 77
Wilson, K. 82, 99
Wind shear 47
Woolf, S.H. 109, 118, 134, 139
Workplace Health and Safety 63
Works Progress Administration 113
World Bank 135
World Health Organization 133, 139
World War II 113

Xerox Alto 77
Xerox Corporation 77
Xerox management, copier heads 77
Xerox management, fumbling the future 78
Xerox Palo Research Center 77
Xerox Star 77
Xerox 5, 10, 73
Xirallic 64

Yu, X. 18–19, 26–7, 92–4, 96–9, 156, 159